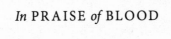

In PRAISE *of* BLOOD

In PRAISE of BLOOD

The CRIMES

of the RWANDAN

PATRIOTIC FRONT

JUDI REVER

RANDOM HOUSE CANADA

PUBLISHED BY RANDOM HOUSE CANADA

Copyright © 2018 Judi Rever

Published in 2018 by Random House Canada, a division of Penguin Random House Canada
Limited. Distributed in Canada by Penguin Random House Canada Limited, Toronto.

www.penguinrandomhouse.ca

Random House Canada and colophon are registered trademarks.

Library and Archives Canada Cataloguing in Publication is available upon request.

ISBN 978-0-345-81209-4
eBook ISBN 978-0-345-81211-7

Book design by Rachel Cooper

Cover image © Carolyn Fox / Arcangel Images
Interior image © Maksym Filipchuk / Dreamstime.com

Printed and bound in the United States of America

10 9 8 7 6 5 4 3 2 1

Penguin
Random House
RANDOM HOUSE CANADA

For their courage, this book is dedicated to

Théogène Murwanashyaka
Manzi Mutuyimana
Mulinzi 21-00

CONTENTS

Those who have been once intoxicated with power, and have derived any kind of emolument from it, even though but for one year, never can willingly abandon it. They may be distressed in the midst of all their power; but they will never look to anything but power for their relief.

—*Edmund Burke*

Introduction

AGAINST THE GRAIN

ON A COLD DAY IN MARCH 2015, I OPENED AN E-MAIL FROM A PERSON named Clarise Habimana. The message read:

> Dear Judi,
>   This document should be kept secret and not divulged to a third party.
> Good luck.
> —Clarise.

I'd been documenting crimes committed by Rwanda's post-genocide government off and on for years. I'd collected detailed testimony from victims, perpetrators and contextual witnesses across three continents. The Rwandan genocide stands as the most tragic and misunderstood event of the twentieth century. The ethnic and political violence that engulfed the country led to the eventual loss of millions of lives in Rwanda and neighboring Congo, forever changing the landscape of central Africa. The man who emerged triumphant amid the bloodshed was Paul Kagame, who seized power in Rwanda in July 1994 after routing the Hutu extremists who had exterminated Tutsis. He was hailed as a hero for stopping the carnage and rebuilding a shattered nation from the ground up. That is the narrative of light and dark forces that has been told in most history books and mainstream media. The real story is more complex and frightening.

I'd been on the trail of the complete story of the genocide since 1997. Though I'd never heard of Clarise Habimana, I immediately downloaded the attachment. I soon realized she was a whistle-blower, someone who could not accept either the erasure of history or the perversion of justice that has resulted from that erasure. She had sent me an official compendium of crimes against civilians committed by Paul Kagame's Rwandan Patriotic Front (RPF) during the genocide.

The document, dated October 1, 2003, and labeled top secret, had been compiled by criminal investigators in the Office of the Prosecutor of the International Criminal Tribunal for Rwanda (ICTR).[1] The ICTR was set up in the aftermath of the genocide to try Rwandans accused of the most serious violations of human rights. The thirty-page report was so explosive that it had remained buried for more than a decade. It revealed that the tribunal had opened several files on RPF massacres throughout Rwanda in 1994. It revealed too that the ICTR prosecutor at the time, Carla Del Ponte, had opened an investigation into the assassination of Hutu president Juvénal Habyarimana. The attack on his presidential plane on the night of April 6, 1994, was the event widely seen as triggering the genocide. A previous inquiry by the ICTR's Michael Hourigan had been shut down by Del Ponte's predecessor, Louise Arbour, who said the tribunal had no mandate to investigate the plane crash.

The report Clarise leaked to me revealed that tribunal investigations had been opened on the RPF's military intelligence wing, whose members stood accused of committing acts of savagery against unarmed Rwandans, both Hutu and Tutsi. It provided evidence that commandos in Kagame's army had not only infiltrated the Hutu militias but helped murder Tutsis at roadblocks in Kigali in a bid to fuel the genocide—one of the most chilling revelations in the report. Investigators identified massacre sites across the country and assembled evidence that thousands of Hutu civilians had been slaughtered by Kagame's Tutsi-led army. And finally, criminal investigators listed potential targets for indictment, including Kagame himself and several of his top men.

At the time the report was delivered to the prosecutor, the investigative team had recruited a hundred sources; forty-one of these people had given the team signed statements, though they risked their lives by coming forward. The team listed a total of 518 potential witnesses across four continents. In 2013 and 2014, I had obtained and read dozens of other ICTR witness statements, many of which provided harrowing details of crimes committed by Kagame's army. In those statements, witnesses claimed that RPF soldiers and intelligence agents had lured Rwandan Hutus to execution sites where they killed them with hoes, grenades or guns, or transported victims to kill zones aboard trucks. Many witnesses admitted to their role in these crimes. The witness statements described a parallel universe to the "Kagame as savior" narrative, yet until now these stories of what his army did during the genocide have been told only through unofficial channels, by victims' families and renegade Tutsi soldiers.

Amid the suffering and grief in post-genocide Rwanda, most people simply wished to believe a more palatable construction of history: the story of a morally disciplined RPF rescuing Rwanda from the brink, having fought to save Tutsis from a genocide that was centrally planned by the former Habyarimana government and carried out by willing Hutu executioners. This story was easier to comprehend than what actually happened, especially by those trying to create moral sense out of the madness of war. The accepted version exploited the suffering of Tutsis, demonized Hutus and wrote off crimes perpetrated against Hutus by the RPF as justified, because they were considered retaliatory. It also allowed Kagame, his political party and his armed forces to consolidate power, pocket billions of dollars in aid and take credit for an economic miracle. Its belief in this narrative of the genocide allowed the international community to stand by as RPF commanders unleashed war in neighboring Congo, where millions have died from violence and war-related diseases since 1996. It also allowed Kagame to operate with impunity at home, where his regime has shut down free speech, killed and jailed critics, and targeted opponents abroad for censure or death—even journalists such as myself.

But the dynamics of violence in Rwanda have been much more complex than what we know from mainstream literature and media. After the presidential plane went down, Hutu elites in rural areas—drawn from military, political and administrative structures—operated in a political vacuum at first. Some of them resisted the call to kill Tutsis, but many others urged Hutu militia and civilians to murder and rape. These crimes were committed publicly, in broad daylight, and with little or no sense of remorse or concern about repercussions.

In areas seized by the RPF or already under its control, its soldiers and intelligence agents worked with similar ethnic zeal, but they were more discreet:

they cordoned off areas and killed Hutus secretly, with great precision. They operated mobile death squads, massacring Hutus in their villages. They brought large groups of Hutus to areas where NGOs and the UN agencies were not permitted to go. Under the cover of night, they transported displaced Hutus by truck, killed them, and burned their bodies with gasoline and gas oil. These atrocities took place mainly near Gabiro, a military training barracks in Rwanda's Akagera National Park. Portions of the park became outdoor crematoriums, and human ashes were spread in its lakes. It was mass murder leaving barely a trace.

While there have been various attempts to estimate the number of Tutsis killed during the genocide—historians and rights groups put the figure between 500,000 and one million—the scale and scope of violence meted out against Hutus at the hands of the RPF is largely unknown and will likely remain so for years to come. There continues to be a conspiracy of silence around the issue. But one would be hard pressed to find a more radically violent regime that is as internationally admired and showered with praise as the government of the Rwandan Patriotic Front. By their actions, Kagame and his apparatus forfeited their moral authority to govern and should have been indicted for crimes as soon as UN investigators had collected the evidence. That did not happen. When Carla Del Ponte made it clear that she intended to indict RPF commanders, she was removed as prosecutor, at the behest of the United States.

In an act that was extraordinarily deferential to Kagame, her successor, Hassan Bubacar Jallow, employed delaying tactics over pursuing those indictments. He eventually endorsed the idea that the RPF had waged a liberation war that had ended the genocide and therefore had earned the right to prosecute itself, no questions asked. He also recommended that key cases against the RPF should be transferred to Kigali, Rwanda's capital. He made it equally clear that in the interests of "national reconciliation" he would use his extensive prosecutorial discretion to target for indictment only Hutu *génocidaires*, whom he believed bore the greatest responsibility for the violence. In effect, he granted Kagame de facto immunity from prosecution, which was something the United States, the RPF's closest ally after the genocide was over, had angled for.

Months after Clarise Habimana sent me the first e-mail, my ICTR whistleblower sent me another document, which revealed the 2003 deal brokered by

Rwanda and the US ambassador for war crimes, Pierre Prosper.[2] The agreement effectively gave the RPF a free pass. The legacy of the ICTR as it wound down in December 2015 was clear: the United Nations had successfully protected an elite group of mass murderers and allowed the court itself to become an instrument of injustice.

The UN documents leaked to me amount to historical vindication for Kagame's victims. They also stand as a testament to the courage of young Tutsis who had been part of a brutal regime yet broke free, risking censure and death to tell the truth. Kagame has grossly miscalculated the mix of fury and shame that many of his men felt after committing acts of depravity. A soldier who was part of a mobile killing unit in Ngondore told me that before they were shot, dozens of Hutu men, women and children were tied up and forced to sit on the edge of a steep hill near a tea plantation, their backs facing the soldiers.[3] He admitted that, day after day, it was the same operation: he and the other soldiers methodically unloaded their guns into the bodies of a total of two thousand civilians on that hill in April 1994. The memory of these executions has never left him.

In 1997 I went to Congo and met refugees in the forests south of Kisangani and in transit camps. I traveled to the equatorial town of Mbandaka then down to the capital, Kinshasa. Then I went back to Goma and crossed the border on foot to Gisenyi, Rwanda, before going through Ruhengeri to Kigali and its surrounding rural areas. That trip, in particular my foray into the Congolese jungle, was a crucible where I discovered a level of suffering that overwhelmed me. For a very long time, I doubted if I could ever truly tell the story of what I heard and saw.

It took me two decades to reorient myself, to shake down the emotions and observations from that trip. But I continued to speak to victims and observers of the violence that has gripped the region. Over the last five years I have devoted myself full-time to understanding the dynamics of Kagame's violence prior to, during and after the genocide. What has inspired me throughout my reporting is the power of memory and the way it works to conquer fear. This book is a testament to the courage of some two hundred direct and contextual witnesses of RPF crimes, including officials who worked at the UN tribunal set up in the aftermath of the genocide. I am grateful to all those who shared their stories and let me into their profound inner world. As their testimony reveals, Kagame did not commit these crimes alone. He operated—still operates—with significant political cover. I continue to be astonished by all the ways he has got away with it.

Violence is never abstract for the victim or the perpetrator. *In Praise of Blood* puts a human face on the violence in Rwanda and Congo. It names those alleged to have orchestrated the most heinous of crimes. For reasons of safety, however, I cannot identify by their real names most of the witnesses who talked to me or provided me with documents for this book. Kagame remains a powerful, protected and dangerous figure.

1

KAGAME'S INNER STATION

The soldiers chased us across the country. They had guns and bombs. We ran and fell over each other. We crawled. Some refugees suffocated. Many of us could not go any further. People would stop along the road. They would give up and die slowly. A mother would lie down with her baby. Her heart was still beating—I could see her chest rise—but her eyes would close. I had my baby on my back. I couldn't hold her in my arms. I felt dead. I was starving and sick. I could not move anymore. We had almost no clothes on, and nothing on our feet except sores. We were dirty. We smelled. I wanted it to be over. I wanted to die.
— Elise, a Hutu survivor from Kasese camp

ELISE AND HER BABY WERE RWANDAN REFUGEES IN ZAIRE. FOR MORE than six months they were human prey, hunted across swamps and hostile jungle.[1] The soldiers chasing them were Tutsi forces from Paul Kagame's army. His troops, backed by allies in Uganda, invaded in October 1996 and attacked Hutu refugee camps inside Zaire's border—an act that formidable intelligentsia in the West deemed inevitable and wholly justified.[2] About half the population in the sprawling camps—at least 500,000 refugees— went back to Rwanda to face their fate. The other half fled westward, pushed by gunfire and fearing slaughter.[3] The refugees who fled deeper into Zaire poured onto paths and into forests they did not know; they ran and hid. They ate shrubs and battled snakes. They settled into makeshift camps, con- tracted cholera, typhoid, diphtheria, dengue fever and malaria. Eventually Kagame's soldiers, with their assault rifles and rifle-launched grenades, would find them again and massacre as many as they could. Those who managed to survive and escape were chased again.[4] Elise and her daughter trekked several hundred kilometers from Kashusha camp, near Bukavu, to Kasese, south of Kisangani.

Imagine being stalked from Frankfurt to Paris. Starving, stripped of every shred of dignity and hope a human being can cling to, with a child to carry. How did it come to this? Who committed this massive crime against Elise and thousands of others?

On May 18, 1997, Kagame and his allies overthrew Mobutu Sese Seko, whose thirty-two-year reign in Zaire had come to symbolize moral decay. But there was more to Mobutu's demise than retribution for his villainy. He had outlived his usefulness. The Cold War was over and he had gone from being a Western stooge in the 1960s to a pariah in the 1990s. The West wanted Zaire open for business. And so did Rwanda, whose natural resources were scarce in comparison with Zaire's. But the invasion came at a steep human price. Hundreds of thousands of Zaireans were displaced during the military sweep and another 200,000 Rwandan Hutu refugees were unaccounted for.[5] At the end of May, a week after Mobutu was toppled, I headed for the region, now renamed Democratic Republic of Congo, to cover the humanitarian crisis. At the time, I was a reporter for Radio France Internationale (RFI), born and raised in Quebec but living with my new husband in Paris.

If I had not crossed a broken bridge in northeastern Congo, I would never have had a clue about Elise's ordeal. Weeks after she had given up hope but still miraculously survived, I traveled south of Kisangani, on the Congo River, with a group of Congolese volunteers from the United Nations, Doctors Without Borders (MSF) and the Red Cross. We were headed to the abandoned camps north of Ubundu, a river port along a railway line where Hutu refugees had scattered into the dense equatorial jungle after a series of attacks in April 1997. The Congolese humanitarians I was with were part of ongoing search and rescue missions to find survivors in the jungle; the volunteers were there, day in and day out, to provide the means of life to people on the edge of death.

When we arrived at the dilapidated bridge south of the river that spanned a deep gorge on the edge of the jungle, I lost my nerve. The bridge was treacherous and wounded from years of neglect. It was everything that was wrong with the country. Its base was a metal grid that had gaping holes in it. That structure was covered with rough wooden planks, but there didn't seem to be enough of them for a vehicle to get across. I stared down into the gorge, at the snakelike tree roots and the sharp rocks along its verge, at the black abyss far below.

"We'll just have to move some planks," our driver said matter-of-factly.

"We can't get across this," I said.

"Yes we can. We do it all the time. We just move the planks as we go. They're not nailed down." He wiped beads of sweat from his forehead.

"No way. I'm not crossing this."

The driver and aid workers looked at me and at each other. I could either go back the way I had come—alone and with nothing—or risk the crossing.

Nyana, one of the aid workers, shook her head. "You won't go anywhere in Congo if you're scared." She was dressed in a plain, oversized white T-shirt and loose-fitting acid-washed jeans. She had tightly coiled hair and cheekbones that were sharp and wide.

"I'm not crossing this bridge in the truck," I said.

"Hold on to the railing and walk along the side, then. It's narrow, but you can do it," the driver suggested.

"I'll walk behind you," Nyana offered.

I stared at the bridge. I didn't want to let them down and I couldn't turn back. I needed to get hold of myself.

I set off along the slim metal beam at the side of the bridge, grasping the railing tightly with one hand, setting one foot in front of the other, hoping my boots wouldn't get tangled. I scouted for places where there were more planks, spots I could land if I fell. My palms were so slippery, I curled my fingers around the railing's rusty underside where I could feel something wet and mossy. Nyana kept pace behind me.

When we reached the other side, I was lightheaded and out of breath. We turned to watch the driver edge the truck over the loose planks, at times getting out to lift the planks he'd just crossed to fill in the gaps ahead. Suddenly his back tires spit out two planks, one of which fell into the gorge. The back end of his vehicle immediately dropped into the hole. But he kept his calm as he revved and swerved slightly to pull the vehicle's hind end back onto the bridge, then made it the rest of the way.

We got back into the truck and traveled for another twenty minutes until the road became a sunken track and the jungle narrowed in on us, its giant trees and ferns forcing us to abandon our ride and continue on foot.

The ground cover had a curious smell that reminded me of lighting matches. Woody vines snaked their way up trees and broad, arched leaves bent into our faces. We had to use our hands and arms to clear the way. It was so damp and dim I delighted in any random beam of light that shone through on us. At times the sounds were deafening: the crackling of termites, like dry twigs thrown into a campfire, the purr of mantids, the birdlike songs of crickets, the chittering of bats and the screech of a lone monkey. It was the most fascinating place I'd ever been.

Lines of sweat dripped down my back. My underwear and pants, soaked as though I'd jumped into a pool, chafed my crotch and waist. I didn't dare complain as my companions trudged along without a word.

We walked for an hour and a half until we reached a clearing in the forest where an aid worker wearing a UN sash appeared. He was a husky man with a raspy voice, who carried a walkie-talkie and a megaphone. He'd been doing his usual rounds in the jungle, searching for refugees who were still in hiding.

"Rwandan refugee, Rwandan refugee," he called. "It's the Red Cross and the United Nations. We have food and medicine for you. Please come out of the forest. No one will hurt you."

He told us to walk a few kilometers farther, toward the railroad tracks along the river, where we'd find a makeshift camp for refugees who had emerged from hiding. "It's been a busy morning," he said.

And so we did, bearing east for another hour, until at last we came upon dozens and dozens of survivors—mostly women and children—sitting or lying on patches of tarpaulin in a clearing. A few aid workers were already at the site. Smoke curled from two campfires. It was eerily quiet, the scene like a film unraveling in slow motion before me. The refugees were barely clothed. Some sat with wool blankets over their heads and shoulders and tucked under their chins. Others lay with their legs splayed and their forearms covering their eyes to block the sun. One boy was swaddled, only his eyes visible, staring somewhere, never seeming to blink. Several people were eating beans and rice from a large aluminum pot near one of the campfires. Beside that were bowls and a jerry can for water. A few aid workers carried very young, naked children into a tent.

In the surprise of coming upon the refugees, I lost Nyana and my bearings. For a few minutes I didn't know what to do, who among these refugees would be well enough or willing to talk. I was an intruder here. At last I began to walk around, the only voices the low murmurs of Congolese aid workers. A few of them were able to speak Kinyarwanda, the language of Rwandans, but most spoke Swahili.

I introduced myself to Jean-Bosco, a 10-year-old boy with a round face and dull eyes. He told me that when Kagame's troops surrounded Ubundu and began to shoot at them, he and his father ran with several hundred others to the Lualaba River. As they crossed the river, his father was unable to keep his head above water. He let go of Jean-Bosco's hand and drowned before his son's eyes. These deaths on the river, I learned, were a tragedy the refugees had endured only a few weeks before coming to Kasese, where they were attacked again. After the refugees had desperately thrown themselves into the water, some tried to save others who could not swim. Others gave up on life entirely and let themselves drown. Countless children and babies died. Jean-Bosco had no idea where his mother was. They'd become separated more than eight months earlier, when the camps in eastern Zaire were first attacked. He didn't know his mother's family name. "I don't want to go back to Rwanda," he said, staring at the ground. He said he felt dizzy and his chest hurt.[6]

I didn't want to ask him any more questions. I didn't know what else to say. I turned to the aid workers, who whispered to me in French about some other children, including Eugène, an orphan from Butare. He was small-boned, had bloodshot eyes and suffered from scabies, a contagious, parasitic infection that inserts itself in the armpits, behind the knees and around buttocks, and causes relentless itching. An aid worker looked at him and wondered in French if the problem was jiggers, chigo fleas that burrow under the skin and lay eggs. Jiggers, he told me, can cause infection that leads to amputation and in some cases death.

Eugène's Hutu mother had died during the mass exodus from Rwanda to Zaire in 1994. He never knew his father. He'd lived in a refugee camp in Bukavu and had fled attacks there in October 1996. "I ran with the others, then ran again in the forest. It has not stopped until now," he said, his voice thick with emotion. Eugène told me he wanted to find a family in Zaire to take him in.[7]

Nyana reappeared just then to check on me, then led me to a little girl on the other side of the camp. She crouched down to the girl's level and wrapped her arms around her blanketed shoulders. "This is Mutesi. Her name means 'princess.'"

Mutesi leaned her head against Nyana's arm. Her eyes, glazed as a porcelain doll's, were deeply seated in their sockets. The corners of her lips were cracked and she had wrinkles, little lines that radiated from her mouth to her cheeks, like scars. There were red, scaly sores on her feet.

"Mayi," Nyana called to one of the aid workers, motioning for water.

Mutesi was malnourished. Her tongue was white, her woolly hair reddish. She was lacking protein. Her skin was raw and flaky and sunken. When she drank, I saw that her fingernails were like spoons. Nyana stayed close by Mutesi's side, talking to her in hushed tones. I imagined her telling the girl stories the way you would with any child that age.

Some of the children looked as though they were on the verge of death, and I did not dare approach because of a stupor in their regard that frightened me. I tried to take stock of everything and contain my emotions, even as my insides were roiling. I had a job to do, and these aid workers were counting on me to get the news out.

I turned and saw a frail woman, hunched on a tarpaulin, looking at me with expectant eyes. I went to her and introduced myself. She nodded and said something in Kinyarwanda. I called over an aid worker, who translated. The woman's name was Vestine. She was a teenager, barely seventeen years old, and said she had survived an RPF attack on Biaro. Her hair was brush-cut and she wore a dirty tank top that showed her skeletal chest. The skin under her eyes and around her mouth was worn and thin, making her look decades older than she was.

I asked her what had happened in Biaro.

"The soldiers approached the other side of the camp. They fired on us and we began to flee. I was not caught in the line of fire. My family was, though. They all died ... my parents, brothers and sisters. I have no one now. I am all alone."[8]

Her voice was shaking, yet she kept eye contact as she told her story. Her steady regard stirred a kind of chaos in me that I have never forgotten. I would look for Vestine when I returned to Kisangani. I found her in a transit camp there, waiting for the UN's planned transport of refugees back to Rwanda. Her stoicism frightened me. The last time we spoke, she took my hand and said, "I don't care where I go."

Vestine had been among an estimated eighty-five thousand Hutu refugees who had settled in Biaro and Kasese I and II camps south of Kisangani. Many of them were too sick and weak to move, much less run, Nyana and her colleagues said. The children were malnourished, some of them severely. The elderly were drawing their last breaths. Women and babies suffered a range of problems, from cholera or malaria or scabies or infections from leech, vermin or snake bites. Sometimes Nyana slept in the camps because it took up to half a day to reach these remote areas in the forest. Rwandan forces had occupied Kisangani since March, and several detachments of soldiers were stationed in strategic areas in the bush.

More than a month earlier, in late April, RPF forces had cordoned off the camps and ordered Nyana and the other Congolese volunteers out. The RPF had already recruited several local villagers to attack the refugees with bayonets and machetes, which prompted counteraccusations that refugees had attacked the locals first. Nyana refused to leave the area, staying on in a village just outside the RPF-demarcated zone because she had developed close friendships with several refugee families. On April 22, RPF soldiers moved in, spraying the camps with machine-gun fire and tossing grenades, killing thousands of people and scattering an unknown number of others.[9] Detachments of RPF troops searched for survivors in the jungle who were wounded or terrified. When men were caught, they were interrogated to determine if they were educated or successful. Many of these individuals were taken away and butchered, refugees told me. The troops had brought tanks of gasoline and bundles of firewood to secluded areas, and fires were reported to have burned for several days.[10]

Despite the influx of aid workers and some international staff, when I arrived, weeks later, the forests south of Kisangani remained dangerous. Two young aid workers told me they knew where the mass graves were but that Rwandan soldiers were still monitoring these spots. Zaire, renamed the Democratic Republic of Congo, was still at war, just at a different stage.

On the same day in the forest, I met a refugee in his late twenties who'd been shot in the buttocks. His wound had become infected and he could barely walk. He said that RPF troops had fired at the refugees, and after he was hit, he ran into the jungle to hide. Within a few hours a Tutsi soldier speaking Kinyarwanda found him lying in a glade and told him to get up and run as fast as he could. He hobbled away obediently, wondering if this soldier was too troubled to actually kill him or whether he wanted the renewed pleasure of a hunt.[11]

His question haunted me for years. After having interviewed a number of Rwandan soldiers from intelligence units and regular battalions, my sense is that many of them did not want to commit murder, but that it was RPF policy to eliminate Hutus. By May 1997, Doctors Without Borders announced that some 190,000 people in the camps I visited, and in other areas of the forest, were missing.[12] There was growing evidence that these missing refugees had been slaughtered. Years later I would interview a man named Jean-Baptiste about what happened beneath the canopy of that equatorial jungle. The brutality he described—that he was part of—recalled Kurtz's inner station in Joseph Conrad's *Heart of Darkness*. But the demigod behind these crimes was not a colonial figure nor a creature of fiction. Paul Kagame, who sent the kill teams into Zaire, was a venerated Rwandan refugee raised in Uganda, an African whose ambitions turned out to be as bloody as they were expansionist.

Jean-Baptiste was a Tutsi from a killing unit in Kagame's army. He told me that after RPF troops overran UN camps on the eastern border with Zaire in October 1996, units like his moved westward across the length of the country, chasing refugees and creating inner stations in the jungle. Jean-Baptiste said he committed unspeakable crimes with his unit, crimes he would later regret so much he would have to confess. One of the first major killing grounds was Kasindi, which sits on the edge of Congo's lush Virunga park, just south of the Rwenzori Mountains.[13]

"We stopped in Kasindi and conducted cleanup operations throughout the area. We got rid of everyone considered an enemy: that meant all Hutu," Jean-Baptiste said. "We found the refugees in the forest. They were starving and sick. There was no water or food for these people. But we were told to eliminate them. So we killed them all. We even killed those who were dying, with perhaps only a few minutes to live. We didn't use guns on the weakest. We used traditional weapons like *agafuni* [hoes] to finish them off. Most of the killings of refugees took place in the jungle. But if refugees tried to hide in towns, we identified them and went after them. At this stage, there were no ex-FAR [Hutu soldiers] in the area. There were only civilians."

By January 1997, Jean-Baptiste had moved with other mobile units to Bafwasende and Waine-Rukula, on the north bank of the Congo River, where he says more than ten thousand refugees were killed in one month alone and dumped in mass graves. To his horror, orders soon came to dig up those bodies and bring them to Banalia, a region farther north.

"I was part of a team that unearthed corpses from mass graves. We worked day and night for a long time to take bodies to other locations to be inciner-ated. It was about the time when people were calling for an investigation to confirm whether indeed there had been massacres of Hutu refugees in the area. Rwanda of course was denying the allegations and we had to destroy the evidence. We needed to hide the proof.

"Bodies were decomposing. We did this with our own hands, with no protection or gloves. Our superiors were behind us. These commanders hit us from time to time. It's hard for you to imagine, but we had to put corpses on our backs and dump them onto trucks. When we were discouraged, they would beat us and force us to carry on. I became ill afterward."

An RPF soldier familiar with my research on Congo had introduced me to Jean-Baptiste, and we met at an undisclosed location outside Rwanda. Every day, he lives with the fear that Kagame's agents will find and eliminate him. It was excruciating for him to reveal these horrifying moments to a stranger like me. Yet he wanted to do so. His courage was sobering. From him I got the briefest, clearest glimpse of our capacity for depravity and good, how it can coexist in the same soul.

We were in the forest, south of Kisangani, for what seemed an interminable moment that day. The experience left behind a series of images that still come back to me when I least expect it. As the heavy sun started to fall, we headed back to the city the way we had come: under the cover of bush and amid the hiss of insects and the cackle of birds and other animals I could not see. We found our truck where the driver had parked it, surrounded by bamboo, and crossed the bridge again. I once again walked along the edge, gripping the rail tightly but trembling less.

We reached the port, said goodbye to our driver and waited for the ferry to take us to the right bank of the Congo River. When we finally boarded the rusty barge, it was dark. There were only a few passengers on board, and none of the boxes of dried fish, sacks of grain, wheelbarrows and goats and chickens that we had pressed up against as we'd crossed in the morning. I could no longer see the clumps of purple hyacinth along the water's swampy edge or the hovering butterflies. I breathed in the engine oil and felt a clammy breeze against my cheek.

Nyana and I were mostly silent on the way home. We were exhausted. We'd known each other for only a few days, but I already admired her. She had an empathetic imagination that enabled her to assess people's needs in extraordinary ways. She had a broad conception of humanity and no patience for the persistent whining of the expatriate workers with the NGOs and UN agencies. She reminded me that we are all connected; it doesn't matter where we are from. In her, I saw hope amid the turmoil. Both of us were young. She had been trying to finish her agronomy studies in the dying months of Mobutu's reign; I had only begun my career as a journalist a few years earlier. We could not have been more culturally different, yet we understood each other in subtle ways and shared the most private details of our lives. With me she was also able to express her fear. "Look at what the Rwandans have done to their brothers and sisters here," she said. "They came all this way just to kill them. What will happen to us?"

She understood I was struggling to tell an important story and that I had my doubts as to whether I could truly convey the agonies I'd witnessed in the jungle. I believed I had also seen the true face of the Rwandan Patriotic Front. I'd seen how efficient it was at annihilating human life. I wanted to reveal how refugees had been chased, injured, dehumanized and destroyed by a regime the West was holding up as a model for a new era in African politics. But my own shortcomings—coupled with a physical fear of the RPF and a strong sense of its moral invincibility in the wake of the genocide—began to overwhelm me. Fear conspired against my best intentions. I have continued to try, though, even when I have paid dearly for my efforts.

I awoke the next day still tired. I dragged myself out of bed and explored Kisangani, its dirt roads lined with palm trees, which gave way to wide colonial avenues, its white stucco buildings streaked with gray. The city was full of diamond counters—little shops where people traded mostly under the table. *The King of Gems is Here* read one sign. A car showroom for Peugeots and Mercedes was abandoned, its windows smashed. Gas stations were empty.

The sizzle of the forest still stirred in my head. Within thirty-six hours of returning, my body began to explode, as though I'd been poisoned or bitten by a spider. More likely I had picked up a violent gastrointestinal flu, yet it seemed more than that. My back and buttocks broke out in welts. My eyelids became red and swollen, and spilled mucus. My body shook and my temperature soared. I became delirious. It occurred to me that I might die in Kisangani without saying goodbye to the people I loved, all of whom wondered why I had left them in the first place.

Nyana checked on me regularly. At first she seemed alarmed, but reassured me on the second day when I began tolerating rehydration salts. On the third day I emerged from my bed and began to work again. We made shorter excursions into the forests and visited transit camps. I met more orphans getting off ferries along the river, and talked to dozens of displaced Congolese housed in an abandoned hospital called Site H. I conducted a series of nonstarter interviews with Western NGO and UN workers in Kisangani, who were unwilling to state unequivocally how this horrifying situation had come to pass. They simply would not point fingers. I did not blame them. The entire country had been taken hostage by Rwanda, and Kisangani was now occupied by the RPF.

I contacted my colleagues at the Africa desk at Radio France Internationale in Paris by satellite phone. Initially I filed reports to RFI on the humanitarian relief and repatriation efforts in Congo. In those reports I made only oblique references to Rwanda's leading role in the rebel alliance that had overthrown Mobutu—the Alliance of Democratic Forces for the Liberation of Congo-Zaire (AFDL). I highlighted the attacks on refugees south of Kisangani but did not directly refer to Kagame's soldiers being behind the killings. James McKinley and Howard French had already done impressive reporting on the AFDL massacres of Hutu refugees for the *New York Times*.[14] And there was brief coverage by the *Washington Post* and the *Boston Globe*. I was concerned about how much I could say while I was still in Kisangani, highly visible as I moved around with Congolese aid workers. I did not want to put Nyana and her colleagues in more peril. And yet I wanted to report on what I had seen. I decided to go alone to Mbandaka, a quiet fishing town near the equator on the western edge of the country. AFDL troops, led by Rwandan soldiers, had killed and dumped the bodies of hundreds of refugees in the river there on May 13. The slaughter was still fresh and the entire village was raw and reeling from the carnage.

I visited a gruff Belgian priest named Père Herman at his home on the outskirts of town. He'd lived in Zaire for decades, maintaining his faith and surrounding himself in his dank, screened-in porch with transistor radios and walkie-talkies on which he kept track of the world. He loved his Congolese parishioners but was now contemplating returning to Europe. He could barely contain his moral outrage about the country's new reality. "There was a trail of dead here, kilometers long," he said, shaking his head. "We warned everyone about the AFDL's arrival. The international community did not do a thing to stop it. We asked the United Nations for help. They did not come. We asked the World Food Programme and the International Committee of the Red Cross. Nobody came. We had to deal with this ourselves."

After I left the priest, I came upon a nervous, middle-aged fisherman on the desolate streets who had witnessed killings near the port. He said soldiers speaking Kinyarwanda announced that refugees should come out of the forest, promising to organize passage home to Rwanda for them. "As soon as the refugees appeared, the killings [began and] lasted for two days," he said. "The AFDL warned Congolese villagers that if they were caught sheltering Rwandan refugees in their homes, even babies, we could be killed too. So the people we were taking care of had to leave our homes. We feared dying ourselves." He said he had never witnessed such brutality in his life. One soldier took a Hutu baby and smashed her head against a tree, killing her instantly.

I also found a Rwandan survivor from Mbandaka, a 14-year-old boy named François who was later transferred to a transit camp in Kisangani. "What did I see, you ask?" he began. "I was coming from the market when I saw the AFDL firing on people. I fled into the woods with the others. We saw many dead bodies. The soldiers were killing men, women and children. There were mothers leaving their babies. Some babies were buried. [But for most] there was no one to take care of them."

François's account of the trail of corpses was lucid, harrowing and first-hand. Using a satellite phone from Kisangani, I called CBC Radio in Toronto and filed a short item that was aired on *World Report*, broadcast through-out Canada. I reported that AFDL troops had entered Mbandaka, along the Congo River, and killed some 200 men, women and children, all refugees, in mid-May at the town's port. I also reported that between 500 and 700 other refugees had been slaughtered in nearby Wenge, along the Ruki River. Finally, I said, the people behind the slaughter were Rwandan members of Laurent Kabila's AFDL forces.

I was staying in one of Kisangani's old, roomy villas on the right bank of the river. My bedroom, which smelled of mold, was at the back of the house and gave onto a garden. The streets were empty after dark because there was a curfew in place. It was so quiet that every little noise was startling. I was up late one chokingly humid night reading Shiva Naipaul's *North of South: An African Journey*, a collection of essays and travel writing, the room light jar-ringly bright against the pitch-black sky.

Around midnight, I heard a pop just outside my window, then another pop and another—sounds that melted into each other, like a motor spitting. It took me a moment to realize it was a machine gun firing, tinny popcorn bursts of sound, like scary, quick taps against a strip of aluminum.

I hit the floor and crawled to the light switch on the wall, where I stood up quickly, legs shaking, and turned off the light. I hit the floor again and lay there, barely able to breathe, wondering if someone was about to enter my room. No one did, but the popping kept on. I got up and ran into the main area of the house to search for my roommate, an international aid worker from Switzerland who been in Kisangani for months. A guard who'd been standing watch outside soon joined us. He was terrified. When the shooting stopped, we all shook our heads in bewilderment. Kisangani had been taken in March without a fight. Why had someone shot at this house?

My thoughts were racing. It was possible that the shooting was totally unrelated to me. But I feared it was not. I took it as a stark warning to shut up and get out of Kisangani as soon as possible. I did not want to put my friends in jeopardy, so I began packing my bags.

One of the hardest moments on that trip was saying goodbye to Nyana at the airport. As we hugged each other, I told her I'd be back someday, although I didn't know if that was true. At the entrance to the terminal, I glanced back to see her still standing there. I put my bag back down and made a circle sign with my fingers, trying to tell her that life was a cycle and that we'd see each other again. She nodded, but her eyes showed me what she was feeling as I walked away to a safer place: terror of what was in store for her and others in Kisangani who had nowhere safe to go. I thought I might embarrass her if I kept looking back, but I couldn't stop. She had taught me not to turn away from people's suffering.

I flew to the capital, Kinshasa, and checked into the Memling, one of two hotels in the city with electricity, running water and TV. I was grateful to take a warm bath. The eight-story building had a view of the muddy Congo River and was crawling with soldiers, mercenaries, US businessmen, Russian pilots and Middle Eastern diamond dealers. Men with paunches hanging over their belts did business in the dimly lit bar and women made money there, dressed in tight skirts and spike-heeled boots in an array of colors, their polyester knit tops bursting open to reveal lacy bras and bustiers, yellow-gold chains around their necks and wrists. Some wore wigs of shoulder-length straight hair with spiky bangs.

The Belgian embassy and the local Rotary Club were holding an event together upstairs in a banquet room the day after I arrived. I had no suitable clothing in my luggage, but I got myself in by saying I wanted to do a story on business in Laurent Kabila's new Congo. I was so hungry I attacked the food table, scarfing down slices of roast beef, Gouda, deviled eggs and soft rolls, topping it off with Haut-Médoc and sparkling water. I couldn't manage to pry myself from the buffet and didn't care who noticed. Eventually a man in a smart suit approached me. He was francophone but eager to show me he also spoke English, and said he was a Congolese of Portuguese descent, born and raised in Zaire.

I introduced myself and told him I wanted to write some business stories.

"You've come to the right place," he said, explaining that he'd worked for Mobutu in "import-export"—in what area of commerce, he would not divulge. He said he had no particular allegiance and was now easily getting contracts with Kabila's new government and its Rwandan backers.

He clearly knew a lot of people. I told him I wanted to meet some mining executives.

"I can help you with that."

He seemed too eager, though, and making my excuses, I left him in order to talk to others.

Thirty minutes later, he found me again at the buffet table, filling my dessert plate.

"Enjoying the spread?"

I nodded, then asked: "What about America Mineral Fields? It's listed on the Toronto Stock Exchange. And another outfit called Bechtel. Any officials from those companies here?"

He laughed. "Not so fast." He suggested we could meet later to discuss his contacts. "Tonight, downstairs, 6 p.m."

I reluctantly agreed, and later I waited for him at the edge of the bar, where I could watch the main desk and entrance. He showed up at 6:10 and waved me over. When I reached him, he said he had a car ready to take us to a restaurant. He was wearing jeans and a casual shirt. His waist was thick. His face was oily and pocked.

"Oh no," I said. "I'd rather stay here. There's a curfew and it's getting dark. I don't want to get into a car at this hour."

He insisted. He said he knew everyone in Kinshasa and could give me a list of contacts a mile long. He suggested a good Italian restaurant just down the road and I told him I'd meet him there in ten minutes but only to talk about mining deals, weapons dealers and gunrunners. When I arrived, he had already ordered a bottle of red wine, and wasn't interested in talking about business or politics. He was interested in women. After making a disparaging comment about my looks, comparing me to a teenager from the Peace Corps, he began to talk about his sexual exploits.

I told him I had to leave, and I did. When I got back to my hotel room, I got into the shower to wash off his aura. I watched some TV, sulked at my own naïveté and went to bed. After midnight, the phone rang. It was him. "You fucking bitch. You insulted me. I know everyone in your hotel. I know the Memling's owners. I can get into your room. I'm coming for you now."

I slammed the phone down and called reception in a panic. Then I contacted Pierre, an AFP reporter who had a room down the hall on the same floor. He came running and was kind enough to watch over me for a few hours. I called my husband. I wanted to hear his voice, but I didn't have the nerve to tell him what had happened that night. I was afraid he'd worry and urge me to come home right away. We talked about other things. I fell asleep after 4 a.m. I never heard from the man again.

I wanted to leave Kinshasa as soon as I could. But I also wanted to flesh out some troubling details on how the Rwandan-led rebel alliance had swept across Zaire so quickly, and do a profile on their financial enablers. Details were emerging as to how the United States government and Western-backed business had assisted the rebel army at the height of the refugee killings. The information was limited but solid: On April 16, 1997, more than a month before Mobutu was toppled and less than a week before Rwandan troops were to machine-gun and slash refugees south of Kisangani, Laurent Kabila's finance minister, Mwana Nanga Mwampanga, signed a $1-billion mining deal with America Mineral Fields (AMF), whose headquarters was in Hope, Arkansas, President Bill Clinton's hometown.[15] Jean-Raymond Boulle, the company's CEO, was close enough to Clinton to receive an invitation to his first inauguration. Boulle gave rebels the use of his Lear jet and advanced $1 million in mineral taxes and fees to Kabila in return for a contract to rehabilitate and develop the country's zinc and copper mines, a project that was estimated to be worth $16 billion.[16]

On April 17, the New York Times ran a story boldly stating that the Zairean rebels' new allies were men armed with briefcases:

A week after Shaba Province fell to Laurent Kabila and his rebel troops, mining company executives are swarming around this region of mineral riches and signing lucrative deals despite the uncertainty hanging over the nation's future. Less than two days after Lubumbashi was captured last Thursday, the executives were already flying into the city aboard private jets and setting up shop in the Hotel Karavia.

They could be seen meeting at poolside and over meals with the rebels' finance minister and the newly appointed Governor of the province. The stakes here are enormous. The province has billions of dollars in untapped mineral reserves. The rolling fertile land holds millions of tons of cobalt, copper and zinc.

A few days after Rwandan soldiers massacred refugees in Mbandaka—and a week before Kabila seized the capital—Boulle flew a group of investment bankers, market analysts and US officials to an area of Congo under rebel control. The US officials were Robin Sanders, Director of African Affairs for the National Security Council, and Congresswoman Cynthia McKinney, a Democrat from Georgia.[17] In a matter of weeks, I'd get hold of a promotional video from AMF aimed at investors interested in making a profit from mining deals in the war-riven country, sent to me by a market analyst friend of mine in Vancouver.[18]

"The government alone is not going to be able to resolve all the problems that the area possesses," Congresswoman McKinney stated in the video. "It's going to take a public-private partnership and it's going to take a strong business climate, and strong investment. Investment, though, with a social conscience. Investment that cares about the environment and work environment, and, of course, the government and people in the area." At the same time, just prior to the fall of Kinshasa, the Canadian group Tenke Mining paid $50 million to Gécamines, the state mining outfit that was already under the control of the rebels. That these business deals were all being negotiated in the wake of serious bloodletting did not seem to register with the US administration or Canadian and American business interests.

During the rebel advance across Zaire, I'd kept in close contact with a mining analyst in South Africa who worked as an intermediary between investors and rebels selling mining concessions. His company was tracking political and military developments in the country, and regularly fed news agencies and rich investors with detailed updates about the AFDL's territorial gains. The mining analyst had an acute grasp of history and knew all the major players. He never wanted to be quoted by name, but he was willing to give me deep background and never minced words. He would eventually tell me flatly that Western investors knew but did not care about the body count.[19]

"The expression being bandied about in political and financial circles was that these refugees were dead men walking," said the analyst. "Those people are gone. It's disgusting, but they [the Rwandan soldiers] killed them. Kabila allowed himself to be at the forefront of ethnic cleansing. The Rwandans clearly had as their chief agenda to create a *cordon sanitaire*. You have to remember that those Rwandans [the bulk of Kagame's army] had spent many years living in Uganda waiting for their chance to get back in Rwanda." He was referring to the decades in exile Kagame and his military colleagues spent after their Tutsi families had been forced to flee violence in Rwanda in 1959. "The last thing they were going to do is let displaced people from Rwanda [the Hutu refugees in Congo] do the same thing they did. They were going to get rid of these guys."

The AFDL, he said, was "never a domestic political force, it was a grouping of foreign powers." Kabila's army comprised "Rwandans, Ugandans and Angolans. That's it. Kabila was a front. He was always just a creature of the foreign powers underneath him."

The market analyst predicted a complete geostrategic restructuring in central Africa, with Rwandan Tutsis, an ethnic group that had faced existential threats for decades, now steering affairs. "You'll see a de facto 'Greater Tutsi Land' there. What you've got is a situation where Rwanda and Uganda are clearly now the dominant military powers in the region. They will do pretty much what they want."

But what did that mean for the Congolese? I asked. What was going to happen to them? And what could possibly justify such a dramatic shift?

"The real truth about Zaire is that it was potentially very rich. Even though it was hugely corrupt and a very violent place, it was quite probably not as violent and was not as corrupt as Russia. But in Russia [business] people were dealing with a legitimate regime and they were able to do business. In Zaire, the difficulty was that everybody knew Mobutu was going to collapse, but didn't know when. And as a result, investment just didn't happen. Now he's gone and you've got a government that is legitimate in the eyes of the Americans. And the Americans, like or lump it, are the people who count at the moment. And that means that investment will take place. People will go in, they will develop the assets in Congo, which are world-class. They may do so from behind barbed wire, they may do it from fortresslike enclaves, but Zaire will be developed."

My source was unable to predict the extent of Congo's future collapse in this reconfigured "legitimate state." And the mostly invisible hand of the US government was hard to see at first too, though there was already some brilliant reporting on its role.

Before I left for Congo, I'd contacted Kathi Austin, who was tracking weapons dealers and war profiteering networks for Human Rights Watch. She told me to follow Bechtel, a US-based company that had reportedly helped the rebels unseat Mobutu. I was unable to unearth much in Kinshasa, but Robert Block, a journalist from the *Wall Street Journal*, had already looked into this shadowy yet powerful engineering giant.

He reported that Bechtel was drawing up a "master development plan" for Congo and providing high-tech intelligence for Kabila's new government, free of charge. Bechtel commissioned and paid for US National Aeronautics and Space Administration (NASA) satellite studies of the country and for infrared maps of its mineral potential. Some of the satellite data gave Kabila useful military information before Mobutu was toppled, Block pointed out. In exchange, Bechtel, which designs and builds projects for mining companies, became first in line to win contracts.[20]

Bechtel's links to US intelligence officials, former politicians and military personnel have made it one of the most powerful and secretive corporate entities in the world. The company had been accused of being a US shadow government.[21] In Congo, the satellite data it provided on mineral deposits were considered part of supragovernmental "black projects"—highly classified military or defense initiatives.[22] And all these secret deals were being struck in 1997 amid the tremendous loss of human life that the involved governments refused to acknowledge.

In Kinshasa, I got an interview with Kabila's finance minister. Mwana Nanga Mwampanga was a confident, US-educated Congolese man who was at the center of the new regime. When I arrived at his spacious villa in the morning, his assistant told me he was talking to the president on the phone and that I should wait in the living room adjacent to his office. I sat down on a leather sofa. The office door was open and I could overhear Mwampanga swearing at Kabila and issuing angry directives, if it indeed was Kabila on the other end of the phone. The minister eventually glanced my way and shut the door to his office, but I could still hear muffled shouting. When he came out to meet with me, though, he was unruffled. During our talk he dismissed most of my detailed questions about companies or foreign governments being behind the AFDL victory. Congo is open for business, is not beholden to anyone, not a country or corporation, he insisted. "We will develop Congo for the Congolese."[23]

At least I had gathered one piece of crucial information: this free marketeer and his Marxist president were already at odds, weeks after forming their government.

After a week in Kinshasa, I realized there was only so much I could accomplish there. The high-stakes decision to replace Mobutu with Kabila had been made in global capitals. The dealmakers and financial backers weren't here but in South Africa, the United States and Britain. I wanted to get back to the refugee story. I had planned to go to Goma, briefly, before heading to Rwanda to visit refugee transit camps. I had been told by several journalists that once I was in Kigali, which was well run and calm, no one would bother me. There were too many NGOs, UN officials and Western embassies there. It was safe.

But there were no direct flights from Kinshasa to Kigali as war had broken out in Brazzaville, across the river. I was told at a travel agency that I'd be able to get a flight to the Rwandan capital from Gisenyi, a city just inside the Rwandan border. I'd already been reassured by a security official with a top aid organization that I could stay overnight in their gated, secure compound in Goma, on the Congolese border, within walking distance of Gisenyi. I gave the security official my time of arrival and was told a driver would pick me up after I landed.

At the Kinshasa airport, as I waited for my flight, with my knapsack and jeans likely making me look more like a student than a journalist, a white man appeared out of nowhere and sat down beside me and flashed his diplomatic passport. He was Canadian and his name was Charles. I didn't ask him what he was doing in Kinshasa because he did not give me the chance. But he asked me why I was there, where I had been and where I was going. I was tired, and a bit exasperated, but he seemed sincerely concerned, so I gave him the broad strokes of my journey. I told him I'd come into the country through Goma, had traveled to Kisangani, then Mbandaka, before returning to Kisangani, where someone had unleashed a machine gun outside my villa. He nodded.

We got on the same flight and he sat beside me. He wouldn't reveal much about his activities and I was in such a bad mood I didn't press. The flight was due to stop in Kisangani, and he tried to persuade me to get off with him there, promising to find me a safe place to stay and to help me get to Rwanda another way. He told me bluntly, "Don't go to Goma."

"Why?" I asked.

"It's too dangerous. We don't have a presence there."

I told him I understood the risks but that I had stayed in the iron-fenced compound of an international agency there before and everything had been fine. I would stay at the compound again and someone was picking me up at the airport. He wanted to know who exactly would be at the airport. I didn't know the name of the driver, but I gave him the name of the security official I had spoken to in Kinshasa, and the head of mission in Goma. He nodded but still seemed concerned.

We discussed a high-profile incident that had occurred in Goma a few days before I had arrived. A 25-year-old American woman working for UNICEF had been gang-raped by a group of AFDL soldiers. The word was that these soldiers were Rwandans. Rank-and-file RPF soldiers were known to be highly disciplined and not prone to raping women, especially expatriate aid workers. But that was true in Rwanda, where they were held accountable. In Rwandan-occupied Congo, it was the Wild West, and there appeared to be no rules, no laws and no accountability. The woman was taken by helicopter to a Nairobi hospital and then flown back to the United States. The United States was said to be furious with the AFDL and Rwanda. Many European women, and a Canadian aid worker I had met in Goma weeks before, planned to leave the city within days.

As we talked, I weighed the circumstances. But I decided I could not return to Kisangani. I was heading to Goma then Rwanda.

During the stopover in Kisangani, Charles gathered his belongings and urged me to call him once I arrived in Goma. He handed me his card and said: "Now you know what I do." Charles's last name was Branchaud and he had been in Congo gathering intelligence for the Canadian government. He already had considerable experience in the Middle East and would later work with Western intelligence in Libya and Mali.[24]

Goma, a city tucked just inside Congo's border with Rwanda, smelled of smoke and must. Its roads were deeply rutted, its concrete buildings cracked or cratered from mortar shells, and its market stalls pillaged or flattened.

Pickup trucks and four-wheel-drive vehicles painted in brown-and-green camouflage swerved by, mounted with machine guns and carrying soldiers wearing berets with AK-47s strapped to their chests. The airport was dark, with puddles on the floor and holes in the wall where weeds sprouted through. I got through the security check with no problem. But when I looked around for my driver, no one was there. No international agency vehicles—from MSF, the Red Cross or the UN.

I waited for a while, but it was getting dark. A few shifty taxi drivers had asked me if I wanted a lift, and after about twenty minutes of waiting I asked one of them to drive me to a well-known aid agency. But when we got there, all the lights were off. I buzzed at the gate several times, but no one came. I didn't know what to do. I had no phone and no way of contacting anyone in Goma. There was no point in going back to the airport. There were no streetlights and it was now pitch-black.

I asked the driver, "Do you know of a decent hotel where foreigners go?" He nodded.

We drove along bumpy roads to a dilapidated guesthouse surrounded by lush tropical grounds. I had no idea where I was, but I didn't want to be driving around Goma at night any longer. The entrance of the guesthouse gave onto a spacious room that looked like a brasserie, with the reception desk— which was really a bar—at the far end. Before I let the driver go, I asked the clerk whether he had rooms available and he said yes. I paid the driver and he left. There were hardly any people downstairs as I filled out a form, paid cash for one night's stay and left my passport with the clerk, as was customary in places like this. My room was on the ground floor, the third door down the left corridor.

I was famished and thirsty. For years I had suffered from hypoglycemia, and became very weak when I didn't eat regularly; if my blood sugar dropped, I also was prone to acute anxiety that would occasionally escalate to panic attacks. I went back to the lobby area and ordered a Coke and a *croque monsieur*. Just then a tall, clean-cut young man came over to my table and sat down next to me. "Hello," he said in a soft voice, smiling at me. *Not again.* He asked me what I was doing here and I told him I had come to Congo to interview Congolese civilians displaced by war. I told him I was Canadian. He spoke English and told me he was a Rwandan student. My Coke arrived and as I was downing it, he began peppering me with more questions. There was only one thing on my mind now: I needed to eat.

Just then I heard a commotion outside, and saw headlights through the window. There was shouting and laughing as dozens of soldiers in camouflage fatigues got off some trucks and poured into the hotel. I could not breathe. I grabbed my knapsack and ran to my room, closing the door, then fitting the old-fashioned hook through the rusty eye. A few of the soldiers had seen me as soon as they walked in. If I was going to leave, I needed my passport, which was at reception. So I'd have to reclaim it, and then wait for a driver to come, in plain view of the soldiers in the bar. There was no phone in my room. Only satellite phones worked in places like this, and I did not have one.

I sat on the edge of the bed, trying to control my thoughts and breathing. I could hear the soldiers in the bar and in the hallway outside my room. I began to pace, then stopped myself and lay down on the bed, staring at the dirty ceiling. My head was spinning, but if I stayed here and kept quiet, maybe everything would be fine. Then soldiers started to enter the garden off my room. I got up and shut off the light. There was no screen on the window, and I couldn't get the window to shut fully. I wanted to scream but couldn't. Several men were standing close to the window, talking loudly in a language I didn't understand. I backed up to the wall and followed it toward the bed, where I'd placed my backpack. Opening it, I dug out the box of digital audiotapes on which I'd recorded my interviews about the killings in the jungle. I needed to hide these. My hands were shaking and my eyes were welling up as I stuffed the box of tapes and my recorder with the microphone under the bed.

I sat on the floor, leaning against the bed and listening to the music outside, a tinny grind, and to the voices in the hallway and garden. I heard bottles break against the building. Then came banging on my door, pounding, laughing and shouting.

I started to sob. How many would come in? What would they do? I would kill myself after this. Why had I ever come here? I stood up in the dark, took a few steps toward the door. The last thing I remember was falling. I lost myself in that instant. I ceased to exist.

2

THE RATIONALE FOR WAR

A FAINT LIGHT WAS COMING FROM THE WINDOW. THE FLOOR AGAINST my cheek felt moist and smelled like camphor. My eyes were crusty and sore, and my head hurt. I pulled myself up slowly. I still had my clothes on from the night before. I felt a wave of nausea and dragged myself to the bathroom, where I dry-heaved for several minutes. I sat on the floor, with my back against the wall facing the sink, listening to the light murmur of voices and birds chirping outside. It was quiet and calm.

I tried to piece together what had happened. I had believed rebels were breaking into my room to attack me and I had blacked out. I felt numb, but I had not been beaten or sexually assaulted. Yet I was so confused about so many things that I couldn't trust my judgment. I checked the door. The hook was still fastened to the eye. They hadn't come in through the door. But the window, which I had not been able to shut properly, was now wide open.

I gathered my things, retrieving the box of tapes, digital recorder and microphone from under the bed. I stuffed everything into the backpack. I checked my money belt, loosely wrapped around my waist. Inside the belt was a zipped compartment with US bills folded carefully into thin strips. It all seemed to be there.

I needed to get out of Goma immediately and I had no faith in my contacts at the aid agency since they hadn't bothered to show up at the airport. I went out to the main reception area, which was empty except for the clerk at the desk, slumped asleep in a chair. I woke him up and told him I wanted my passport and a driver to take me to the border. I didn't see any telephone behind the counter. He wandered off, then came back to say that a car would be here in five minutes, which it was.

I slipped into the car and got to the border crossing within minutes. The Rwandan border guards were taciturn but efficient and let me through to Gisenyi with no problem. The sun was crawling over the horizon as I walked with my heavy bag from Congo to Rwanda. I needed to get to the airport there, but there were no taxis. I placed my bag on the ground and sat on it and put my head in my hands, dizzy and discouraged. Just as I wondered how long I would have to sit there, I looked up and saw two men in a white jeep, parked at the border crossing.

I approached the driver and introduced myself. His name was Luiz and he worked for the Dian Fossey Gorilla Fund. "Are you all right?" he asked. I nodded and asked if he could take me to the airport. I must have looked as desperate as I felt, because even though he was headed to Kigali, he agreed to take me. But when we got there, the airport was closed. The only way left for me to get to the capital was by road, which was risky. At the time, the route from Gisenyi through Ruhengeri to Kigali was so perilous it was called Death Highway. There were daily reports of ambushes and attacks in villages throughout northwest Rwanda. Kagame's troops were battling Hutu militia whose forces launched raids from their bases in Congo.[1] The crackdown on Hutu insurgents was a pretext for a wider, more brutal campaign in which the RPF killed unarmed Hutu civilians and other targets—including foreign aid workers and UN staff—who were witnesses to these human rights violations.[2]

Luiz and his traveling companion, a Congolese student named Paulin, had been conducting conservation work for the Fossey fund in Gisenyi and had asked the local United Nations office to provide a security convoy for their return to Kigali. The UN flatly rejected that idea. Recently one of its vehicles had been ambushed and they had lost staff members. As far as I was concerned, anything was better than the last twenty-four hours. I could not, would not, go back to Goma. So I asked if I could hitch a ride to Kigali with them, and Luiz agreed.

The highway moved through misted hills and valleys full of banana, papaya and eucalyptus trees. I gazed at the beauty around me, but the violent sounds and images of the rebels pouring into the bar and garden leaked into my thoughts. When I glanced in the side mirror, I realized that blood vessels under my eyes and on the top of my cheekbones had burst. From crying, or were they bruises? I needed to get to Kigali and eat, then sleep, but Luiz insisted we stop in Ruhengeri to check on one of Fossey's villas and a research center.

Ruhengeri, a town in the foothills of the Virunga volcanoes, was at the center of the RPF's counterinsurgency campaign. While Luiz took care of business, Paulin and I walked around. A peasant we met on a potholed road pointed out Mount Karisimbi, the highest of the eight mountains of the Albertine Rift. Paulin and I found a place that sold sandwiches and Fanta by the roadside and after I ate, my hands stopped shaking. When Luiz rejoined us, he said he needed a nap before he continued the drive, so we returned to the vehicle, climbed in and locked the doors. It sank in how eerily quiet it was in Ruhengeri. There was no one in the fields. There were no children outside playing. I assumed people were hiding.

A few hours later, we were on the road again, winding around the edge of cliffs that overlooked impenetrable valleys. Within a half hour of Kigali, as we were coming around the corner at a slow clip, a group of villagers came out of nowhere and jumped on our vehicle. One landed on the windshield and pressed his face to the glass. For a split second we thought it was an ambush but then realized they were all smiling and full of goodwill. It turned out they wanted to sell us some food. Luiz bought some fish from them and we carried on.

Luiz and Paulin dropped me off at the Auberge de l'EPR, a Presbyterian guesthouse in Kigali. The hotel was peaceful, at least. My room had a phone and I was able to relax for the first time in a few days. It was the end of June.

I was already grateful to Luiz for the ride, but he also helped me find a driver who worked as an interpreter. The next day I headed to Runda, a town west of Kigali where Hutus returning from Congo were being registered at a transit camp set up by the United Nations. The UN had agreed to Rwanda's demand that all Rwandan orphans be returned home even if Congolese families had taken them in. I wanted to explore the fate of these children. What happened if they could not be reunited with their surviving relatives? Would these under-age boys and girls become wards of the state? Many children I'd interviewed in Congo, even very young ones, told me they did not want to return to Rwanda because they had been traumatized by the genocide and its aftermath.

The camp was teeming. In theory, it's against international humanitarian law for state military forces or militia to be present in UN-run refugee camps. But clearly the regime did what it wanted, because Rwandan soldiers inside the camp shouted and pointed guns at mothers struggling to carry young children and their belongings; I saw a soldier hit an old man with his gun butt. The military personnel also seemed to be listening to conversations, and questioned me twice as to why I was conducting interviews, each time taking down my name and glaring at me as though I were trespassing.

I noticed a man with slumped shoulders and dirty pants standing in line waiting to be registered who returned my gaze. Every Rwandan had a story; the question was whether this man felt he could tell his. When I approached him, he wordlessly indicated the soldiers, who were everywhere. I backed off and approached him again after the soldiers had moved away, and he whispered that he was an educated man but was hiding this fact because intellectual Hutus were targeted by the RPF as potential enemies of the state. He told me where he'd gone to school and what he'd studied. He'd even gone abroad. But he warned me that writing these details about him—identifying where he had studied and what village he was from—could get him into trouble.

I told him I wanted to hear how he'd survived. "I survived twice, and lost everything twice," he said in a low murmur. In Kigoma, south of Lake Edward, he and his family tried to escape when Rwandan soldiers speaking Kinyarwanda moved in. "I was there, ten meters away from my wife and little girl, when they were massacred in front of my eyes," he told me. They were his second family, he said. He'd lost his first wife and five children during the genocide. I asked him who killed his first family—an extremist neighbor or Interahamwe militia? Had he been a Hutu opposition member, someone who had opposed the former Habyarimana regime? He broke eye contact and would not say. I shut off my tape recorder. "There are things you want to know. Yes, I see," he said. Which, to me, meant there was something he wanted to explain but could not.

I would not walk away from him. I don't think he wanted me to walk away from him. His story was important. We knew it. Why had he fled to Zaire in the first place? This was something I kept asking refugees in Congo, and now in Rwanda. The vast majority said the same thing: they fled because the RPF was killing Hutus, and had killed them during the genocide. It was hard for me to accept this explanation. I thought I knew what had happened during the genocide—that the RPF had swooped in and routed the Hutu extremists who were responsible for killing Tutsis and moderate Hutus. The perpetrators were Hutus. The people who stopped the genocide and were its principal victims were Tutsis.

I'd seen what the RPF was capable of in Congo, and yet I still framed their crimes as retribution killings, possibly genocidal but ultimately acts of revenge. It wasn't until months later—when I listened again to my taped conversations from the trip, and thought about this particular educated man who was shaking but unable to tell me how he'd lost his first family—that I began to question everything I had read about the Rwandan genocide. Perhaps this educated man feared I would not believe him. Most likely he was worried that someone might overhear what he was telling me. I was afraid that just being seen talking to me was endangering him. I believe he was willing me to understand more than he could tell me. When I listened again to his voice much later, I realized that he was trying to tell me that the RPF had killed his first family during the genocide, that his wife and five children had been slaughtered by Kagame's army. In fact he *had* said it. "No, the Interahamwe did not kill them. Hutu soldiers did not kill them either," he'd insisted, shaking his head.

I went over the testimony of others who'd told me that they'd fled en masse to Zaire or to the French-occupied Zone Turquoise because RPF forces were killing Hutus. I realized I believed what these refugees were telling me: both Tutsis and Hutus were covered in blood. Yet only one side had been allowed to tell their story. Only one side was believed. What I did not know then, of course, was how organized, immediate and successful the RPF killing campaign had been in 1994.

I traveled farther south, to Gitarama, where I interviewed dozens of people, most of whom were uncomfortable speaking about their experiences. It was proving nearly impossible to do candid interviews in Rwanda. I found one young woman who was resettled in her rural village after her ordeal in the Congolese forest. She had lost relatives, yes, but she would not say who they were or what had happened. What was her reintegration like now? Was she getting support from other relatives or authorities? She would not look at me when she answered. "Things are fine, good," she said. I worried she was hesitant to elaborate on her experiences in the presence of my interpreter-driver, a Tutsi. But perhaps she felt other eyes and ears were open too, and any revelation could get her into trouble.

Meanwhile, every time I had breakfast at the guesthouse or went to a restaurant in Kigali on my own, I'd be approached by a friendly person who would sit down next to me, offer to help in some way or ask me how my work was going. No one threatened me, but I became afraid to leave my interview tapes in my room and carried them with me everywhere I went.

I talked to senior officials with the United Nations High Commissioner for Refugees (UNHCR) and a few mayors, but I opted to avoid meeting any senior RPF officials. I was afraid of them, to be honest. Deciding it was impossible to do serious reporting in Rwanda, I got a flight out of Kigali to Entebbe and then home to Paris.

My husband was relieved to see me, though worried that I was so haggard and skinny. I didn't want to talk about what I'd witnessed or what I suspected—which was the beginning of a long pattern of me pretending to be fine as I pushed anguish to a place where I thought I could control it. I eventually tried to tell him about small incidents, but they were conversations I'd begin and never finish. He never asked me to tell him more, which seemed fine at the time. He was the love of my life, and we were young and living the dream in Paris, with his aunts, uncles and cousins nearby, providing that extra bit of familial comfort. On Sundays we often sat at the family dining table all day, enjoying each other in a country we hadn't grown up in. But after that first trip to Congo, the security I felt with my husband did not insulate me from hidden thoughts and troubled memories of what I'd seen there.

I took only a few days off before I returned to the Africa desk at Radio France Internationale. I poured myself into producing documentaries that flowed out of my trip, and sent some material to Vatican Radio and more to the CBC. But I found that I was unable to fully exploit what I'd collected because, though I believed what I'd seen, I still somehow couldn't accept it. I needed to better understand why it had happened, and why such atrocities were still happening. I grew increasingly disturbed by the narratives coming to us through the mainstream media and circulating in political and humanitarian circles: what was in the making in the Congo was an African renaissance—the dawn of a new era of peace and security. These stories and interpretations were diametrically opposed to what I'd seen myself. That the West continued to dole out money to Kagame and Kabila fueled my outrage. How had it become accepted wisdom that Kagame had the right to invade Zaire and go after "armed Hutus" there?

As the weeks wore on, I kept working but could not sleep. My husband insisted it was physically impossible to not sleep for so long. Surely I was sleeping and not realizing it. I tried melatonin and sleeping pills. They did not work. If I kept my eyes open, I would stare at the shadows on the wall or a sliver of light from the street. If I closed my eyes, I'd see lifeless faces and bodies. I'd hear the hiss of jungle, the voices in a camp. Sometimes I imagined hands around my neck or covering my mouth and I could not breathe. Clothes ripped and body shoved. I continued to keep these thoughts to myself because they shamed me and I assumed my husband would not understand.

I did more research. Beyond drinking red wine into the night, it was the only thing I could think of doing. I wanted to understand, first of all, why the international community had failed to protect the refugees in October 1996, when the RPF had invaded Zaire.

Bait and kill—the phrase in itself is chilling, and the reality worse. When Rwanda had invaded Zaire, I discovered, the RPF used humanitarian organizations, the United Nations and journalists as a means to locate and kill refugees.[3] As the war progressed, there was mounting evidence that Rwanda had gained access to satellite equipment that enabled it to intercept the texts as well as voice and video communication of NGOs, media and other personnel in the field.[4] As soon as aid workers found refugees and got them to stay in one place so they could bring them food and medical care, Rwanda-backed rebels and RPF forces would move in, cordon off the area and attack, or chase the refugees into more remote, denser areas of the jungle in what they called "bait and kill" operations.[5]

Nik Gowing, a British journalist who conducted a study of information management and media coverage in eastern Zaire, quoted Kagame himself saying that humanitarian information exchanged by aid workers was militarily valuable. "NGO information is not just humanitarian information,"

Kagame said. "It is also military information."[6] One NGO worker told Gowing that as soon as they sent their situation reports to the agency's headquarters, "we were challenged by army commanders on the ground" about the contents of the messages. "We were strongly advised by UN Security that all calls by satellite phones [were being] recorded."[7] A Western diplomat told a physician with Doctors Without Borders that the organization's radio traffic in the towns of Tingi-Tingi, Kisangani, Goma and Bukavu was being monitored by Tutsi fighters in eastern Zaire.

There was also disturbing evidence that the RPF had used deception to infiltrate the UNHCR and other humanitarian organizations, along with sightings of AFDL soldiers traveling in trucks bearing false UNHCR logos.[8] A number of refugees in the jungle told me that the UNHCR had been infiltrated by "Rwandan spies." A priest gave me a handwritten account from a witness who claimed the UNHCR had provided Marc Kazindu—a Tutsi who had received military training and was working for the AFDL—with transportation, handsets and money to locate refugees in the areas of Bukavu, Walikale and Shabunda. Kazindu allegedly passed that information on to the AFDL, whose fighters would enter these zones and massacre Hutus.[9] Other humanitarian agencies complained that they were forced to use AFDL "facilitators" in order to operate in certain zones, and that these facilitators would later inform their military commanders of "concentrations of refugees to expedite their killings."[10]

There is no evidence to suggest that senior officials from the UNHCR and other aid agencies knew about this infiltration when it began. But they did know that their aid workers were operating in a climate of fear. The rape of the American woman working for UNICEF in Goma, which occurred a week before I arrived, had sent shockwaves through the humanitarian community. "I was scared to speak," a senior UN official admitted to Gowing. "In May 1997 a UNICEF delegate was raped and beaten up just after UNICEF condemned the [AFDL] Alliance."[11] The official added, "A journalist was seriously intimidated, persecuted to the point of fearing imminent death in a faked road accident, then left the country terrified, whereupon it was discovered that agents for the Alliance were stalking the reporter into a neighbouring country."[12]

When I was in Congo, I hadn't realized how dangerous it was for journalists to cover the conflict critically until that machine gun opened up outside my bedroom. Had I known, I would never have filed reports while I was still in the country.

I was following another, equally troubling, thread: evidence that the CIA had provided covert aid to Kabila and Kagame in the form of satellite imagery and communication. Stephen Smith, a reporter for the French newspaper *Libération*, was in eastern Zaire during the refugee crisis. Two independent sources had told him that the United States provided assistance to the AFDL. In an interview with me, he said the CIA had put up a satellite dish at Mobutu's residence in Goma after it had been seized by Kabila. The feed from the dish allowed the rebel alliance to read license plates off vehicles and register all movements of convoys. "This was of tremendous help to Kabila for military movements but also for movements of civilians, especially the Rwandan refugees."[13]

Gregory Stanton, who worked for the US State Department's Human Rights Bureau, was in Rwanda when the Rwandans invaded Zaire. When he checked in with the US embassy in Kigali in late October, he noticed a new satellite dish in the compound. He was also surprised that the US ambassador, Robert Gribbin, and his second in command, Peter Whaley, were bothered by his unannounced visit and told Stanton that he did not have the appropriate clearance to visit. "You shouldn't be here," they told him.[14]

The US chose to side with Rwanda, not the humanitarian organizations on the ground, over how many refugees had returned to Rwanda versus how many had been pushed deeper into Congo by AFDL forces. The United States insisted in November 1996 that most of the refugee population, about one million people, had gone home, and that those who ran westward were family members of armed Hutu forces and therefore considered *génocidaires* or their sympathizers. Pro-Kigali journalists, academics and diplomats seemed to consider such refugee camps fair targets for Tutsi forces.

The debate over refugee numbers was central to whether the UN Security Council would approve the deployment of an international military force to protect the refugees in Zaire. Canada's prime minister, Jean Chrétien, had announced in November that Canada would lead the multinational force, whose main task would be to provide humanitarian aid to refugees "with military assistance if necessary." Chrétien appointed Canada's Chief of the

Defence Staff, Lieutenant-General Maurice Baril, to head the mission in Zaire. Baril had run the military division of the UN Department of Peacekeeping Operations (DPKO) during the Rwandan genocide and was familiar with the region's geopolitics. But as soon as the discussion progressed to logistics, refugee movements and needs, Washington began to claim that there was a dwindling urgency for the mission because most of the refugees had safely returned to Rwanda.

Nicholas Stockton, who was emergencies director of the global charity Oxfam, said he might have been able to swallow Washington's claims had he and his colleagues not been given privileged access to highly credible information that told a different story. On November 20, 1996—as US officials were claiming that one million refugees had safely returned home—Oxfam staff were shown the original US aerial reconnaissance photogrammetry, which were measurements from photos, that confirmed, in considerable detail, the existence of more than 500,000 people distributed in three major and numerous minor groups inside Zaire.[15] The information was also shown to the United Nations. "Yet, incredibly, in a press conference in Kigali on 23 November, the US military claimed that they had located only one significant cluster of people which by the nature of their movement and other clues can be assumed to be the ex-FAR (Hutu army) and militias."[16]

Stockton and his colleagues at Oxfam were outraged. That December he wrote:

> We were asked to believe, and many did, that all the missing refugees and displaced persons simply did not exist. However, on the basis of the quality and authority of the information received by Oxfam on 20 November, we feel bound to conclude that as many as 400,000 refugees and unknown numbers of Zairean displaced persons have, in effect, been air-brushed from history. If this is the case, why was it done and why have so many experienced journalists and other seasoned observers not noticed?

During this debate over refugee numbers, Maurice Baril was meeting with Kagame, Kabila and Ugandan president Yoweri Museveni. On November 18, Baril saw Kagame at his home in Kigali for what he described as a "pleasant" few hours. "It was a great honour that is bestowed on very few people," Baril said about his visit with Rwanda's strongman. Baril then went to Goma to meet with Kabila in Mobutu's former residence, and in December he encountered Kagame again in Entebbe, where the Rwandan leader was holding meetings with Museveni.[17]

In the report Baril tabled at the United Nations on December 13, he advised that the multinational force was not needed.[18] Baril reported that the 150,000 refugees he'd initially observed in Zaire had later dispersed into smaller groups and were "untraceable" under the triple-layer jungle canopy. He claimed that the fighting in Zaire had not moved as quickly as expected and the rebel alliance had not come into contact with the refugees. This was incorrect, but he went further: "To date, there had been no evidence of AFDL mistreatment of Rwandan refugees who wish to be repatriated to Rwanda."[19] Baril also wrote that there were no signs the refugees were being forced to move west and that they appeared not to be in urgent need of assistance. He claimed that the hundred thousand refugees he estimated were left wandering around in Zaire did not want to go back to Rwanda because they were Interahamwe, former Hutu government soldiers and civilian accomplices responsible for the 1994 genocide.

After Baril delivered his assessment to the UN, I interviewed Marius Bujold, Canada's envoy to central Africa, who had been involved in negotiations over whether the multinational force should go ahead. He told me he agreed with the American position that the multinational force would have stopped Kabila from "moving farther out." Meaning, the Canadian-led mission could have posed an obstacle to Kagame's victorious sweep across Zaire and the final ousting of Mobutu.

"I'm not a humanitarian agent," Bujold said. "My concern was to reach a political solution in Zaire. And the refugee situation was part of the political problem. The Americans and other countries, with a few exceptions, had come to the conclusion that Mobutu had to go."[20] It was what I suspected, but still, I was surprised that he admitted it to me. My interview with Bujold was testy. He denied that the policy he supported meant the extermination of human life and said he believed that the United Nations had inflated the numbers of Hutu refugees to begin with.

Less than two months after Baril's report caused the UN to shelve the protection force, hundreds of thousands of Rwandan refugees were seeking

shelter in Zaire's hostile jungle. Many were still running from Kagame's soldiers; others had given up running and were dying from wounds or illness.
Emma Bonino, the European Union's commissioner for humanitarian affairs,
was one of the rare voices to express moral outrage. She said the United States
and Lieutenant-General Baril were wrong when they insisted that the only
refugees left in Zaire were *génocidaires.*

"We find ourselves faced here with individuals who no longer exist," she
said indignantly, "who could not be detected by the world's most powerful
armed forces with ultrasophisticated satellite equipment at their command.
We were told last December that there was no point in going there, as virtu-
ally all the refugees had returned home to Rwanda. We were accused of
having overheated imaginations when we continued to insist that hundreds
of thousands of refugees were missing. The International Community has to
admit it made a mistake."

In early February 1997, Bonino went to Tingi-Tingi camp, where more
than 100,000 refugees were huddled together in deplorable conditions. "I've
just come back from hell," she said when she got home.[21] On the heels of
that visit, the UN High Commissioner for Refugees, Sadako Ogata, visited
makeshift camps inside Zaire and concluded that 500,000 Hutu refugees
and displaced Zaireans were in desperate need of help.[22] But the international community continued to believe that its inaction was justified.

In October 1997, five months after Mobutu was overthrown, the *Boston Globe*
reported that European intelligence claimed US Special Forces had participated in the fighting in eastern Zaire. A French military officer said that
France's secret service had detected as many as one hundred armed American
troops engaged in the conflict, and alleged that the US government actively
participated in Mobutu's ouster.[23] Reporters had also learned by then that
the US had provided military aid—both psychological operations and tactical training—to the Rwandan government.[24] The evidence was fairly compelling that the United States had steered political events in Africa's Great
Lakes region, at a steep human cost, in order to put an end to Mobutu's
necrotic regime. It wanted multinationals to be able to move in and exploit
the country's immense mineral resources. Any international force sent into
Zaire to help protect the refugees would slow or stop Kagame's advance, and

that would be a bad thing for the region. While the United States had developed close relations with Paul Kagame and his RPF, it had refused to intervene in the genocide in 1994, and it also did not care to intervene to protect the lives of the Hutu refugees who had fled to Zaire. The United States government and most reporters and media outlets bought the Kagame version of the genocide, and few were prepared to thoroughly investigate and understand why so many Hutus had fled to Zaire in the first place.

Many reporters covered the humanitarian crisis in Goma in 1994, but few interviewed the refugees themselves about their plight. Among the explanations the reporters offered as to why more than a million Hutus ran away from their homeland was that their militias and military had told them to; another was that Hutus as a whole feared retribution because many of them had committed genocide against Tutsis. The United Nations High Commissioner for Refugees, meanwhile, estimated that 93 percent of the Hutus who fled deeper into Zaire after the Rwandan invasion were genuine refugees deserving protection.[25]

Nik Gowing wrote:

> The ready fixation of many reporters that all Hutus in eastern Zaire were extremists or genocidal maniacs remains a central concern. One senior NGO worker went so far as to describe many experienced Africa-based journalists as "brain damaged" by what they saw as their moral failure during their 1994 Rwandan experiences. This repeats the complaint of distorted reporting in the official, multinational analysis of the 1994 Rwanda genocide.[26]

Kagame's allies weren't only fudging the cause and the size of the postgenocide refugee crisis. Reports of Rwandan-led rebel troops killing refugees emerged as soon as they invaded the border camps in October 1996. UN aid workers said dozens, possibly hundreds, of refugees had been killed at Kibumba camp on October 27.[27] In November, Amnesty International highlighted disturbing killings by AFDL forces in Chimanga, a refugee camp near the border. Witnesses told Amnesty workers that a "Tutsi dominated army" had killed hundreds of refugees and buried the victims in mass graves.[28] In early December, French newspapers reported the discovery of mass graves in Zaire's Virunga Forest.[29] And in an interview, the US State Department's Gregory Stanton told me that aid agencies and governments were aware of massacres in 1996.

"I kept asking [my superiors in the US government] for facts about the alleged massacres that had been reported to me by human rights organizations and others, and I was stonewalled," Stanton said. "The main deputy assistant secretary at the US Africa bureau responsible for central Africa, in addition to the coordinator for central Africa, Richard Bagosian, told me to stop asking those questions. I told them it was my job to ask those questions."

Stanton eventually got authorization from the State Department's Human Rights Bureau for $50,000 to fund an investigative team that found evidence of the cremation of bodies south of Kisangani and of refugees killed in Mbandaka. The results of that investigation were not released by the State Department because the findings were politically explosive. Stanton said he nevertheless got backing from his boss, the assistant secretary of state for human rights and humanitarian affairs, to hand over the information to Human Rights Watch.

Stanton said he was not permitted to tell me who the investigators contracted by the State Department's Human Rights Bureau were. But he was sure that senior Washington officials knew about the crimes as they were happening, and tried to conceal them for politically expedient reasons. "I think it was a case of a cover-up by the American government," he said. "I think the American government helped plan the invasion of Zaire."[30]

In 1996 Stanton had attended meetings at the State Department in which officials from the Pentagon and the National Security Council (NSC) discussed the security situation in eastern Zaire and Kagame's plans to "force" the refugees home. At the NSC at that time, a man named Richard Clarke was driving US policy on Africa. Clarke and Susan Rice, who was a special assistant to President Bill Clinton and senior director for African Affairs, had a decisive role in how events played out in central Africa. Rice supported the Rwandan invasion of Zaire. "Anything's better than Mobutu," she is reported to have said.[31] In a meeting in mid-1996 at the State Department's African Affairs bureau, Stanton raised his objections about Kabila's murky past and questioned support for a group of people that the United States knew little about. The discussion eventually coalesced around the question of what needed to be done to dismantle the refugee camps. An official at the meeting, whom Stanton did not identify, made the somewhat facetious comment, "I think it's time to give war a chance," referring to the title of a book by P.J. O'Rourke. But the group did view war as a realistic solution to the instability in the Great Lakes. Kagame visited Washington in August 1996 and told officials he would be forcing the refugees home in due time. He not only got the green light he wanted, the United States was willing to assist him in his efforts.

My worldview changed forever when I discovered the degree to which Western officials acquiesced to—and at times actively assisted—a regime that butchered women and children in the forests I'd visited. Even now, when politicians in the West speak of the democratic values they hold dear, my heart turns cold.

3

RWANDA DIGS IN

BY 1998, CONGO'S NEW PRESIDENT, LAURENT KABILA, WAS FED UP WITH the foreign regimes that had brought him to power and was ready to kick them out. But by then it was impossible to take on Kagame. Rwandan and Ugandan soldiers were firmly entrenched inside Congo's borders and feeding off the country's resources. Théogène Murwanashyaka, a former RPF soldier, remembers how James Kabarebe, the brash commander who led Rwandan troops to the Congolese capital, became invincible after the victory. "He had girls, he had his own jet, he had limitless cash at his disposal. He had absolute power, and made sure that everyone knew it," Murwanashyaka said.[1]

There was no way men such as Kabarebe were going home; they owned the place. Rwanda and Uganda had also created a militia called the Rally for Congolese Democracy (RCD), which eventually spun off into several splinter groups that fought to control territories rich in coltan, a mineral from Congo's black mud that is used in the manufacturing of electronics and aeronautics. The battles over ownership of mining rights and trading relationships became a motor of war.[2]

As the price of coltan rose spectacularly from $65 per kilogram in late 1999 to a peak of around $530 in late 2000, profits from its sale contributed to the continuation of the conflict in eastern Congo. The Rwandan army, RCD-Goma and other armed groups that effectively controlled the trade sustained their forces on the profits they made, and killed and tortured local people, as well as driving them from their lands or forcing them at gunpoint to work in coltan mines.[3]

And it all devolved into a looters' war called the Second Congo War of 1998, which drew in the armies of nine African nations and more than a dozen armed groups. This conflict would eventually kill several million people, mostly through starvation and war-related diseases, and it eviscerated what remained of the country. Soldiers and militia raped women and girls, often in front of family members, shoving rifles, knives, wood, glass, nails and stones into their victims. Some attackers shot women in the vagina at point-blank range after raping them. Women who survived such assaults needed treatment for fistulas—tears of the tissue between the vagina, the bladder and the rectum that leaked urine or feces.

Even though the survival mechanisms of the Congolese people were extraordinary and its civil society had long been a refuge of resistance and strength against a history of domination, families could no longer function as they once had. Land disputes and ethnic rivalries—longstanding local antagonisms—now intensified, tearing the social fabric even more. By late 1999, Rwanda's army was reaping revenues of at least $20 million a month from the export of coltan alone, through its company Rwanda Metals, because of the tech boom in international markets.[4] In 2001, experts and dealers estimated that the Rwandan army had made at least $250 million from coltan over a period of eighteeen months.[5] And former RPF officials say Rwandan commanders were pocketing significantly more than UN investigators could document.

Rwandan dissident Theogene Rudasingwa, who for years had headed the RPF Secretariat—the government's political authority—said he and his colleagues were constantly surprised when the United Nations estimated its Congo revenues in the millions, when Rwandan commanders had already sucked out "a billion dollars' worth" of coltan, diamond, gold, tin and copper, along with the revenue from timber and extortion networks.[6]

By 1999, Rwanda and Uganda, longtime allies, were competing for control of the mineral resources and other riches in northeastern Congo. Their armies turned on each other and began tearing apart Kisangani, which was economically strategic, situated as it was on the Congo River, and rich in diamonds, coffee and timber. In a six-day battle between the two armies in June 2000, more than 1,200 civilians were killed and thousands were wounded.[7]

As the conflict escalated, I became desperate for news of Nyana; her worst fears were coming true. I couldn't get through on the phone numbers I had for the international agency she worked for in Kisangani. I wrote letters and e-mailed contacts asking for information on her whereabouts. No one was able to help me. And she could not reach out to me. Not only had I moved to another address in Paris, we had never exchanged e-mails since she did not have access to the Internet. I had no idea whether she was alive or dead. I eventually discovered through a third party that she'd been gang-raped and forced to flee to Uganda. I had dared to hope that somehow she would be spared the evil descending on her country. But she was no exception. It was another moment of ugly reckoning: barbarity is not aberrant or isolated to certain areas or certain people. The violence in Congo was committed by many actors against everyone, but in particular against the givers of life and the future generation. Targeting its women and children broke the heart of Congo as a nation.

In 2002, a UN panel of experts issued a third scathing report laying out the economy of war in Congo. The UN named eighty-five companies and elite networks that had ransacked the country or violated international regulations. The majority of the firms were based in Europe and North America. Five Canadian companies were cited for failing to respect responsible and sustainable business guidelines, as set by the Organization for Economic Cooperation and Development (OECD). Those Canadian companies were First Quantum Minerals, Tenke Mining, International Panorama Resources, Harambee Mining and Melkior Resources. The United Nations estimated that up to 70 percent of coltan exported from Congo was mined under the direct surveillance of the RPF and transported to Rwanda using Rwandan military helicopters, small airline companies and planes belonging to the world's most notorious arms dealer, Viktor Bout.[8]

Whenever Rwanda needed to establish sovereignty over a particular territory, it entered into agreements with its enemies, even Hutus it considered *génocidaires*. The UN panel was in possession of a letter from the Rwandan-backed militia, RCD-Goma, that urged "all army units to maintain good relations with our [Hutu] Interahamwe brothers, and further, if necessary, to let them exploit the soil for their survival."[9] The Rwandan army entered into local alliances with such armed political groups as the Interahamwe and

Mai-Mai militias in the territories of Walikale and Masisi. In 2002, leaders from a Mai-Mai group known as Mundundu 40 were incorporated into Rwanda's political administration in the province of South Kivu.[10] In Ituri, a gold-rich province farther north, a resident complained that a myriad of rebel groups were controlled by the Rwandan and Ugandan armies. "Let's not hide the facts: there are only two principal actors in the area controlled by the rebels. On the one hand there is Uganda and its army, the UPDF. And on the other, there is Rwanda and the RPA.[*] The others you call rebels are only the local servants in the service of Kigali and Kampala. And since they also find wealth in this way, they join up with these forces and all we poor people can do is die," the resident told Amnesty, after more than two hundred people were killed in intercommunal violence in September 2002.

Congo had become a hotbed of military commercialism, stoked by powerful states and their clutch of local militia and politicians. The manifest brutality, terror and looting at the heart of this conflict severed hopes for a free, stable and independent nation.

At the start of the Second Congo War, I knew I didn't have the psychological stamina to return to Congo and report from the ground while the country was torn into even smaller pieces. And despite my pitches to several magazines, I could find no editor who was interested in an article on the political underpinnings of the Hutu refugee crisis in central Africa. But I was restless in Paris and wanted to be on the move, so in 1998 I went to work for Agence France-Presse as a correspondent in west Africa, based in Abidjan, leaving my husband to hold down the home front. Over the next couple of years, I covered conflicts in Sierra Leone and Liberia, elections in Nigeria, and the Christmas Eve coup in Ivory Coast, and then I was briefly sent to the Middle East to reinforce AFP's bureau in Jerusalem during the Second Intifada. I loved the work, but it did occur to me that there was a reason I hopped from one place to the next, one conflict to the next, never settling. When at last I returned to Paris, in the summer of 2001, the distance between me and my

---

[*] The Rwandan Patriotic Army was the armed wing of the Rwandan Patriotic Front. In 2002 it became the Rwandan Defense Force (RDF). Since the RPF is the public face of Rwanda's military regime, in most places this book will describe military and other operations and groups as RPF-led.

husband had grown into a wall I wasn't sure if either of us had the energy or desire to breach.

One day in the summer of 2001 my husband suggested we have a rare lunch together, so we met at a pizzeria with a terrace on the sidewalk. We ordered our food, barely talking and only occasionally glancing at each other. He wanted to discuss something but was hesitating. I thought I knew what was on his mind, and before he could say it to me, I blurted, "I think we should move on."

"Yeah, maybe," he said, but breaking up wasn't what he had wanted to talk about. Instead, after our pizza was delivered, he told me that he would like to become a father. "I don't really see that happening with someone else," he said. "I don't expect to meet someone in the short term, someone I would trust."

It hit me that he was treating having children together as a transaction between us, and I was hurt. "That's not the way I wanted to start a family. I thought being in love might have something to do with it."

He didn't argue or try to explain himself further, but just seemed vulnerable and sad. As I was walking back to work, I wondered whether this had been his clumsy way of trying to reach me. I also knew that I was mostly responsible for the way things had played out between us. By the time I was opening the door to my office, I had decided that I didn't want to leave him. I would take a leap of faith and try to get pregnant.

So many changes resulted from that choice, the most important by far being two healthy, beautiful human beings—daughters, born five years apart. I went freelance, and we moved back to Canada, settling in Montreal, the city of my birth, close to my parents and grandparents, who were living in the Quebec countryside. My husband had never been happier, and some of the fatalism and cynicism that had invaded my soul began to fade, or at least shift. Sharing my life with children also restored a small measure of the idealism I believed I'd lost for good in Congo and Rwanda, and allowed me to care, for the first time in a long time, about smaller, daily things.

But the thoughts and memories were always there, floating to the surface at unexpected moments. In October 2007, a few months after I'd had my second daughter, I covered a global conference sponsored by McGill University on preventing genocide. At that event I met Gregory Stanton in person, after having interviewed him on the phone during and after the invasion.

I also met, for the first time, Alison Des Forges, an American historian who had done extensive human rights research on Rwanda (and who was killed two years later in a plane crash near Buffalo, New York). It was Des Forges who told me that the UN human rights commission in Geneva had at last authorized an investigation into atrocities in the Congo from 1993 until 2003. It turned out that the head of that probe was a Montreal human rights lawyer named Luc Côté, who had a lot to tell me. And soon Congo, and the untold story of the Rwandan genocide, once again had me by the throat.

The son of a construction worker and a Catholic feminist, Luc Côté grew up in a working-class neighborhood of Montreal called Ville-Émard. Eventually he became a public defender, providing legal aid for thieves, drug addicts and the mentally ill. After the genocide, when the United Nations needed bilingual lawyers in Rwanda, he was among the first wave of French-Canadian lawyers to arrive in the country.

In areas outside the capital of Kigali, bodies were still rotting in rivers, outhouses, churches and mass graves. Corpses that had been piled along roads and in fields had dried stiff under a parching sun. "They gave me a jeep and a shovel and I was going around the country visiting massacre sites, opening graves, talking to people," Côté told me in his kitchen on the top floor of a three-story walk-up in Montreal's Plateau district. "The smell of death is something you never forget. It's so peculiar. It's something you come to know. I was soon able, like many others, to walk around the bush and smell a corpse nearby." [11]

In 1995, Côté joined the Office of the Prosecutor at the International Criminal Tribunal for Rwanda. As head of the legal office for four years, he wrote indictments and helped organize the arrests of genocide organizers and perpetrators. At the same time, he saw firsthand the dark shadow of oppression that Kagame's post-genocide government was casting, under the powerless gaze of the international community. Prior to joining the tribunal, Côté had worked as a UN human rights monitor in southern Rwanda, investigating the arbitrary arrests and disappearances of Hutus at the hands of Tutsi forces. It was there, after he'd witnessed a number of appalling incidents, that he discovered that "these people [in Kagame's regime] were as bad as the others." He meant as bad as the Hutu *génocidaires*.

In April 1995, he and his UN colleagues were in Kibeho monitoring a sprawling camp for internally displaced Hutus that the RPF wanted to close. The camp was located in a humanitarian safe zone set up by French military forces during the genocide that was later monitored by UN peacekeepers. On April 22, RPF forces opened fire on the camp, sending tens of thousands of Hutus running for their lives. UN staffers saw Tutsi soldiers shooting women and children in the back as they tried to flee, and many Hutus died in the stampede.[12] Australian medical personnel put the dead at more than 4,000, but Rwandan officials said only 338 people had been killed. Three days after the Kibeho massacre, Côté wrote an opinion piece for Montreal's *Le Devoir* in which he questioned why Hutus who had fled to Zaire and Tanzania did not want to return to Rwanda even though the war was over. He pointed out that many Hutus in displacement camps had tried to go home, but had ended up returning to the camps because of insecurity in their villages. He warned that the human rights situation in Rwanda was deteriorating fast. "In each commune, you'll find an *amigo*, a kind of dungeon usually under military control, where justice is expeditious and hidden. Here, the rule of law is named *Kalashnikov*, and it wears green"—referring to the RPF's khaki uniforms. Côté described Rwandans as "hostages" in their own country.

In 2009, more than a decade after his first stint in Rwanda, Côté returned to central Africa, this time to Congo, where he headed a 34-member investigative team that worked with villagers, victims' families, human rights groups and child soldiers to collect evidence of some of the worst crimes against humanity in recent history. During an interview over a cup of espresso after he got back, he told me that he had not expected the violence to be "so devastating, so extensive, and so brutal."

Côté said, "I thought I had seen the worst with the genocide in Rwanda. We have testimony in the Congo that it was just as bad or worse than what happened in Rwanda. In Rwanda, it happened in three months. In the Congo, it never stopped." His voice grew hoarse. "I saw a pattern in the Congo that I'd seen in Rwanda. There are dozens and dozens of incidents where you have the same pattern. [The killing] was systematically done."

In August 2010, a month before the UN planned to officially release the investigation's findings, a draft report was leaked to the French newspaper *Le Monde*. Within hours, I filed a story for AFP.[13]

The 560-page report, which covered the period from 1993 to 2003, was titled *Mapping Human Rights Violations*. In UN legal jargon, the term "mapping" means providing an inventory and classification of crimes. The investigators found evidence that the Rwandan Patriotic Army (RPA) and its rebel allies used hoes, bayonets and axes to butcher Rwandan and Congolese Hutus, often rounding them up beforehand and killing them in groups. In many cases, the victims were raped, burned alive or shot. The report indicated that the vast majority of Hutus who were killed were "women, children, the elderly and the sick, who posed no threat to the attacking forces." The authors concluded that Kagame's troops may have committed genocide in Congo: "The systematic and widespread attacks described in this report . . . reveal a number of damning elements that, if they were proven before a competent court, could be classified as crimes of genocide."[14] The UN called for a full judicial investigation.

Rwanda reacted swiftly and with fury. Its government called the findings "immoral and outrageous" and it persuaded Western sponsors to attack the UN team's methodology. Kigali also threatened to withdraw troops from UN peacekeeping missions. The pressure likely quashed any hope that the UN would ever support a tribunal in Congo to prosecute Kagame and his killers.

At the same time, a renowned forensic investigator was already in Congo training a team of local scientists, police officers, army personnel and human rights activists to investigate mass graves found there. José Pablo Baraybar, a Peruvian forensic scientist who had worked in Srebrenica, Haiti and Ethiopia, had received financial backing from the American Bar Association and the US State Department for the three-month training program. Baraybar said his team got considerable help from Congolese villagers too. But when it came to opening up the mass graves in Rutshuru—a town in north Kivu where Kagame's mobile killing teams had committed some of the worst atrocities at the beginning of the invasion—the provincial governor blocked the investigation. "And Kinshasa would not give its approval either," Baraybar told me.[15] Joseph Kabila, who had taken over after his father, Laurent, had been assassinated by a bodyguard in 2001, "was evidently playing both hands."

"On the ground, a forensic analysis was not possible, anywhere," he said. "It was clear that Rwanda had used its influence in Congo and abroad to quash a full investigation." More than a decade after Kagame had built his inner stations in Rutshuru and other Congolese villages, his ability to define reality and influence people's lives remained intact.

My interview with Baraybar left me wondering what to do next. The United Nations had exposed the crimes—odious acts that had been committed by Kagame's troops in Congo—and yet no international authority had the courage to hold Kagame or his commanders accountable. It was as if no one could imagine prosecuting the man credited with stopping the Rwandan genocide, no matter what he did. The injustice was staggering. And at last I realized that the only way to live with what I'd witnessed in Congo was for me to backtrack into the heart of the genocide and examine what exactly the RPF had done. And then to publish what I found.

4

GOING FOR BROKE

THE OFFICIAL GENOCIDE NARRATIVE CAST A LONG PSYCHOLOGICAL shadow, even over me. One of the earliest, most startling glimpses of the RPF's actions during the genocide came in 2005 from a French investigative journalist named Pierre Péan, author of the book *Noires Fureurs, Blancs Menteurs* ("Black Furies, White Liars"). The book unmasked the RPF's propaganda and gave readers insight into more than a decade of violence the party had aimed at civilians. As important as Péan's work was, his book was not translated into English and was considered controversial even in Europe, where the Kagame regime and its Western backers worked to discredit Péan's findings. Any new charges coming from French and Belgian authors, even institutions, were considered suspect right off the top, as both countries had supported the Habyarimana regime.

In 2006, a French inquiry made headlines around the world when it issued arrest warrants against several senior RPF officials after it concluded that RPF commandos were responsible for shooting down the plane carrying President Habyarimana on April 6, 1994—the event that set off the genocide. In 2008, a Spanish judge issued indictments against forty senior RPF commanders for genocide and crimes against humanity committed in Rwanda and Congo during the 1990s, in part spurred by the murder of several Spanish nationals at the hands of Kagame's intelligence network.[1] And in 2010, a long-buried UN report by a US refugee consultant named Robert Gersony was leaked. Gersony's report revealed that the RPF had committed systematic massacres in 1994 in areas of Rwanda that it controlled. Yet many of Kagame's senior officers continued to travel freely to Britain, the United States and

South Africa because countries that supported Rwanda refused to respect the international arrest warrants.

The evidence from these European sources corroborated the anecdotal testimony I'd collected in 1997 from Hutu refugees who had fled to Zaire. But the mechanics of the killings in 1994—how they were organized, how extensive they were and who ordered them—were still unclear. How many people did RPA troops slaughter, and how planned and methodical were the murders? What sparked these crimes? And how did Kagame hide them? The only way to answer these questions was to go inside his regime and interview soldiers and officers who had been part of it.

I began reaching out to senior RPF officials who had fled to Europe and North America. Then something remarkable happened. A former RPF High Command soldier who had testified against Kagame at the ICTR and for the Spanish court reached out to me, unprompted, in 2012. His name was Théogène Murwanashyaka, a man whom investigators and lawyers viewed as a highly credible witness. Théo, as he soon urged me to call him, was familiar with some of my earlier reporting on the RPF, and wanted to speak to me about what he knew. While there were many things he did not know, he also introduced me to other former soldiers who spoke to me of their experiences. Then, independently of Théo, I found more former RPF members, many of them officers, who had never dared to testify before a court. At last, as people long silenced by fear found their voices, I began to put together a picture of the RPF's operations in all their savagery.

I collected testimony from men who had worked in the RPF's Directorate of Military Intelligence (DMI), in its Training Wing, with the Gendarmerie, the Military Police, the High Command and regular battalions. Yet, of all the former RPF members I've spoken with, Théo has been the most consistent and trustworthy. He lives quietly with his wife and children in Spain. He has never joined an opposition group in exile. Above all, he is patient and believes that truth, justice and reconciliation will come to Rwanda eventually. I could never have done this work without him. So, before I describe what Rwandans experienced at the hands of the RPF, before and during the genocide—scenes he helped me put together—I want to pay tribute to Théogène Murwanashyaka and his courage in standing up to a modern tyranny.

Théo grew up in Kigali in a well-to-do Tutsi family. Though his mother died when he was four years old, his father, Stanis Mukulira, carried on and managed to provide his children with opportunities most Rwandans could only dream of. Mukulira was a successful Tutsi in Habyarimana's Hutu-dominated Rwanda: he built a construction business, owned a number of properties and a soccer team. Théo—lean and fast—became his star player.

In the 1980s, Rwanda was a good place for people with means. "I did not suffer. I was lucky," Théo admitted. Yet the young man could not shake his existential angst over what it meant to be Tutsi in Rwanda. The country had been an ethnic state since 1959, when it transitioned from a Belgian colony with a Tutsi monarchy to a Hutu-dominated republic. The Hutu revolution was marred by anti-Tutsi pogroms and sent hundreds of thousands of Tutsis into exile. Théo remembers Hutus and Tutsis being identified by their ethnicity in primary and secondary schools. "'You are Tutsi, you are Hutu,' we'd hear in class. It was humiliating. Tutsis who were poor suffered the most. It bothered me profoundly. I was frustrated, idealistic, and I wanted things to change."

In October 1990, the rebel Rwandan Patriotic Army invaded from Uganda, where the largest diaspora of Tutsis had lived as displaced people for three decades. The Habyarimana regime immediately arrested high-profile "interior Tutsis" such as Théo's father—the term for Tutsis who hadn't fled their homeland—interrogated and then released them. Then reports emerged of Tutsis being killed in western Rwanda, and that news was enough for Théo, who by then was in his early twenties. "I believed the Hutu government did not need us and I thought Tutsis as a group would eventually be massacred," he said. "I thought the RPF knew what it was doing. They had fought to overthrow despotic governments in Uganda. They were experienced at war. They wanted power and I thought they would protect Tutsis." In 1991, he joined the rebels.

One of Théo's sisters, who now lives in Holland, told me their father's heart was broken when Théo went off to fight. "Our father wanted him to get an education. But my brother had other ideas," Espérance Mukashema said.

In 1993, after two years on the front, Théo received a letter from his father, personally delivered by a senior RPF cadre who knew the family. It made painful reading. His father told him that he dearly hoped he would stay safe but that it was increasingly dangerous for Tutsis in Kigali. He wrote that he did not believe Tutsis would survive the rising violence. He worried they would never see each other again. He was right.

Once the genocide began, Théo's father stayed alive for nearly two months, literally buying time by bribing Hutu neighbors and signing away some of his assets. He was killed at the end of May 1994. Théo also lost three brothers during the slaughter: Joseph, who worked at a government ministry; Jean Baptiste, a doctor for the Red Cross; and Jean Claude, a student at the University of Butare. They were butchered by Interahamwe and other Hutus they knew. Though five of his siblings survived, Théo's family was shattered.

In the immediate aftermath, the young man was seized by despair and hatred. He loathed Hutus for what they had done. "What eventually saved me [from extremism]," Theo said, "is remembering my experiences before the war. When I played soccer, I felt utter joy. It was a joy I shared with Hutus who played on our team. We were friends; we were united. These moments held me together. My memories of good times sustained me. Past relationships with teachers, classmates, neighbors, friends, got me through."

Still, he gazed at the wasteland that Rwanda had become and was overwhelmed with disgust. He took stock of everything he knew, everything he had witnessed during the war and the genocide. The disgust turned to anger and he finally understood where to direct it, which was not only at Hutu extremists. "I realized in fairly short order what had actually happened: the RPF had sacrificed interior Tutsis. There was no doubt about it. Their campaign was well planned. They wanted power and were willing to resort to every deception and crime to attain it." But why would a diaspora army, which had entered a country in order to liberate it from ethnic-based rule and defend the Tutsi people, kill its own?

By the beginning of April 1994, it seemed as though blood was the only fuel powering change in Rwanda. There was still a pretense of peace: under the Arusha Peace Agreement, negotiated in the wake of the 1990 invasion, Hutus and Tutsis had agreed to share power in a new transitional government on the way to the goal of a free and democratically elected one. More than 2,500 UN peacekeepers had been sent to the country to ensure that the Hutu

government and the Tutsi rebels—who had invaded the country and soundly
defeated government troops before agreeing to hunker down along the
border with Uganda, north of a demilitarized zone (DMZ) that was only sixty
kilometers away from Kigali—respected the deal. But in fact a new, much
dirtier war was in the making.

Even as the peacekeepers of the United Nations Assistance Mission for
Rwanda (UNAMIR) took up their duties, youth wings of Hutu political parties
were arming and training recruits.[2] Though most of its army remained
sequestered above the demilitarized zone, as part of the peace agreement,*
members of the RPF had been allowed into the capital for the first time.
Rebels who had been appointed to serve in the transitional national assembly
were assigned security, which meant six hundred soldiers from the RPA's
Third Battalion came with them to the capital, where they were housed in
a government building known as the Conseil National de Développement
(CND). This was the official arrival of the RPF on the political scene, but
Kagame and his formidable intelligence apparatus also used these new
headquarters as a Trojan horse, secretly caching military reinforcements
and weapons in the CND. The RPF strategy to achieve power in Rwanda had
three objectives: to infiltrate, instigate and obfuscate.[3]

As 1993 turned to 1994, attacks escalated in the capital and demilitarized
buffer zones in the north. Hutu political figures were assassinated. Innocent
civilians—Hutus and Tutsis—were killed. No one knew who was telling the
truth and who was lying, and the assailants proved impossible to identify.
International observers were unable to see what was really going on. For the
United Nations peacekeeping force, it was a dangerous and uncertain mess.
In *Shake Hands with the Devil*, his account of the genocide, the commander
of UNAMIR, the Canadian general Roméo Dallaire, described going to meet
for the first time with RPF officials, including Paul Kagame, on the technical
mission that preceded the mission's deployment. On the way, he passed
through a camp for people displaced from the demilitarized zone, a place of
despair, starvation and illness; he wrote that he could smell it before he could

---

* Under the provisions of the Arusha Peace Agreement, no military forces were allowed to
enter the demilitarized zone. But several sources have confirmed to me that the RPF indeed had
a presence there, unofficially, and carried out violent attacks there prior to the genocide.

see it. He described the zone itself as eerily depopulated, dotted by empty villages that had been deserted by the displaced people he had seen in the camps. He writes, of his first meeting with Kagame and the other RPF leaders, that "the RPF was unanimous in its support of Arusha." But after expressing their support, the RPF leaders stressed that, for security reasons, until the Arusha accords were fully implemented, they did not want the people from the camp that had so shocked the Canadian general to return to their homes in the zone. Dallaire wrote, "Later on, the thought crossed my mind that the reason the RPF raised the issue had less to do with security and more to do with the resettlement ambitions of Tutsi refugees then in Uganda." He also noticed that the RPA officers he met "were good at giving the impression of full cooperation, but they offered very little information about their force structure and true capabilities." This reluctance did not make much sense to the man who was supposed to oversee, under the Arusha agreement they claimed to support, the demobilization of the rebel army. Dallaire was being sent to Rwanda to lead a force whose mission was to help implement the peace deal, but even at the end of his first brief foray into Rwandan reality, he had the unsettling sense that though he was the one meant to be assessing the situation, he and the UN were the ones being assessed by all parties to the conflict. With the benefit of hindsight, he writes, "They had calculated that the West would deploy a token force and when threatened would duck or run. They knew us better than we knew ourselves."

Once the UN force landed, things became even more murky. "We didn't know why assassinations were occurring, why grenades were exploding, why daily protests degenerated into violence. We had trouble understanding and interpreting these events," said Luc Marchal, the Belgian contingent commander and Kigali sector commander with UNAMIR.[4]

Marchal said the United Nations contingent initially dismissed as propaganda Hutu military claims that the RPF was illegally transporting weapons and soldiers in trucks meant to carry firewood for cooking purposes. But when the RPF repeatedly refused to allow UNAMIR to inspect its trucks, Marchal began to have doubts. His personal relationship with Colonel Charles Kayonga, head of the RPF's battalion at the CND, was tense and, he said, "Colonel Kayonga refused to cooperate with UNAMIR in any way." The UN peacekeeping force was unable to monitor the RPF's movements as closely as it might have liked because it spent the first three months of 1994 trying to provide security for transitional government members, calming riots, and dealing with the aftermath of murders and grenade blasts. "It was an explosive situation," Marchal said.

What the United Nations and the UNAMIR peacekeepers did not know at the time was that the RPF had already set Rwanda on fire. Kagame and his colleagues had figured out how to divide and rule Hutus to dramatic effect. The RPF had infiltrated the Hutu political parties who were vying for and squabbling over power, along with their respective youth militias, with an estimated 150 RPF political operatives called "technicians." These infiltrators, many of whom had been trained in commando tactics, were mainly Tutsi soldiers from RPF High Command units and from its Directorate of Military Intelligence.[5]

As well as these technicians, about a hundred Tutsi civilians, known as *abakada*, had come from all over Rwanda to be trained at the CND and then sent back into the population.[6] They constituted a fifth column, who, along with the technicians, were charged with wreaking havoc throughout the country. The technicians ignited violence and stoked extremist sentiment among the Hutu militias and parties they infiltrated, sparking political assassinations and reprisal killings against Tutsi civilians. By the beginning of 1994, the RPF had successfully infiltrated all four Hutu militias: the Interahamwe (the youth wing of the ruling MRND party), the Inkuba (the youth wing of the MDR party), the Abakombozi (the youth wing of the PSD party) and the Impuzambugambi (the youth wing of the CDR party).[7]

RPF commandos staged attacks in the demilitarized zone, placed grenades and land mines in public places, and were ultimately responsible for the brutal slayings of the Hutu government minister Félicien Gatabazi and the Hutu hardliner Martin Bucyana in February 1994.[8] Gatabazi was killed by two experienced technicians named Kiyago and Mugisha, who reported to Emmanuel Karenzi Karake—also the RPF's liaison officer with UNAMIR. Bucyana was then lynched by members of Gatabazi's PSD party, which the RPF had infiltrated.[9] The murders sparked the beginning of war in Rwanda's southern region of Butare and led to clashes among Hutu militias in Kigali that left thirty-seven people dead. Habyarimana's allies were blamed and the RPF benefited from the chaos. In fact, that was the point of infiltration in the first place.[10]

RPF hit squads eliminated two other prominent Hutus—Emmanuel Gapyisi, a moderate who wanted to unite northern and southern Hutus, and the militia leader Alphonse Ingabire, whose alias was Katumba. Their murders unleashed a spate of bloody reprisals, most notably against Tutsi civilians. In some cases, RPF technicians actively killed Tutsi villagers in staged attacks that were blamed on Hutu mobs or civilian defense units.

By April 1994, the RPF decided to go for broke by killing Rwanda's president, Juvénal Habyarimana.[11] His assassination set the stage for a level of mass killings that Rwanda has not yet recovered from. It was the catalyst that effectively destroyed the old order and changed the course of central African history. Which is what Kagame and the RPF were aiming for all along, while paying lip service to the UN, to UNAMIR and to the peace process.

The following account of the shooting down of Habyarimana's plane is based on separate testimonies from former RPF to the 2006 French inquiry under Judge Jean-Louis Bruguière and the International Criminal Tribunal for Rwanda.

Kagame and his inner military circle held a series of three meetings in late 1993 and early 1994 to plan to shoot down the plane.[12] The commanders present at the meetings were Colonel Kayumba Nyamwasa, Colonel Steven Ndugute, Colonel Sam Kaka, Lieutenant Colonel James Kabarebe and Major Jack Nziza. The RPF agreed to train a team to handle two surface-to-air missiles that the RPF had secured from its ally Uganda. This team brought the weapons from northern Rwanda into the capital to a farm in Masaka. On the night of April 6, after attending a summit in Dar Es Salaam, Tanzania, the presidents of Rwanda and Burundi, along with key members of the Rwandan military, boarded a French-piloted Falcon 50 jet and headed to Kigali. At 7 p.m., RPF colonel Charles Kayonga told his battalion at the CND to be on "stand by one"—in full battle dress and ready for an attack. By 8 p.m., the missile team in Masaka was in place, waiting for the plane to arrive. The first missile was launched but missed the plane as it approached the airport. A second missile, fired by Sergeant Frank Nziza, hit the mark, damaging the aircraft's wing and fuselage.

The jet exploded, killing all twelve individuals on board, including the two heads of state and the three French crew members. Most of the plane's debris landed in the backyard of Habyarimana's presidential home.

Luc Marchal was astounded at how fast RPF forces—between 25,000 and 30,000 troops—moved into position after the plane was shot down. "The RPF launched a major offensive, which would have required weeks of preparation," he told me. To undertake such an immediate, large-scale offensive, the RPF would have had to formulate orders, issue those orders, and ensure that the military leadership transmitted the orders to troops so that soldiers got into position fast. He points out: "They launched a systematic attack and had enough ammunition and other supplies—including equipment and food—to fight immediately. They had [already] brought it over from Uganda. The downing of the presidential plane was directly related to the RPF's military offensive. You cannot improvise such matters. It is impossible."

A day after the president was killed, all hell broke loose. Hutu soldiers assassinated Prime Minister Agathe Uwilingiyimana and her husband and then kidnapped the Belgian peacekeepers who had been sent to protect her, taking them back to the main military barracks, where they lynched them. Tutsis living in Hutu-controlled zones were targeted and slain, but also, while that was going on, Hutus living in RPF-controlled areas were tracked down and slaughtered.

By April 12, only six days into the large-scale slaughter, Marchal saw at least four RPF battalions in Kigali. He believes that with such military capacity the RPF could have easily organized security zones inside the capital where Tutsis could have sought refuge. But they never created safe havens for Tutsis. Instead, they told the Belgian, Italian and French troops to get out of the country. The Italian and French troops were part of a coalition of elite paratroopers and special forces sent to evacuate foreign nationals. The same day, April 12, a dozen senior Hutu officers from the Rwandan armed forces formally requested the RPF join forces with them in a bid to stop the carnage. The Hutu officers called for an immediate ceasefire. But the RPF would not agree to it. Three days earlier, on April 9, the RPF had issued an ultimatum to the UN's Ghanaian contingent: get out of the demilitarized zone in the north or your soldiers will face artillery fire. "Not only did the RPF not show the slightest interest in protecting Tutsis, it fueled the chaos," Marchal said. And he is unequivocal about Kagame's intentions: "The RPF had one objective. It was to seize power and use the massacres as stock in trade to justify its military operations. This is what I saw."

The carnage and human suffering from the genocide brought about a new political era. Rwanda was no longer a Hutu nation; the country would be run, as it had been before independence, by a Tutsi minority.

5

THE DEEP STRUCTURES
OF RPF VIOLENCE

IF THE RPF HAD BEEN SINCERE IN ITS SUPPORT OF THE 1993 PEACE agreement reached for Rwanda, the leaders who met with UN peacekeepers would have been more forthcoming about how they were organized. But they weren't sincere. It's clear from the way the genocide unfolded that the RPF was not preparing to move into a peaceful future in which all Rwandan political parties vied in democratic elections, but, as Luc Marchal observed, for something else entirely. The key to understanding both how the RPF attained power in the region and, crucially, how they were able to hide massive crimes against humanity in plain sight and largely escape censure for their actions is to recognize the power and influence of the Directorate of Military Intelligence under the ultimate sway of Paul Kagame. Kagame had developed his intelligence skills in the late 1980s in Uganda, where he earned a reputation for being a ruthless spy chief for President Yoweri Museveni.[1] Central to the RPF's political and military efforts both when it was a rebel force, throughout the genocide, and now that it is in charge of a one-party state under Kagame's tight control are its intelligence operations at home and abroad.*

Former DMI agents have confirmed to me the pervasive nature of the directorate within the RPF. Not only does the DMI run counterintelligence, criminal investigations and prosecutions, as well as a Research, Records and

---

* For a more detailed look at how the RPF was organized and wielded violence, please refer to Appendix A, Structure of RPF Violence from 1994 through the Counterinsurgency.

Registry department, it has officers and lower-ranking staff in the Republican Guard, a military unit formerly known as the High Command that provides bodyguards for Kagame and his top aides. It also has people in the Gendarmerie, the Military Police and the army's Training Wing, where new recruits are inducted into the armed forces. Its agents have thoroughly infiltrated the regular army, with representatives at every level of each battalion, from the company to the platoon to the smallest section. The result is a kind of a military matryoshka structure, recalling the Russian dolls you open only to find another one inside. For example, every army battalion has an intelligence officer (IO) from the DMI. During the genocide, the RPA consisted of eleven battalions, so there were eleven IOs at the battalion level. Each of those officers had six to a dozen lower-ranking intelligence staff (IS) from the DMI at his side. Each company in every battalion had an IS. Since there were on average ten companies in each battalion, that meant there were an estimated 110 intelligence staff at the company level. Each company consisted of at least three platoons, each with its own intelligence staff member, meaning there were about 330 such staff at the platoon level. In each platoon there were three sections, each of them having two or three intelligence staff.

When, as part of implementing the Arusha agreement, the RPF was allowed to establish a political headquarters at the parliamentary buildings in Kigali, the politicians were allowed to bring a protective force: a small battalion of 600, with about six companies, 18 platoons and 36 sections, which meant that 100 to 140 RPF intelligence staff came with them. The DMI became the main instrument through which crimes were inflicted on Rwandans during the genocide, and is the continuing source of control and violence against Rwandans and Congolese. DMI staff killed, maimed and conducted sabotage throughout Rwanda and the region from 1990 through the genocide, the counterinsurgency and the conflict in Congo. They continue to do these things to this day, at home and abroad.

The DMI was created in 1990 and at first headed by Kayumba Nyamwasa, a man who fled Rwanda in 2010 decrying a "lack of democracy" in the country. Immediately after the genocide, it was run by Emmanuel Karenzi Karake, another shrewd, brutal RPF apparatchik even more skilled at eliminating enemies than his predecessor. It was at its most active in 1994, just before and during the genocide, using its agents to screen for and kill Hutus. Its tapping of Tutsi civilians as a support network inside Rwanda was central to its success.[2] The three-tiered military struggle by the RPF—using civilian militia, guerilla-type DMI units and regular battalion forces—recalls the military strategies of Mao Zedong in China and Vo Nguyen Giap, the Communist general whose forces beat the French and the Americans in Vietnam. The DMI was and still is omnipresent in Rwanda, operating in military, political and civilian realms. Its representatives have infiltrated international organizations and used embassies to attack, kidnap and intimidate people outside Rwanda's borders (more on this in later chapters).[3]

In the top secret report on the ICTR investigation of RPF crimes that was leaked to me, the investigators wrote: "The DMI is hated and feared by most of the Rwandan population, inside and outside of Rwanda, due to its reputation for cruelty and killing. Most of the massacres attributed to the RPA were committed by the DMI."[4]

The investigators concluded that RPF soldiers had slaughtered civilians but that the DMI representatives in the military units initiated these massacres. Reports by these intelligence agents and officers were sent to their superiors at DMI headquarters, bypassing the heads of their military units. It was not unusual for DMI agents to receive instructions from their commanders at DMI headquarters and undertake operations alongside battalion soldiers, sometimes without the knowledge of unit commanders. From July 1994 onward, after the RPF had seized control of the entire country, each company and platoon operated a dungeon (a secret detention center), which was managed by the intelligence staff under the supervision of the battalion intelligence officer. Local Tutsi cadres and civilians, described by the DMI as the "loyal population," oversaw the running of the dungeons, along with intelligence staff. Hutus were also arrested by regular RPF troops. The prisoners brought to these dungeons were executed based on decisions taken by unit commanders and the intelligence officers and staff. After the genocide, when the Red Cross began to inspect prison conditions in Rwanda with regularity, many prisoners were taken by the intelligence staff to other locations and eliminated.

Before and during the war, DMI representatives at the Training Wing are known to have killed young French-speaking recruits—Hutus and Tutsis—from Rwanda, Zaire and Burundi on the suspicion that any recruit who spoke French was a spy. DMI agents were in charge of screening and inter-rogating recruits. During the war, Hutu recruits were screened and trans-ported to sites where they were executed.

The DMI began training military and civilian commandos in July 1992, two years before the genocide began and one month after the start of the Arusha peace talks. The covert group, which carried out some of the most sinister acts before and during the genocide, was initially called the "network" and then became known as the "technicians." The ICTR investigators found that technicians were trained in five main areas:

i.   how to use chemicals to poison water and pharmaceutical products to kill
ii. how to use cords, hoes and plastic bags to kill, how to inject oil into ears to poison victims, how to carry out *akandoyi* (tying elbows behind the back)
iii. how to use bayonets, guns and grenades
iv. how to install mines and use remote control bombs
v.   how to gather intelligence

According to witnesses who testified to the investigators, the technicians reported to the High Command of the DMI, which in turn reported to Paul Kagame, who was the chairman of the RPF's High Command Council.

The following officers are listed as technicians in the top secret summary report. The list is not exhaustive.

Captain Jomba Kakumba
Captain Jean Bosco Muhigirwa
Captain Ntukayajemo, known as Kyago
Captain Herbert Kamugisha
Captain Mugisha
Lieutenant Christian Ibambasi
Lieutenant Alexis Rusuna
Lieutenant Geoffrey Byagatonda
Lieutenant Mahoro Aman
Lieutenant Alfred Karanangwa
Lieutenant Jean of God Ndagije

Lieutenant Geoffrey Gahigana
Lieutenant Eddy Nkuranga
Lieutenant Nurayija
Donat Sebera

At the end of their training, technicians were assigned to three groups tasked with three missions. The first group became, along with other High Command soldiers, escorts for Kagame. The second group went to Kigali and was tasked with providing intelligence for RPF troops in the buffer zone as they eventually moved toward the capital after the genocide began. The individuals in this group also placed bombs and land mines in public places such as bus stations to heighten distrust and tension, and, when the opportunity arose, they targeted and eliminated people opposed to the RPF. They threw grenades at residences and assassinated prominent Hutu politicians.

Their other job was to infiltrate the Interahamwe, the Hutu militia that killed Tutsis at roadblocks, in their homes and wherever they could find them. The technicians chosen to infiltrate the Interahamwe resembled Hutus, were shorter, spoke French and pretended to be servants, drivers, gas station attendants—anyone who could go unnoticed. The following technicians were identified by investigators as having infiltrated the Interahamwe:

Ntukayajemo, known as Kyago
Mugwaneza Jean Baptiste
Mahoro Aman
Gahigana
Kamugisha Herbert
Kanyemera Samuel
Geoffrey Byagatonda
Mugisha

The role of the technicians deployed with the Interahamwe was to assist in actually killing Tutsis and to incite the militia to commit more massacres.[5] The technicians wore civilian clothes but reported to Captain Herbert Kamugisha at the CND in Kigali, who in turn reported to Major Charles Karamba, an intelligence officer from the Third Battalion.

The third group of technicians was assigned to launch attacks in the buffer zone—the demilitarized zone that UN peacekeepers were supposed to monitor. There they received weapons from Uganda and ammunition and created arms caches. Former soldiers who testified to the ICTR investigators said these caches remained secret, even from the RPF.

The investigators listed several people against whom the ICTR could seek indictments in relation to crimes by the DMI:

1) Colonel Kayumba Nyamwasa, who directed the DMI before and during the genocide. "Nothing was done without his knowledge," according to the top secret report.

2) Jack Nziza, the head of special actions at the DMI. Before the genocide began, operatives under him infiltrated government-controlled zones wearing Hutu army uniforms, and assassinated prominent Hutus and Tutsis, in addition to carrying out acts of sabotage. Nziza was also involved, according to informants, in the screening and elimination of recruits from Rwanda and Burundi at the RPF's Training Wing.

3) Jackson Rwahama was head of DMI ground operations and close to Nyamwasa. "At the beginning of August 1994, he thanked new recruits in Masaka for the hard work which they had carried out. By work he meant the execution of Ibipinga opponents." (*Ibipinga* is a Kinyarwanda word for anyone opposed to the RPF.) He also is said to have organized meetings with intelligence staff and ordered them to keep the killings and arrests secret.

4) Dan Munyuza was an intelligence officer in the Training Wing for DMI. He was involved, in particular, with assassinating young French-speaking Tutsis suspected of being spies for the former Habyarimana government.

5) Sergeant Deus Kagiraneza worked under the orders of Munyuza and eliminated those suspected of being spies. According to informants, he was also involved in massacres in Ruhengeri when he was prefect after the genocide in 1994.

For many Tutsi soldiers, the discovery that colleagues had infiltrated the Interahamwe and killed fellow Tutsis at roadblocks gutted their faith in the RPF movement.

"I realized that interior Tutsis were pawns in Kagame's end game. Killing Tutsis and further discrediting the Hutu regime was part of an elaborate strategy to take power with the approval of the international community," said Théogène Murwanashyaka, who had been part of the High Command.[6]

Another soldier, an interior Tutsi who had worked in intelligence, said rumors had circulated early in the genocide that the RPF was killing Tutsis and fueling the killing madness.[7] He discovered it was true in July 1994, when RPA troops seized the capital. Several witnesses came to him with independent stories of what they'd seen, and one of the technicians who directly participated in these acts also confessed to him. The intelligence agent said his superiors talked openly about this infiltration, admitting they had "successfully manipulated Hutu hatred for Tutsis."

When he finally realized the extent of criminality he'd been part of, this soldier felt he was sinking in emotional quicksand. He told me, "The RPF had killed our relatives. I felt ashamed and guilty. It was excruciating. I wish I had died." He wanted to leave Rwanda in 1994 but did not have the means. If he had deserted the army or voiced opposition to these crimes, he would have been killed. He had no choice then but to silently continue being part of what he described as a highly successful "criminal and terrorist organization." He only managed to flee many years later.

These are the images and the actions these former intelligence officers and soldiers want to forget: Injecting syringes of kerosene into ears.[8] Smothering people with plastic bags. Choking with ropes and cords. Impaling women and girls with tools. Using *agafuni*—the RPF's war hammer—to crack skulls and spill brain matter out like porridge. Burying people alive. Forcing victims to dig their own graves. The methods are intimate, sadistic. They were used before, during and after the genocide, and are still being used, on civilians by the Directorate of Military Intelligence. Its signature technique is *akandoyi*, a variation of the strappado torture device used on witches and heretics during medieval times. *Gushyira ku akandoyi*, which in Kinyarwanda means "putting someone under akandoyi," involves tying a person's elbows behind their back so tightly that the head tilts downward. As the rib cage stretches, the lungs and diaphragm become tight and acute respiratory stress sets in. "Crying becomes impossible in this position," said a former DMI agent.[9] Victims' legs are then tied in a technique known as *umunzani*, which means balance. Once they are tied in this way, the victims usually die within an hour.[10] A voiceless, silent, efficient death.

The planning the RPF undertook to infiltrate Rwanda before the genocide, its efforts to keep its agenda hidden while appearing to go along with the peace process, the mask of innocence it wore in front of the international community as it achieved its ends—which was gaining absolute power in Rwanda and the region at a huge cost in human lives—the mask of the victim it still wears to prevent too close a scrutiny of its crimes: the seeds of the RPF's continuing impunity are all there in the party's basic structure, with the intelligence wing at its heart. And all of it flowed from the ruthlessness and cunning of its leaders, who, as the following chapters will demonstrate, committed war crimes to rival those of the Hutu *génocidaires*, yet are still unpunished.

GETTING AWAY WITH MASS MURDER AT THE BYUMBA STADIUM

THEY WERE BAREFOOTED HUTU PEASANTS—THOUSANDS OF RWANDAN men, women and children. "We called them *les va nu pieds*: weak, power-less people who worked in the fields and knew nothing about politics," said Théo Murwanashyaka.[1] They were hungry and cotton-mouthed from having been kept for three days in the courtyard of Byumba's town hall surrounded by a Tutsi-led army. Théo, an RPA High Command soldier who was stationed in Byumba at the time, said, "It was awful to watch. They were suffering. I thought we were going to let them go."

It was April 1994. The genocide had begun about two weeks earlier, unleash-ing a malignant ethnic killing fervor that spread across Rwanda's steep hillsides and luminous green plateaus with an efficiency and speed that would later surprise scholars who had also studied the ways the Holocaust had unfolded.[2]

The Hutu peasants had arrived in Byumba at the barrel of a gun. Kagame's forces had bombarded the sprawling refugee camp known as Nyacyonga, north of Kigali, where thousands of them had been living in makeshift shel-ters after being uprooted by war. After blasting the camp with mortar and gunfire, the troops left a path open for refugees to go north, announcing on Radio Muhabura, a station operated by the RPF, that the war was over and refugees could return to their homes and reclaim their belongings.

So the events in Byumba started with a plan. After the refugees had trekked to Byumba on foot, RPF soldiers ordered them to gather in front of the town hall and wait. Finally, the RPF promised food, drink and cooking supplies if they proceeded to the town's soccer stadium. The refugees did not know what lay in store or what else they should do, given that the RPA was everywhere—nor did a soldier like Théo for that matter—and they followed instructions to the letter.

It would take Théo a while to comprehend what he was about to witness in Byumba, let alone its purpose. Only later, as the genocide wore on and the bodies piled up, would he understand what Kagame's political ambitions really were.

Théo and his comrade Pina, another High Command soldier, had been ordered to stand guard outside the stadium. They watched the Hutus file in slowly, noting the mothers with babies strapped to their backs and the old people dizzy with exhaustion. As the sun edged below the horizon, the peasants settled in, began preparing the food the RPF had given them and looked forward to a night's rest. Soon the air grew cooler. The smoke from the cooking fires rose and children brought their bowls to their mothers, eager to fill their stomachs with *ubugali*, a thick porridge made from cassava flour.

Outside, Théo saw a series of convoys arrive and recognized senior figures in the RPF's military echelon among the men who disembarked. Theogene Rutayomba, an aide-de-camp to Kayumba Nyamwasa, the head of the Directorate of Military Intelligence, came and left. Two other DMI officials arrived: Jackson Rwahama and Dan Munyuza. Denis Karera, the ground commander in Byumba, and the RPF's chief political commissar, Frank Mugambage, also showed up. Théo grew increasingly concerned that something was about to occur, but there were so many Hutus inside the stadium he could not imagine what it would be.

Patrick, a young recruit from the RPF's Military Police battalion, was posted inside the stadium and had been briefed on what was about to go down—the first time he'd been privy to something so massively brutal and methodically executed.[3] Around 8 p.m., in the light of cooking fires, Military Police and members of Kagame's High Command unit began picking out the strongest males from the families on the pitch and in the bleachers, leading hundreds of them over to the stadium's dugout, which they'd kept clear of refugees. "It was about crowd control. They wanted to massacre the strongest quickly," Patrick said, shifting in his chair at the restaurant where we met.

Dan Munyuza—who worked for the RPF's Training Wing but assisted in DMI operations—lobbed the first grenade. "It was his way of saying that all weapons were allowed," Patrick said. As other members of the Military Police opened fire on the men, Patrick remembers hearing the women scream and the children cry. The crowd panicked and scrambled; many tried to escape but were blocked by soldiers.

It took more than an hour to slaughter all the men in the dugout. Many didn't die immediately after being shot and were finished off by men wielding the RPF's signature instrument, the *agafuni* or sharp hoe, which soldiers used to crack victims' skulls. Then they used grenades, machine guns and *agafuni* to slaughter the elderly men, the women and the children.

Théo and his friend Pina stayed outside at their post all night, listening in horror to the screams. "It was agony. I will never forget it. It went on until six o'clock in the morning." At dawn, Théo saw some of the first trucks come to haul away the dead. Getting the corpses out of the stadium was an over-whelming task. The stadium was slick with blood and had to be cleaned from top to bottom, Patrick said. But that wasn't his job. "I helped bury the bodies," he admitted.

Some were buried hastily at a flour mill and other locations in Byumba town. About half the corpses were dumped into mass graves in Rukoma, at the edge of Byumba prefecture.* A week after the massacre, Kagame called the Military Police commander, Augustin Gashayija, and was overheard by his bodyguards telling Gashayija that it had been *stupid* to bury the bodies. The French, long supporters of the Habyarimana regime, would be using their satellites to surveil the country and could find evidence of mass graves, Kagame said. Gashayija soon had new orders for his men. "We now needed to exhume the bodies and incinerate them," Patrick told me, his face

* Rwanda's highly organized administrative structure has existed since precolonial times. Before colonization, the country was made up of provinces, districts, hills and neighborhoods. In later years, Rwanda was divided into twelve districts called prefectures, which in turn were divided into 154 communes. These communes were made up of sectors, which in turn were divided into smaller cells. The administrative hierarchy allowed for people to be easily located and murdered during the 1994 genocide.

contorting with the memory of what he had seen, smelled and touched more than twenty years earlier.

The Military Police went back to Rukomo, put on masks and gloves, and dug up the human remains. "At first I refused to do it," Patrick said, "but I was lashed twenty times. Any soldier who still refused was shot. The bodies were decomposing and we were vomiting. It was really difficult. It was shameful to pick up pieces of babies and other human beings. It was inhumane. Many soldiers had nightmares after this."

In Rwanda, death is generally not regarded as the end. If the spirits of the dead are dishonored, many believe evil will befall those responsible. The soldiers would have believed that the intentional disturbing of a corpse was sure to unleash malevolent spirits. They had to tamp down their fears and overcome their cultural prohibitions about the respect due the dead since a program of ethnic cleansing was under way. At twilight's darkest hour, they transported the corpses southeast to Akagera park, a vast wilderness area near the border with Tanzania, far from the scrutiny of the United Nations peacekeepers and the few NGOs still in Kigali. There, they dumped the bodies in pits, and incinerated them with a mixture of gasoline and gas oil. Soon the smell of smoke with death in it issued from the RPF's improvised "ovens."

When the genocide broke out, Kagame's forces already controlled a large swath of Byumba, having seized it during the war of invasion that began in late 1990, and they had pushed up to a million Hutus into displacement camps such as Nyacyonga, where disease and hunger were rife. Within days of the plane crash that killed President Habyarimana, the RPF had claimed and controlled the entire territory, every misty green hill and plot of arable land.

The butchering at Byumba stadium, only days after the genocide began, clearly displayed the operating tactics that the RPF rolled out across the country in the weeks to come: first control access to an area, then round up or lure large groups of Hutus to a designated site with promises of food and safety. Sometimes the groups were kept where they congregated and killed there in the night, as in Byumba stadium, or they were hauled off in trucks to forests to be murdered away from anyone who could see, hear or suspect. The RPF was able to kill with impunity because it concealed much of the evidence by turning human beings into ash. People who had once existed were no longer traceable. Since they were often killed with their entire family, and since the entire country was awash in blood, who was left to register that they were gone? Occasionally, with smaller-scale killings, the RPF buried the Hutu dead in graves with Tutsis who'd been murdered by Hutu militia.

The Byumba stadium massacre was one of many mass murders during the genocide that the international community soon became aware of but clearly viewed through a different moral lens than they applied to killings by the Interahamwe and other Hutu *génocidaires*. When Kagame's Tutsi army killed Hutu civilians, human rights and legal investigators called the killings "massacres." If they were willing to acknowledge these crimes at all, Kagame's supporters referred to them as reprisal killings or as collateral damage. In contrast, when Hutu militia, soldiers or civilians killed Tutsis, the crimes were given their rightful name: genocide.

One side killed in broad daylight, openly and with abandon, without concern for the consequences; the other side mass-murdered meticulously, and covered up its heinous crimes. The RPF planned to seize and hold on to power for a very long time. It recognized that it needed to convince the international community that its members—being Tutsi and sharing the ethnicity of people who were clearly and openly victimized—had the moral authority to rule.

An investigator with the UN tribunal that probed the crimes committed during the genocide later gathered testimony from soldiers who took part in the killing at the stadium, and those who transported the bodies and burned them.[4] "In my life I've never seen a situation where so much evidence was collected and no indictment was issued," he said in one of the lengthy interviews I conducted with him. "The Byumba case is a very good example of how Kagame's regime operated. They would hold 'security' meetings. They'd bring or invite people to a location. They'd kill everybody. Then they'd get rid of the bodies."

The former investigator, who wishes to remain anonymous for security and professional reasons, is frustrated that so much of his work was stymied. In the early years of the UN International Criminal Tribunal for Rwanda, he investigated major cases against Hutu *génocidaires* that went to trial, which was gratifying. Then his expertise in investigating atrocities was put to use by the clandestine team that probed crimes committed by Kagame's army, the one whose report was leaked to me by the whistle-blower Clarise Habimana. It was a dangerous task for everyone involved, not least for the witnesses he interviewed, and fraught with ugly politics.

"We had 108 witnesses on operations that targeted Hutus, transported their bodies and got rid of them in Akagera park. Everyone knows this story. The UN knew," the investigator insisted. "This happened everywhere. The RPA cleaned up. [They] killed children, women and men. Whenever possible all Hutus were killed. They didn't kill the cows and chickens, though, because others were coming back to the country [they cleared]." Those "others" the investigator was referring to were the thousands of Tutsis who had been forced to flee Rwanda in pogroms in the late 1950s and early 1960s as the first Hutu regime was seizing power in the country, post independence. Many of them fled to Uganda, which is where the RPF was created.

The investigator estimated that Kagame's army killed hundreds of thousands of civilians in 1994. But he says that no indictments were ever issued for Kagame or his commanders because the political powers at the UN refused to go after them. "This was the politics of the United Nations," he said. The proof was there; the tribunal lawyers agreed that indictments should be prepared. But the prosecutions were not allowed to proceed.

Over the years, the investigator came to know witnesses such as Patrick— the young man who was inside the Byumba stadium the night of the slaughter—very well. Patrick served in Kagame's army for more than fifteen years. When I interviewed him, he told me, "It took us time to realize that we were not part of any revolution. We did a lot of damage to Rwanda, just like the Interahamwe did. It's shocking. The whole thing became a conflict of principles. We have many questions that we still don't have answers for." The muscles in his neck were so taut as he said this, his voice was strained.

Théo, for his part, came to despise Kagame's enterprise early on. The Byumba stadium massacre was not just about eliminating Hutus, although that was an integral part of it, he realized. It was about claiming land in Byumba, the breadbasket of Rwanda, for those thousands of Rwandan Tutsis who'd grown up as refugees in neighboring Uganda. The majority of these people grew up in squalid conditions, humiliated and nursing dreams of returning home. Thousands joined the RPF, and some of those who rose to power in that movement sought political and military revenge. Théo soon came to believe that the RPF killings were not about reprisals, even though the Hutu extremist radio, RTLM, was urging Hutu peasants to kill Tutsis in Kigali: "The RPF was doing an ethnic screening of Byumba [getting rid of Hutus in the north] so that former Tutsi refugees from Uganda could claim the land." The phenomenon of ethnic cleansing is not historically uncommon. In a case at the International Criminal Court, Croatia accused Serbia of genocide and of seizing lands throughout Croatia in 1991 with the goal of establishing a Greater Serbia. Prosecutors argued that the former Serbian president, Slobodan Milošević, was part of a joint criminal enterprise with other Serbian leaders that led to mass expulsions of Croatians from their homes. Serbia, for its part, made the counteraccusation that its people were victims of genocide after Croatian forces attacked in 1995 and reclaimed territory previously occupied by Belgrade.

In Byumba, the RPF devised and carried out a plan to lure Hutus to the stadium and kill them. Senior military figures from intelligence, Military Police and High Command units encouraged, aided and abetted these war crimes. They were part of a *joint criminal enterprise*, which had a purpose. The RPF officials rounded up refugees and falsely promised them security; they had already devised ways to efficiently exterminate thousands of Hutus and cover up the evidence; and they had a clear mission, which was to steal land for Tutsi returnees who had lost their homes in the pogroms that had pushed them into squalor in Uganda decades earlier.

The difference between what happened in Croatia and what happened in Byumba and other prefectures of Rwanda during and after the genocide is that the RPF did not expel the Hutus. It murdered them, ensuring there would be no reprisals or reclaiming of territory.

Where was Paul Kagame when the Byumba stadium massacre was carried out? According to witness accounts, he was in the town, very close to the bloodletting. Several of his bodyguards in the High Command protection unit told me and tribunal investigators that he was seen in the vicinity and that his military motorcade traveled throughout the town in the days leading up to the slaughter. He even slept in a house in Byumba, a few kilometers from the stadium, according to a soldier who guarded the residence with another RPA High Command soldier who was also a well-known soccer player. He remembered that when Kagame got back to the house one night, he told them both they'd have "a lot more room to play football when we're done here."[5]

Finishing a job efficiently and tying up all the loose ends have always been important for Kagame, who is disciplined and forward-thinking. The morning after the massacre, Kagame stopped by the stadium very early. A bodyguard who broke with the regime years later and escaped to the United States said that a dozen or so Hutus had jumped the fence of the stadium during the night and lay injured on the ground. They were still alive but barely able to move; some of them were children. The bodyguard said Kagame was furious.[6] "Finish them off," he ordered. "And clean this up."

An ICTR document leaked to me identified the Byumba stadium as a "massacre site."[7] "During meetings with the population that had taken refuge in the stadium, the military had gained their confidence," the investigators noted. The document said that Lieutenant-Colonel James Kabarebe, head of High Command, arrived at the stadium, where he talked with his military colleagues. After Kabarebe left, a Lieutenant Masumbuko gave the order to "open fire on the refugees." Kabarebe and Masumbuko, along with senior RPA officials, were named as potential targets for indictment.[8]

Witnesses also testified to the Special Investigations Unit (SIU) that, before the stadium killings, an RPA commander named Colonel Fred Ibingira had reported to Kagame that Tutsi civilians in the area had been murdered by Hutu militias and civilians. On the heels of that communication, "Kagame gave him the authorization to start killing the population in vengeance for the dead Tutsis."[9] Separately, another former High Command soldier, who is familiar with the massacre and now lives in exile in Europe, told me that Kabarebe showed up at the stadium and gave Lieutenant Masumboko the orders, then left the premises. The soldier said the Hutus were then destroyed like "beans in a bucket."[10]

Kabarebe's presence inside the stadium has been independently confirmed by several sources interviewed by the tribunal and by me. His role in briefing the soldiers who went on to massacre thousands of civilians speaks volumes about who is ultimately responsible for this crime. Were the evidence to be presented in a court of law, the Byumba stadium massacre would implicate

Paul Kagame himself, according to a man who was a leading member of the Rwandan Patriotic Front, given that the High Command leader reported directly to Kagame. Major Alphonse Furuma, an exile now living a quiet life in Texas, was one of the most highly regarded founders of the RPF and its precursor political movement, RANU. He is skeptical about the ethics and honor of most of his former comrades-in-arms—even exiled dissidents—occasionally referring to them bluntly as "cold-blooded killers."[11]

"Apparently High Command stepped in and took charge of the operation," Furuma said of the Byumba massacre. "If James Kabarebe came to brief soldiers, it means that James was the highest authority in that operation. That is significant in military terms. The person giving the briefing is the overall commander of the operation. But that doesn't make him the final person . . . James was working under the direct orders of Kagame. It meant that the High Command was getting directly involved in the execution of massacres, which makes Kagame directly responsible because these were his escorts." Furuma says that using High Command soldiers to massacre civilians brings the "crimes of Kagame, as an individual, to another level. Using your escorts is like using members of your household, using your husband or wife or children. These are people directly under his day-to-day management."

There is little doubt that Kagame, as commander of the RPA, had ultimate responsibility for the crimes committed in zones his army controlled in 1994.[12] No one dared to go against his authority, for fear of being executed.

7

KAGAME'S ROVING DEATH SQUADS

ON APRIL 9, 1994, SHORTLY AFTER DAWN—BARELY THIRTY-SIX HOURS after the president's plane was shot down—the Rwandan Patriotic Army arrived with guns blazing in the commune of Gituza, a regional district of Byumba prefecture. When troops neared the village where a man I'll call Daniel lived, Daniel heard people outside shouting, "Inkotanyi" (the common term for the RPF).[1] Within minutes, scores of people from an adjacent town ran into the village in a wild panic, some of them with bloody limbs and faces. Many of the first to die when the RPA advanced were educated Hutus whom Daniel knew very well: civil servants, teachers, businessmen and community leaders, along with their spouses and children. But peasants were not being spared. He and his wife and three sons ran south on a main road then headed east toward the commune of Rukara, where they joined thousands of other Hutus from neighboring communes who were also fleeing for their lives. After ten days of flight, staying one step ahead of the killers, Daniel along with his family and an estimated three thousand other displaced Hutus finally settled at the Karambi Trading Center, worn out from hiding and scrounging for food.

On April 20, RPA soldiers invaded the village and surrounded them. At about 7 a.m., sixty men brandishing machine guns and rifles told the hordes of people to gather in the garden at the back of the trading center, where they would be given information about returning home to their communes. Suspicious and terrified, Daniel shouted, "They're going to kill us!" As soon as he uttered the words, an RPF soldier took hold of his arm and ordered him to stay with him as he and the others herded the Hutus into the garden. Next the soldiers ordered them to sit down so they could listen to the RPF's plan for them. Though Daniel's wife and three sons were only a few meters away from him, he could barely see them in the crowd. Men and women around him clasped their hands and began to pray, fearing the worst. The pretense that this was a benign gathering didn't last long: the shooters surveyed the human beings before them, took aim, and began to spray the crowd with machine-gun fire. Some threw grenades. Victims who tried to run were shot and fell on the already injured. The blood of others gushed onto those still alive.

Daniel took a bullet in the leg, and was hit by shrapnel in the stomach, buttocks and forehead. After he collapsed, he did not move or yell. At one point he thought, "This is what dying is." The gunfire stopped, but he realized the killers were only pausing to reload. Daniel staggered up from the mass of corpses around him and ran as fast as he could, hoping the soldiers would not shoot him in the back. He'd picked his moment well, and got away.

He sought refuge in Akagera park, among the grevillea and sausage trees and papyrus swamps. He had worked for an international aid agency before the genocide and had picked up enough rudimentary medical knowledge to remove the bullet from his leg and the bits of shrapnel from his other wounds, and bandage himself. It would have been safer to stay where he was, but Daniel needed to know what had happened to his wife and sons. If they were dead, he wanted to bury them properly so their souls would not wander in anguish.

On April 22, two days after the slaughter, he made his way back to Karambi Trading Center. He saw that the soldiers had left and that civilians he took to be Tutsi were coming and going, pillaging the shops and homes. With trepidation, Daniel headed around the back of the trading center, where he found an immense garden of the dead. Victims' limbs were severed, their bodies riddled with bullet and shrapnel wounds. Many were burned. He began to search, and at last found his 28-year-old wife among the corpses. She'd been shot in the head and her torso and face were scarred by fire. Beside her were their three sons—aged six, five and three—their bodies also charred. He couldn't leave his family there. But no one would help him without being paid, and he had no money. He was afraid the soldiers would return or that the Tutsi civilians would denounce him. "In the end," he told me, "I was not able to bury my family." Daniel has borne that sorrow ever since.

He left them where they lay and returned to his home village, where he found his 17-year-old sister, Jeanne, hiding. The rest of the place appeared deserted. They decided to gather food and a few of their belongings and escape through the park to Tanzania. Jeanne said she would run quickly to collect some food and other essentials while he packed. Shortly after she left, he heard a crowd coming up the road. He looked outside to see a gang, most of them Tutsi civilians he recognized, holding his sister. "There were at least a dozen of them. They had traditional weapons, machetes and hoes." (He gave a list of their names to a refugee rights organization after he fled the country.)[2]

As they got closer, he ran outside to hide behind the mango and avocado trees in his yard. He knew if he stayed in the house he'd be caught and sliced to pieces. The men brought his sister into his house and proceeded to rape her, one after the other, while Daniel hid, listening to her agony. His powerlessness to stop them and save his sister still haunts him. As soon as they were finished assaulting her, they torched the bedroom with Jeanne still in it and left. When they were out of sight, Daniel rushed inside, but his sister was already dead. On May 8, he managed to cross the border into Tanzania, joining other Hutu refugees in overcrowded camps.

There were only a few survivors of the Karambi massacre of April 20, but I found another one: Malik from Murambi commune, who was seventeen at the time. Malik, whose forehead is scarred and whose buzz-cut hairline is severely dented, told me his story calmly, if haltingly. He also has significant scars on his left shoulder blade, which he showed me.

When the RPF arrived, he and his family fled to the neighboring commune of Rukara. After two days of rest, they made their way to Karambi Trading Center, which was already full of displaced Hutus but seemed quiet. When the Inkotanyi arrived and summoned everyone to the meeting, Malik said many were afraid. A few lucky ones managed to escape, but Malik and his family were surrounded, and herded along with "thousands" of others to the garden.[3]

All of a sudden, Malik said, "one of the killers gave a signal, then they started to fire and throw grenades." As he tried to scramble away, he felt a hot, piercing blast to his body and fell with a thud. He could barely breathe. He'd been struck on the forehead and his left shoulder blade by shrapnel, and shot in the arm, wrist and right thigh. In those first moments, which seemed to go on forever, he closed his eyes and pretended to be dead. The shooting eventually stopped. His ears were ringing. People whimpered and moaned. Time wore on and on. He could hear soldiers talking and moving about. He opened his eyes and saw them pour gasoline on the victims at the edge of the pile he was in. But he was in the middle where the soldiers could not reach without climbing over the bodies, so he was not doused. When they set the pile on fire, many were still alive but were too wounded to get away; they writhed and screamed in excruciating torment amid the swirl of black smoke. The fire twisted slowly toward Malik, who tried to lie stock-still. "I was petrified," he said, "and I stood up. I held my arms in the air in surrender. Then an Inkotanyi hit me with a hoe. It struck the top of my scalp. He then struck my left cheek. I fell unconscious."

He somehow survived. When he came to the following morning, he realized it had rained, because there were puddles everywhere. The rain had put out the fire before it reached him. But around him, his entire family was dead: his parents, three sisters, two brothers, an aunt and an uncle. What would he do now? What was the point? Still, he pulled himself up and staggered to hide in the banana plantations in a place called Ngumeri, where a man named Joseph gave him shelter and treated his wounds. A number of other Hutu refugees slept outside Joseph's home so they could better hear if the Inkotanyi were coming for them. A week later, they got word that the RPF was fast approaching, so they all fled to Tanzania, including Joseph.

I interviewed an RPA intelligence officer who was in Byumba prefecture in April 1994 and confirmed Malik's and Daniel's account of the slaughter at Karambi Trading Center. He told me that at least three thousand Hutus were killed there, and that it was only one of "many" large-scale massacres throughout Rwanda in 1994 in which the RPA rounded up Hutus, promising them they'd be safe, then butchered them.[4] The RPF didn't always clean up right away in areas firmly under their control. And occasionally they left the evidence of the killings in place if they saw a political or propaganda advantage in doing so.

In June 1994, Major Alphonse Furuma was the RPF's Commissioner for Inspectorate and the job required him to travel freely in the east, from north to south, then westward close to the Burundi border—from Gabiro to Rwamagana, down into Kibungo and then up to Gashora.* The RPA had entered those zones and cleared out former Hutu forces. "Essentially the whole area was littered with bodies. I could see old bodies, and I could see fresh bodies. I could tell which bodies had been there since [the start of] the genocide, and which bodies had been [killed by] the RPA. What was most striking is that in the south, in the area between Kigali and Burundi, you could see evidence of massacres. Although the Interahamwe and government forces had left much earlier, I could see recent military activity in terms of bodies and belongings left on the streets. That showed me that the RPA had been targeting civilians. It was easy to look at those bodies and know that they had been there for about a week." He said the bodies of Tutsis killed earlier in the genocide had been removed by the Hutu *génocidaires*. "They were cleared as they were killed. The Hutus did not expect to run away. They carried out the massacres with the confidence that they would stay in place. They dumped them in mass graves or elsewhere to make their lives comfortable." He said at that stage in June, at the height of the genocide, "the RPA was killing and going. The idea was nobody was going to differentiate between these victims [of the RPA] and the victims of the genocide.

"Who was going to know the difference? There were bodies left and right. Come to a primary school, more bodies. Come to a church, more bodies. Come to a training center, more bodies. I knew these were not bodies of Tutsis. From their appearance, I could easily tell."

Who was going to know the difference? Who was going to tell? These are crucial questions to ask in light of what I was learning about the killing record of the RPF before, during and after the genocide.

Since the genocide, Joseph Matata, a Rwandan farmer of mixed ethnicity, has done his utmost to shed a clear light on the violence that engulfed his

---

* In August 1993, Furuma was promoted to the rank of major and appointed the RPF's Commissioner of Inspectorate. The appointment, he said, was in recognition of his abilities, but it was understood that he would not criticize what he witnessed. As commissioner, he was allowed to enter territory seized by the RPA and would report back on what he saw, in addition to liaising with RPF civilian cadres. When I pressed Furuma on whether he witnessed actual killings as they were taking place, he would not elaborate. He referred me to the public statement he issued to the Ugandan authorities and the press after he fled in January 2001. The substance of that statement is given in Chapter 15.

homeland. In the process, he has become something of a legend in the field of human rights. In the 1970s and early 1980s, Matata worked at the National Bank of Rwanda in Kigali. A voluble man who was openly critical of Habyarimana's one-party rule, he grew tired of life in the capital. He loved the outdoors and eventually moved to Murambi, a village near Rwanda's eastern border with Tanzania, where he had a farm. In November 1990, when Kagame's troops first invaded northern Rwanda from Uganda, the Hutu government accused Matata of aiding the rebellion, a charge he denied, and briefly threw him in jail. In 1991, alarmed by the illegal detention and mistreatment of civilians under the Habyarimana government, he became a founding member of ARDHO, the Rwandan Association for the Defense of Human Rights. (After he moved to Belgium, he became the head of the Brussels-based Center to Fight Impunity and Injustice in Rwanda and has become a tireless chronicler of the complex, unrepentantly violent history of his country.)

In April 1994, when the genocide began, he was in Belgium at a conference. But his children and his wife, an ethnic Tutsi, were at home in Murambi. At dawn on April 12, a group of Interahamwe arrived at the house looking for blood. The attackers quickly forced Matata's family outdoors, where they sliced his wife's back with a machete and then went after his 12-year-old daughter, cutting her neck and face. The girl fell to the ground and soon lapsed into a coma from blood loss. A Hutu neighbor named John intervened as the militia started beating the three other children with clubs, and the attackers moved on, likely figuring they'd at least killed two Tutsis. With the help of a local gendarme who knew the family, John managed to get Matata's wife and daughter to the nearest hospital; the rest of the children found refuge with a neighbor who kept them safe by paying off the marauding bands of killers. A week later, the RPF swept into Murambi and brought Matata's wife and daughter to a better hospital in neighboring Gahini, a village in the commune of Rukara, on the shores of Lake Muhazi. "For that, I have to thank the RPF," Matata said dryly, as we sat talking at a restaurant in central Brussels in 2013.[5]

When the RPF formed an emergency coalition government at the end of the genocide in late July, flights resumed to Kigali and Matata was finally able to get home. His children were safe with his neighbor, so he headed straight to Gahini to pick up his wife and daughter, who had moved into a house near the hospital. It was then that he heard a litany of the horrors that had occurred in Gahini and in villages throughout the prefectures of Kibungo and Byumba, including the systematic large-scale killings of Hutus perpetrated by the RPF. "I was grateful to the RPF for helping my family, but I couldn't ignore what I was hearing," said Matata, who was unable to finish a single glass of beer during our three-hour interview. "As someone who believed in human rights, I felt obliged to investigate the allegations."

Within days, Matata had interviewed dozens of villagers, many of whom would later disappear. He also visited ten mass graves in three nearby towns.[6] Some of the bodies of Hutus in those graves were later dug up and burned, or reburied in mass graves containing Tutsis killed by the Interahamwe. One of his former employees on the farm assisted Matata with the investigation. This man, a Tutsi, told Matata he'd had the ghastly job of transporting corpses for the RPA in a *fourgonnette*—a kind of African taxi minibus the RPA had seized—to mass graves. Matata said, "He was traumatized. Sometimes the victims loaded into the taxi weren't even dead. They would still be moaning and crying." (This man, whom Matata described as a sensitive person, eventually had problems with the RPF and was forced to flee the country.) Witnesses told Matata that "the RPA hunted people down like they would rabbit or other prey. The soldiers did clean-up operations in the hills. They went from house to house, shooting people." Some people hid in banana groves or escaped to the Akagera park. "Quite a few victims would see the soldiers coming and throw themselves into the lake and drown," he told me. At that time, he also documented the entrapment method used by the RPA to kill larger groups of people. "They asked people to gather in certain areas, in schools and markets. Those who showed up at these meetings were given cooking equipment, clothes and food. These people were told to spread the word about other meetings. When larger groups of people showed up, the RPA used grenades or guns to kill them." Matata described the way the RPF tried to instill trust before going in for the kill: "They caress their victims before they kill them. It's appalling. Not even the Nazis did this."

Matata contended that the RPF committed similar slaughters in other areas of the country too. But he was unable to complete a full investigation—with names and numbers of victims—because his life was soon in danger. When local authorities he knew threatened his safety if he carried on, Matata and his family went to live in Kigali, where it was safer and international agencies and UN staff had poured in. In early 1995, he and his family had to leave Rwanda for good.

Before he fled the country, Matata tried to ascertain who was specifically responsible for the slaughter in the area where he and his family had lived. Eventually, he discovered that the orders had emanated from a lieutenant colonel who would later go on to lead the world's biggest UN peacekeeping operation. "That commander was Patrick Nyamvumba," Matata told me. "The soldiers who massacred civilians were under his responsibility."

Today, Nyamvumba is Rwanda's chief of defense staff and a highly respected figure on the international military stage. In 2009, UN secretary-general Ban Ki-moon appointed him commander of UNAMID, the joint United Nations and African Union peacekeeping mission in Darfur, set up to stop ethnic cleansing in Sudan. Nyamvumba held the post of UNAMID commander until June 2013, and when he stepped down, Ban praised the general for his "dedication and invaluable service" provided over four years.[7]

In extensive interviews, more than a dozen former members of the RPF's Training Wing, High Command unit and Directorate of Military Intelligence shared with me their knowledge of Nyamvumba's supervisory role in RPA massacres in Rwanda. They also shared crucial information about Nyamvumba's former comrade-in-arms Jean Bosco Kazura, a man who led one of Nyamvumba's death squads yet eventually became the peacekeeping chief of the UN's stabilization force in Mali, in 2013.[8]

Others, too, have come forward with stories about Nyamvumba's actions during and after the genocide. A young man named Kamanzi—a Tutsi genocide survivor who was a teenager at the time—related to me chilling memories of Nyamvumba and some of his men operating in an area on the western rim of the Lake Victoria basin, a seeming paradise of red rutted paths, papyrus reeds and bourbon coffee trees that belies its history as a killing ground. In late April 1994, Kamanzi was entrusted by the RPF with collecting livestock on abandoned properties seized by the RPF, because of his acquaintance with some of the young Tutsi soldiers who were based nearby. He remembers Nyamvumba as a pleasant man with a limp: "He presented well. He was calm and often smiling. He was the ground commander. Soldiers were definitely comfortable around him."[9] Nyamvumba often stayed in the

most beautiful house in Gahini, overlooking Lake Muhazi—the first dwelling on the left on a road leading to the top of the hill. Kamanzi went to Nyamvumba's residence several times, and said he often saw young women there; one well-known local woman became Nyamvumba's girlfriend. Kamanzi told me he regularly accompanied soldiers when they ransacked buildings, grabbing merchandise, food and money. "It was wartime. We were trying to get by," he explained.

It was while going house to house and into the fields with these men that the teenager saw firsthand what the RPF soldiers' actual objectives were. Over a period of two months, from late April to June, Kamanzi accompanied soldiers on their missions two to three times a week. The soldiers referred to the work as "screening" or "cleaning out" the enemy. "I saw soldiers kill people. Sometimes I stayed back in the vehicle because I really did not want to see what was happening," he said. "I was frightened to see someone killed in front of me." The soldiers, many of them barely out of their teens, said the unarmed Hutus they killed were Interahamwe. "But what is sad is that these were villagers," Kamanzi said. "They weren't Interahamwe. Many of them were working in the fields. Sometimes the parents had fled and children were left at home alone. Unfortunately, the soldiers killed the children."

Kamanzi remembers one traumatic incident early on, in a village near Akagera park. "We went into a house. No one was there except a little girl about five years old. The soldiers asked her where her parents were. She told them they had gone into the fields. A few of us headed back to our vehicle, but one soldier stayed behind. After a few seconds I heard a gunshot. The soldier shot her dead. He later told me she was the daughter of an Interahamwe. He didn't even think that she was just a little girl. At that point I wondered: 'Did these people come to save us?'"

Nyamvumba rarely accompanied his soldiers during such operations. But there was one incident, Kamanzi recalled, where they'd received word that Hutus in a particular village might be armed. On that day, the ground commander, his escorts and a team of soldiers went in separate vehicles to the location, eventually surrounding a house there. Kamanzi went along too. He heard Nyamvumba give orders in Swahili, a language the teenager did not understand, and then saw him retreat a few meters away from the action, while soldiers fired for an extended period of time. As in every mission

Kamanzi witnessed, the soldiers met no resistance, no fighters: the RPA soldiers just proceeded to kill.

Former soldiers and officers told me that before April 1994, Nyamvumba was the chief instructor of the RPA's Training Wing, which provided military instruction to new recruits—a middle-ranking officer with very little, if any, command experience. After the genocide was unleashed, he was put in charge of creating clandestine units to (euphemistically) screen, mop up and otherwise rid the hillsides of Hutu civilians. The death squads made two geographical swoops: they started in the north of Rwanda—which the RPF largely controlled in early April—then moved down the eastern edge of the country to the southern tip near the Tanzanian border during the remainder of the month and throughout May. Some units stayed in the east while others fanned out into Gitarama in June, then headed south to Butare in July, before going back up to the northeast of Rwanda at the end of the genocide. They operated principally in areas already under RPF control in the rear of the army's 157th mobile force, led by Colonel General Fred Ibingira, and the Seventh Brigade, under Colonel William Bagire.

Nyamvumba composed his mobile units from young soldiers drawn principally from the RPF's High Command—Kagame's bodyguards—and soldiers from the Training Wing and the DMI. Many former officers told me that the operations were conceived, planned and coordinated by Kagame and his High Command Council and the DMI, along with intelligence staff from High Command and the Training Wing. Several sources confirmed that these operations were approved by the RPF's political body, the RPF Secretariat. According to senior officers familiar with the death squads, Nyamvumba received direct instructions from Kagame. One intelligence officer who worked directly for Kagame was Silas Udahemuka, who also helped coordinate these operations, assisted by three other Kagame bodyguards: Innocent Gasana, Jackson Mugisha and Charles Matungo.

At the time, the DMI was headed by Kayumba Nyamwasa, who was second to Kagame in the RPF's military hierarchy. (Nyamwasa fell out with his boss in 2010, fled to South Africa and survived an assassination attempt by suspected Rwandan agents.[10]) Another central figure from the DMI who helped execute the cleansing was Jackson Rwahama. "Rwahama was a senior killer from the Ugandan army, who had worked in intelligence for Idi Amin,"

one officer said, referring to the ruthless dictator whose 1970s Ugandan regime was marked by egregious human rights abuses and political repression. "Rwahama helped coordinate the killings. Remember, Nyamvumba was young at the time and had little experience. They asked themselves, 'How are we going to kill a lot of people in a short period of time before anyone knows about it?' Rwahama was the best person to plan this," the officer claimed, given Rwahama's experience helping to plan and execute crimes under the Idi Amin government.

At least three deputy commanders overseeing death squads reported to Nyamvumba. They were John Birasa, Emmanuel Butera and Jean Bosco Kazura. Kazura was an intellectual with a passion for soccer and little battle experience. Originally from Burundi, he spoke fluent French, English and Kinyarwanda. Commissioned in 1992, he joined the RPF's High Command, where he became a translator for Kagame. But as soon as Habyarimana's plane was shot down, Kazura was catapulted into new, deadlier terrain.

Immediately after the assassination, Nyamvumba left his official job at the headquarters of the Training Wing, near the Ugandan border, along with three intelligence staff and several members of the rank and file.[11] Some of the first sweeping operations were along the eastern border of the demilitarized zone in the north, where the RPF had gained the upper hand in the pre-genocide war of invasion. The RPF had already infiltrated the area and tried to establish trust with Hutu peasants, promising them salt, sugar, medicine and other basic necessities. These peasants were some of the first people to be caught and killed. And in April, the RPF's Training Wing was relocated to Gabiro, creating a new military base of operations at the edge of Akagera National Park. As the genocide wore on, Nyamvumba's units grew to an estimated eight hundred soldiers, bolstered by new Tutsi recruits from within Rwanda and the surrounding countries. Kagame's translator, Jean Bosco Kazura, became deputy commander of these operations.

Gabiro, along with the killing spots inside Akagera park, became a bona fide death factory during the genocide. The new military base was a 36-square-kilometer site that the RPF declared off-limits to UN peacekeepers and NGOs, ostensibly because Kagame's army needed to remove antipersonnel mines in the area. One of the main killing centers was Nasho, next to a lake of the same name, on the park's southern flank.

David, a former RPF officer now living in exile, listed for me some of the people he knew to be involved. "Kazura was at times in Nasho overseeing those killings," he said. "Sometimes John Birasa was there with Nyamvumba, who was working under Kagame's orders." When he is not talking about Rwanda, David is jovial and ironic, his expressions betraying little of the emotional scars he bears. But when he speaks of the crimes that unfolded around him in his homeland, his mouth contorts and his brow twists. "They had the manpower to dig [mass graves], to burn [the corpses]," David said. "There were some serial killers, people who were trained just to kill, to exterminate. Others were there to get rid of the dead."

One of the first killing spots was Gabiro's House of Habyarimana—a guest lodge of more than two hundred rooms that had once been the home of Rwanda's king.[12] As soon as the genocide started, the RPF began to use the facility for screening, identifying and eliminating Hutus. Other known killing grounds were deeper in the park, five to ten kilometers from Gabiro, and at Rwata, thirty kilometers away, near the Akagera River.

"From Gabiro, Hutus could not escape; they were surrounded by soldiers. They were thrown into mass graves dug by bulldozers. Then soldiers started shooting at them," an intelligence officer who had received daily reports of the sweeping operations told me. "Lieutenant Colonel Nyamvumba . . . was the commander of that operation." [13]

The officer, who now lives in Europe, estimates that the death squads killed many thousands of people. He said that five to ten lorries, each carrying from 100 to 200 bodies, went through Gabiro and into the park nightly for months. The base at Gabiro had bulldozers for digging, stocks of diesel and petrol to burn corpses, and even acid to dissolve the victims' remains. The ashes of the dead were then mixed with soil or dumped into the lakes in the park.

By June, at the height of the genocide, Kazura had moved on to Rwamagana, east of the capital of Kigali, an area that was now under RPF control. A High Command soldier said Kazura was in charge of about one hundred soldiers who hunted down civilians, killed them and dumped them in a pit in neighboring Rutonde. "Kazura was personally involved in carrying out and commanding and overseeing those operations of hunting down and rounding up Hutu civilians [in this area east of Kigali], bringing them to a detention house and taking them to the killing site," said the soldier, who was present during the murders.[14] In one incident, Hutu women and children who had taken refuge in a Catholic church were taken to Rutonde, where they were massacred and thrown into a pit on top of Tutsi victims who had been killed by Interahamwe earlier in the genocide. Other people were captured and detained at a petrol station before being killed and buried in the same pit.

"Women's arms were tied behind their backs with their *pagnes* [wraparound garments] and men were tied with their shirts. They were taken to a detention center at the petrol station in Rwamagana. In the evening they were killed at the station or were taken to the pit and killed there," the soldier said. He estimated that at least six hundred people were killed in this manner in Rwamagana alone, and more than two thousand in total from the nearby area.

A junior officer who was posted there said that, by early July, Kazura was coming to Rwamagana several times a week in his white Land Cruiser. He stayed at the Dereva Hotel, a guesthouse where he had access to women and alcohol.[15] The junior officer, a quiet, self-assured man named Damas, confirmed that Rwamagana was a microcosm of the style of detention and killing the RPF practiced throughout the genocide. Damas was there in July when soldiers at the local Gendarmerie barracks killed an estimated two hundred Hutu men with guns and hoes. Many of the Hutus had their arms and hands tied behind their backs. Some of them were already dead from gunshot wounds they'd received while they were being rounded up. Damas has vivid memories of the slaughter, which took place under cover of night in a tent sent up in the barracks compound. "No one could say no when it was happening or [insist] that it had to stop," he said. "On a personal level, it was shocking, but we were in a killing situation." The bodies were loaded onto three Mercedes trucks and driven to the Akagera park. "After it was over, one soldier said aloud: 'Not all of these bastards are killers. We didn't have to kill all of them!' The soldier was then struck in the head with a hoe and brought to a hospital." (Damas said Kazura was not present that night, and that the forces carrying out those killings were part of the regular army serving under a major named Gahigana.)

As the genocide wound down, both Kazura and Nyamvumba oversaw the transport of Hutu refugees back into Rwanda from the camps in Tanzania to which they had fled. In one instance, an officer witnessed Kazura directing operations in which an estimated 120 women and children were promised food, supplies and a peaceful return home. They were put on trucks at Benaco, a town on the Tanzania border, and brought to Rwanteru, Rwanda, where they were killed.[16]

"I was there when they were collected in trucks. Most of them were ladies and children. The men were very few," the officer told me. "These people were killed under the command of Kazura. They were killed with hoes in Rwanteru."

Immediately after the genocide and in the years that followed, Nyamvumba and Kazura worked with DMI agents to supervise the screening of Hutu men from all over Rwanda, who were rounded up at night or deliberately recruited into RPF military ranks in order to be eliminated at Akagera National Park and in the Nyungwe forest in southwestern Rwanda. "Nyamvumba was chief coordinator of those operations because, after all, he had already done it. He was critical," said an officer. Another officer told me, "After the genocide, Nyamvumba wasn't the only one," noting that brigades led by notoriously violent commanders such as Fred Ibingira also killed or rounded up Hutu civilians.

A soldier at a barracks in Kigali called the Camp Garde Présidentielle (Camp GP) also witnessed Kazura's participation in such operations in 1995. "Kazura was involved in taking people in lorries from Kigali to Gabiro. Those people were young Hutu men that were lured into military training from all over the country then taken to Kigali, to Camp GP," he said. Some of the recruits were actually young men coming back from Zaire who were seized and forced into trucks at the border, in Gisenyi. Others were from families who believed that the war was over and that their sons could stay safe by joining the RPA. "Kazura was personally involved in transporting the recruits. And then those men were taken to Gabiro, where they were killed and burned near the Training Wing, at a place called New Camp, near the house of the former king of Rwanda." Some of these young Hutu men died of carbon monoxide poisoning on their way to Gabiro. RPF senior commanders and intelligence agents shoved Hutu recruits into airtight compartments in trucks and piped in the exhaust while the engines were running.[17]

In 1996, this soldier was in Gabiro for training. He saw that Hutus were still being brought to the barracks, and he witnessed Kazura, Nyamvumba and key members of the DMI on site. "Kazura, Nyamvumba, Jack Nziza and Nyamwasa were personally involved in killing and supervising the burning of bodies," the soldier said.

His testimony is strengthened by the observations of a former ICTR investigator, who told me that the ICTR had enough evidence to indict Nyamwasa, Nyamvumba and others. He said witnesses brought forward evidence against Nyamvumba for his role in killings in the east, and against Kazura with respect to his role in transporting and eliminating Hutu recruits. "Evidence on Patrick Nyamvumba? We had enough evidence to get him twenty-five times over."[18]

Two confidential ICTR documents also provide details of operations led by Nyamvumba. In one document, a witness formerly with the RPF's Training Wing who was involved in operations at Gabiro is quoted claiming that as soon as Kagame's troops seized the Training Wing in April, one of the principal objectives was to eliminate displaced Hutus from the northern communes.[19] The civilians were brought to Gabiro aboard Mercedes-Benz trucks that had been abandoned by enemy battalions. One of Kagame's bodyguards, Lieutenant Silas, was put in charge of operations with a Sergeant Gasana, who was in direct communication with Nyamvumba. The procedure was the following: Civilians were brought to the House of Habyarimana, the former hotel. Soldiers tied the victims' arms behind their backs so tightly that their elbows touched. They then forced them to walk single file to the "cemetery," where they were shot. In some cases, the soldiers ran out of rope to tie everyone, so once victims were killed, they untied them and used those ropes on others. The executions continued day and night for the four to five weeks the witness was on site; he left Gabiro at the end of May. By the end of April, he said, the smell of corpses began to overwhelm the camp. Two bulldozers were used to bury the bodies.

The other ICTR document, featuring sworn testimony from an ex–DMI agent, indicated that between November 1994 and May 1995, Nyamvumba was a commander in the southwestern prefecture of Gikongoro, and that the RPF was still conducting "cleaning operations."[20] The witness participated in these operations, which involved arresting civilians, confining them at the military camp in Gikongoro, and killing them with ropes, knives, plastic bags, hammers or hoes. "We could not use guns because we were too close to the commune and they would have heard gunfire," he testified. Corpses were taken by truck to Nyungwe forest, where they were buried in mass graves. Each truck carried between fifty and sixty corpses at a time. Another vehicle, a green military Land Cruiser, was also used to bring the dead to the forest.[21]

It's clear that the evidence of RPF crimes was everywhere in the days and months after the genocide. So why did the image of Kagame and his forces as the heroes who put an end to the killing of innocents persist? I believe it is because so many institutions and governments needed the story of the genocide to be one of good and evil, with the evildoers simply defined. But the UN in particular cannot claim ignorance when it comes to these crimes.

By August 1994, with the RPF firmly in power, Rwanda had been drastically transformed. Nearly a third of its population had fled to camps in neighboring countries.[22] With Operation Turquoise, France's military had established a safe zone in southwest Rwanda and the UN force commander, Roméo Dallaire, had requested to be relieved of his command and to quit the country, debilitated by what was later diagnosed as PTSD. That same month, the United Nations refugee agency hired Robert Gersony, a US consultant with extensive experience in African war zones, to conduct a survey on the feasibility of Rwandan refugees returning to their homes after the genocide. Like many who came to Rwanda in the aftermath of the genocide, Gersony and his team were initially sympathetic to the RPF, which granted them access to ninety-one sites in more than forty communes around the country, mostly in Kibungo, Gisenyi and Butare, and in nine refugee camps in neighboring countries.[23] They conducted interviews with two hundred individuals and held another hundred small-group interviews. What they discovered was disturbing: RPF soldiers appeared to have carried out genocide against Hutu civilians.

The US State Department sent a cable dealing with Gersony's findings to the US ambassador to the United Nations at the time, Madeleine Albright, and to US embassies in the region. The cable, dated September 1994, read:

Refugees were called for meetings on peace and security. Once gathered, the RPA would move in and carry out the killing. In addition to group killings, house-to-house searches were conducted; individuals hiding out in the swamps were hunted; returnees as well as the sick, the elderly, the young and males between 18–40 years old were victims. So many civilians were killed that burial of bodies is a problem. In some villages, the team estimated that 10,000 or more a month have been killed since April.[24]

Another cable, dated October 14, 1994, and sent by Shaharyar Khan, with the UN peace monitoring mission UNAMIR, to the DPKO at the United Nations, quoted Gersony using strong language to describe the crimes committed by the RPA against Hutus:

Gersony put forward evidence of what he described as calculated, pre-planned, systematic atrocities and genocide against Hutus by the RPA whose methodology and scale, he concluded, (30,000 massacred) could only have been part of a plan implemented as a policy from the highest echelons of the [now Tutsi-led] government. In his view, these were not individual cases of revenge and summary trials but a pre-planned, systematic genocide against the Hutus. Gersony staked his 25-year reputation on his conclusions which he recognized were diametrically opposite to the assumptions made, so far, by the UN and the international community.[25]

(It is worth keeping in mind here that Gersony and his team did not visit Byumba, Rwanda's biggest prefecture, which had been under the RPF's control within days of the start of the genocide and, from the evidence I've gathered, was Kagame's most efficient killing ground.)[26]

Gérard Prunier, a French historian and scholar of Africa, interviewed Gersony later, and said that Gersony admitted that he never wrote a fully developed version of his findings because he knew they were too explosive and would never be made public, even though the substance of his investigation had already been leaked to the press.[27] In his book *Africa's World War*, Prunier claimed that the US Undersecretary of State for Global Affairs, Timothy Wirth, was given orders by Washington to discredit Gersony's findings.[28] "Wirth went to Kigali and New York, reassured the RPF, attacked

Gersony's methodology, hinted at a Hutu conspiracy, and leaked carefully chosen tidbits of information to the press. It worked," Prunier wrote.

Gersony's field notes were ultimately suppressed as part of a concerted effort to protect Kagame's post-genocide regime. In 1996, when the office of the UN's special rapporteur investigating crimes that occurred during the genocide asked the UN refugee agency for more information about Gersony's findings, it received a curt reply: "We wish to inform you that the Gersony Report does not exist."[29] As a result, individuals suspected of being behind the slaughter of innocents were never questioned. Gersony never spoke of his investigation again. Despite numerous requests, I was unable to secure an interview with him.

Other influential groups did have clear proof of RPF crimes. Its practice of luring people to meetings and then killing them fit a pattern that Human Rights Watch recognized in its 1999 seminal account of the genocide, *Leave None to Tell the Story*, coauthored by the late scholar and activist Alison Des Forges.[30]

"RPF forces killed civilians at meetings organized soon after their arrival in the community, a practice which gave rise to the bitter joke that *kwitaba Imana*, meaning to die, had come to mean the same as *kwitaba inama*, to attend a meeting," HRW wrote in their report. *Leave None to Tell the Story* also highlighted a series of RPF summary executions of prominent members of the former Hutu government, army and political parties. And its researchers documented several small massacres by RPF forces but provided few details. The Byumba stadium massacre warrants only a sentence in HRW's nearly 1,200-page work:

> In a number of places, such as in the communes of Ntyazo, Mukingi and Runda, RPF soldiers massacred unarmed civilians, many of them women and children, who had assembled for a meeting on their orders. The people were told to come to receive food or to be given instructions or to gather before being transported to another site. The RPF soldiers also massacred several hundred people in the Byumba stadium in mid-April.

The diction HRW used to describe RPF crimes was revealing. RPF forces killed "civilians" or "people." Rarely does HRW indicate that the Tutsi-led RPF were killing Hutus—that these crimes were ethnically driven. The contrast between how it framed the killings in RPF-held as opposed to Hutu-held zones is telling. Here is how HRW describes the killings of Tutsis by Hutus:

> The prefects of Kibuye and Cyangugu directed Tutsi to assemble in the local stadiums. In Kivumu commune, Kibuye prefecture, the burgomaster reportedly drove a white pick-up truck around to gather Tutsi who were straggling along the road. He was anxious to get them to Nyange church, where they would later be massacred by a bulldozer that flattened both the church and the people inside.
>
> From the start, in Kigali and out on the hills, leaders directed two kinds of killing: that of specific individuals and that of Tutsi as a group.
>
> Patrols searched for Tutsi in and out of their houses, in the fields, in the bush, in the swamps, wherever they might be hiding.

Human Rights Watch clearly—and rightfully—found that Hutu militia, military and government officials targeted and exterminated Tutsis and, in some cases, Hutus opposed to their genocidal plan. But it appeared not to have discovered a similar ethnic dynamic in zones controlled by the RPF.

Meanwhile, in one of its most detailed accounts of an example of RPF violence, HRW researchers said soldiers killed "without regard" to ethnic group. Here is an excerpt:

> The only massacre by RPF forces that was documented in detail at the time was reported by Human Rights Watch/Africa in September 1994, as a result of an investigation carried out in late August. In that case, RPF soldiers arrived on June 19 from the direction of the hill Saruheshyi and assembled both local people and displaced persons from a neighboring camp in a field in the cell Nyagakombe, Rugogwe sector in the commune of Mukingi, Gitarama prefecture. They explained that they wanted to talk about transporting people to Rwabusoro in Bugesera. Without giving any reason, soldiers killed a woman named Sara and a man named Bihibindi. An hour and a half later, they opened fire on the crowd of hundreds of people. Some people fled down the road next to the field and were shot trying to escape by running through the woods on the adjacent hills. Others were caught and then killed with

hammers, hoes, or other blunt instruments. *The soldiers killed without regard to age, sex, or ethnic group [my emphasis].* One of the victims was a Tutsi woman identified as the daughter-in-law of a man named Gahizi.

HRW also documented an attack in Butare by RPF soldiers, describing it as part of "generalized violence" in the zone, even though the victims were Hutus:

> In another case that dates from the early days of the RPA victory, Human Rights Watch/Africa investigated the killing of some sixty persons arrested at a barrier in the Goma section of the town of Butare on the night of July 27 to 28. The victims, who had previously fled to the west before the RPF advance, were en route back to their home communes in four pick-up trucks. After their arrest, they were taken to the Karubanda School for Social Workers, where they were executed. Among the victims were eighteen members of the family of Nkiko Nsengimana, a prominent member of civil society and opponent of the former Rwandan government. Their murder appears to have been part of the *generalized violence directed against passers-by [my emphasis]* rather than a deliberate attack meant to injure and intimidate a politically important leader.[31]

To describe this attack as part of "generalized violence" is misleading at best. I interviewed Manzi Mutuyimana, Nkiko Nsengimana's nephew. He said his family members had sheltered Tutsi neighbors at the beginning of the genocide and were then forced to flee to the French-secured Zone Turquoise when the RPF entered Butare. When his family headed back home, the RPF sent them to the school's premises and supervised their execution.[32] The victims were killed with *agafuni*. The skull of his 79-year-old grandfather was crushed and his seventeen-month-old cousin died when a soldier smashed the baby's head against the wall. Manzi and other surviving family members returned to Butare two weeks later to see what they could find out about what happened to their relatives and spoke to Tutsi neighbors who had also been brought to the school but were not killed. Manzi said the Tutsis told him his grandfather pleaded with the RPF to spare the Tutsis' lives, which they did. (Often Tutsis who had witnessed RPF crimes and opposed the killings were also eliminated.)

Manzi then fled to Uganda and spent a good part of his youth in a refugee camp; he said his family was persecuted for years after that attack. Several relatives who stayed in Rwanda were detained and tortured. Others disappeared after being picked up by DMI operatives.

ICTR investigators looked into several RPF executions in schools in Butare from mid-July 1994 onward. They mentioned the killing of Manzi's family members and other displaced Hutus, who were transported to two local schools, where they disappeared; witnesses in the vicinity heard screaming. Investigators noted that the RPF had carried out "widespread, systematic killings and massacres" of Hutus in Butare city and surrounding areas.[33]

The Human Rights Watch report, too, made a strong concluding statement that RPF atrocities across Rwanda were widespread and systematic, and targeted unarmed civilians and people with political affiliations. It cited Gersony's findings, noting that he and his team were convinced the RPF had engaged in the large-scale killing and persecution of Hutus. But *Leave None to Tell the Story* did not refer to any cable or notes in which Gersony had described the RPF killings as a campaign of genocide against Hutus. On balance, the report's anecdotal accounts, which describe RPF crimes as part of generalized violence rather than ethnically driven, stand in stark contradiction to the testimony I've collected from survivors, from former Tutsi soldiers and officers with knowledge of operations, and from the ICTR's Special Investigations Unit.

To cite one example, in its top secret summary report, ICTR investigators had this to say about RPA killings in the commune of Rambura in Gitarama:

Towards the end of the war of 1994, the 59th battalion of the RPA had established its headquarters in the commune of Rambura-Gitarama, close to UNAMIR positions and opposite the French operation Zone Turquoise. The battalion set up a barrier by which the population returning from the Turquoise Zone had to pass through. This population was screened at the barrier. The majority was killed only because they were Hutu. The soldiers in charge of this task were divided into six groups of eight men chosen exclusively from the Tutsi ethnic group of the RPA. The killed their victims with agafuni. The slowest teams killed between 20 and 30 persons per night, but the specialists of agafuni could kill 100 per night. Towards the end the victims were to dig their grave before being killed. This work lasted four to five weeks, day and night. Other people, Hutu intellectuals and ex-FAR (soldiers with the Rwandan Armed Forces from the former Hutu regime of Habyarimana) preferred not to cross the RPA barrier and established a camp near UNAMIR position. With the refusal of UNAMIR to dismantle the camp, the [RPA's] 59th battalion attacked this refugee camp. The RPA soldiers shot at the occupants without any distinction. The number of victims of this carnage was evaluated at between 2,000 and 3,000 according to the witness who used to be an RPA soldier and who participated in the attack.[34]

During the genocide, a few independent voices had the courage to condemn RPF attacks against Hutu civilians, although this had little impact at the United Nations or on human rights groups and mainstream media. Refugees International, one of the most independent and respected of refugee advocacy groups, reported in mid-May 1994 that refugees fleeing RPF-controlled southeastern Rwanda into Tanzania were being slaughtered wholesale. A four-page cable, written by Mark Prutsalis from Refugees International, contained excerpts from a UN refugee agency protection report on the situation.[35] The UN report cited eyewitness accounts from refugees arriving in Ngara, Tanzania. The cable outlined the following points:

- In Kigarama, in the commune of Rusumo, the RPF called a "peace meeting" at a school, but if anyone refused to participate, they were forced to. Once gathered, people were tied together in groups of three and stabbed. Bodies were put on trucks and dumped into the Kagera River. Some refugees who managed to escape were shot crossing the river into Tanzania in canoes.
- In other sectors in Rusumo, the RPF would wait for villagers to open their doors at dawn and then take them away in trucks. The villagers were never seen again.
- The RPF surrounded the village of Gasarabwayi in Musaza, according to a witness, gathered twenty people in a house and burnt it down with the people inside.
- RPF soldiers shot escaping refugees at crossing points into Tanzania.

Finally, the Refugees International cable cited a staffer at the International Committee of the Red Cross who issued an urgent plea: "Things are getting very bad at the border here . . . someone really needs to do something about all of the killing and torture on the other side. Each day there are more and more bodies in the river and most of them without their heads; the count is between 20 to 30 each 30 minutes."

The grotesque sight of bodies floating down the Kagera River into Lake Victoria in Uganda in May and June 1994 came to symbolize the monstrous brutality meted out by Hutus against Tutsis in the genocide. By the end of May, relief specialists said up to forty thousand corpses had glutted the waters of this giant lake, which provided fish and drinking water for scores of Ugandan villages. On May 21, 1994, Donatella Lorch from the *New York Times* wrote that "cloaking the countryside with the stench of death, the bodies—as many as 100 an hour—are being washed ashore in the Rakai district of southern Uganda or onto islands in Lake Victoria and have been seen as far north as Entebbe." Further down in the story, Lorch pointed out that "the Kagera River flows through southern Rwanda, mostly through government- and militia-controlled territory, and bodies have been carried by the current for weeks. Relief officials say the killers must have dumped the bodies into the river by the truckload. Many are mutilated."[36]

Reporting on May 29, 1994, from Malembo, Uganda, David Lamb of the *Los Angeles Times* said bodies carried by the Kagera River into Lake Victoria had to travel a hundred miles—over thundering falls and winding through fertile savanna—to reach a fishing village called Kansensero. Lamb said fishermen loaded "a ghastly collection of limbs and torsos" onto their boat. "The fishermen, donning masks and gloves, worked quickly to wrap and tie the bodies, never sure what parts belonged together, and to load them into the trailer of a red tractor parked nearby." Grimly, Lamb further noted that

the majority of the victims of the most extensive massacre in modern
Africa's post-independence history appear to be women and children.
Some who reach Lake Victoria apparently were beheaded. Others' arms
were tied behind their backs. One cluster of infants washed downstream

in a tied sack. Three others were joined by a single pointed stick thrust through their stomachs.

He described them as victims of the Hutu *génocidaires*.[37]

And so we are led to believe that the bloated bodies clogging the Kagera and floating into Lake Victoria in May and June were all Tutsis killed by extremist Hutu elements. And yet the wide swath of Kibungo prefecture around the Kagera River, which flows north along the Rwanda–Tanzania border, was under the control of the RPF by late April. Within the first weeks of the genocide, RPF forces led by Fred Ibingira and William Bagire quickly and tidily moved through the prefectures of Byumba and Kibungo, clearing out all Hutu military and militia. Within hours of the plane crash, the RPF sent out its mobile death squads to kill unarmed Hutu civilians in the rear of the fighting battalions. Near the end of April, the most southern prefecture of Kibungo was securely held by the RPF. The refugees escaping to Tanzania were therefore not Tutsis, but Hutus being chased and killed by the RPF. The corpses dumped in the Kagera from late April onward were Hutus. The media's inaccurate reporting only fueled the hurt and injustice Hutu survivors felt.

Richard Dowden, a British journalist who has spent most of his career covering Africa, was in Rwanda during the genocide. His dispatches were undeniably compelling. Of all reporters, he got closest to perceiving the moral quagmire, but on balance he stuck to the official RPF narrative.[38] On May 6, Dowden wrote this for the *Independent*:

> At last we reached the border with Tanzania, the River Kagera at Rusumo Falls. The river, wide as the Thames and flowing fast, swollen with rains, thunders over rapids and falls beneath a bridge. The river is the colour of oxtail soup and there are lumps in it. Above the bridge you see them coming, about one a minute, sometimes more. And that smell returns again. One looked as if it had been crucified, arms outstretched rigid. Another seemed to be clutching something which had slipped away. Beneath the falls the shiny grey lumps bob around in the eddys and pools; children, women, men. Hundreds and hundreds must have passed down the river in the past week and they are still coming.

Who has done these things? The territory we pass through is now controlled by the Rwanda Patriotic Front, the rebel movement which is largely Tutsi. It rapidly advanced after the death of President Juvenal Habyarimana on 6 April and moved down to the border with Tanzania last week. The RPF appears disciplined and does not appear to have been involved in the killings of civilians.

They have been carried out by the government militia, Hutu fanatics, who have killed all the Tutsis in their areas as well as anyone who supported last year's peace agreement between the government and rebels.

But this is not what the people in the refugee camps say. They are mostly Hutus and they say they fled from the RPF which kills all Hutus. Very few say they actually saw the RPF killing people, and only four arrived with bullet wounds according to the UNHCR. Among the refugees are the militiamen who, armed with spears, knives and machetes, have been carrying out the killings and the refugees may be too frightened of them to speak the truth.

Dowden, like so many others faced with these horrors, portrayed the Hutus as unreliable and the Tutsis as truth-tellers.

But there were victims and perpetrators on all sides in Rwanda's genocide. And what made the war even more shocking was how civilians joined in the fury of killing. We've known, almost since the beginning, that Hutu civilians delivered Tutsis over to Interahamwe and Hutu soldiers, or picked up machetes and killed their neighbors themselves. What we haven't yet recognized is how Tutsi civilians also hunted down and denounced Hutus, and sometimes participated in the brutality of slaughter.

8

THE TUTSI FIFTH COLUMN

THE HUTU GENOCIDE AGAINST TUTSIS WAS PARTLY SPARKED BY FEAR:
fear of an army encroaching from the north, but also fear that the rebels had
secret allies on the ground—the so-called fifth column. In the first instance,
the fear was justified: a Tutsi rebel army had invaded Rwanda in 1990 and had
come close to overthrowing the Hutu-dominated government. But the fear
that Rwandan Tutsi civilians were also secretly working with the RPF turns
out also to have been justified—though that fear could never justify the scale
of the killings it set off.

The international community has long viewed Tutsi civilians primarily as
victims. For many, the most horrifying aspect of the Rwandan genocide was
that Hutu peasants killed their Tutsi friends and neighbors and, in some cases,
Tutsi members of their own families. Scott Straus, a US professor of political
science whose academic field is genocide studies, has estimated that 8 percent
of the Hutu adult population in Rwanda actively engaged in killings.[1]

But a growing body of evidence now shows that Tutsi civilians betrayed
and killed their Hutu neighbors in the same way that Hutus turned on Tutsis.
The dynamic at work was chillingly similar. In many cases the Tutsis involved
in the killings were not seeking to avenge the death or mutilation of their
families. Some of the worst Tutsi-on-Hutu violence was preemptive, occurring early and in areas where no crimes against Tutsis had yet been reported,
as in Giti, Rutare and other areas of Byumba. The complex truth is that, in
1994, Rwanda was awash in fear, mistrust and paranoia.

Who were these Tutsi civilians who resorted to crimes against humanity? Some of them were peasants lucky enough to be living in RPF-controlled areas in the early days of the genocide, whose families remained mostly intact. Some of the Tutsis killers were, indeed, genocide survivors whose families had been wiped out and who turned to retribution. But most of them were *abakada*, or civilian cadres—Tutsis who had been recruited by the RPF before, during and after the genocide. These Tutsis—both *abakada* and civilians loyal to the RPF government and army—committed unspeakable atrocities against Hutus, crimes comparable to those committed by Hutu civilians and Interahamwe. They delivered Hutus over to RPF death squads; they helped locate Hutus and lock them in dungeons; they dug mass graves and helped conceal crimes; and in some cases they picked up hoes and guns and joined in the killing.[2] After the genocide, they became the interface between the RPF and UN agencies, NGOs, human rights investigators and international journalists, playing a crucial role in Rwanda's statecraft and propaganda system. Aid officials, war correspondents or academics who needed interpreters, taxi drivers, fixers or escorts were assigned *abakada*, for example, meaning that their whole experience inside the country was mediated by people with strong reasons to be loyal to the Kagame regime. A former RPF official told investigators with the ICTR that before the genocide broke out, a network of "civil intelligence services" was created inside Rwanda at the request of Kagame and Kayumba Nyamwasa, then the head of the DMI. This network worked closely with the DMI to gather intelligence within the civilian population.[3] When, as part of the Arusha Peace Agreement, the RPF was allowed to establish a headquarters in Kigali, they also used it as a hub to train civilian allies. Between December 1993 and the beginning of April 1994, the four-month period before the genocide, these civilians went to the CND in the evening under the pretext that they were going to the canteen. "During the night they would do firearm training," said a former RPF sergeant. "All civilians trained were Tutsis. They were brought to the CND by civilian members of the RPF and came from everywhere, such as Gitarama, Butare, Cyangugu and Bugesera. On arrival at the CND, they were briefed by the RPF's intelligence officer, Charles Karamba. After their training they were sent back into the population."[4] A certain percentage of Tutsis were evidently helping the RPF prepare for war at a time when all parties claimed to be preparing for peace.

A Tutsi civilian from Byumba, in northern Rwanda, who joined the RPF during the genocide gave detailed testimony to ICTR investigators on the role of civilian cadres. As I've already shown, the prefecture of Byumba was largely controlled by the RPF from the outset of the genocide. "As of April 8, 1994, there were no ex-government soldiers in the region of Ngarama, prefecture of Byumba," the civilian reported to the tribunal investigators. "RPF soldiers and cadres were monitoring the region. They began to enlist all young people into their ranks. At that time, murders and disappearances started. They began to target intellectuals and politicians that belonged to the former regime, and former mayors, town councillors, teachers and businesspeople."[5]

The witness provided a partial list of victims killed, people he knew personally, including a Hutu agronomist who worked for the NGO Care International. He said the victims had initially run away from RPF forces but were lured back with promises they would be safe and could remain in their jobs. "In the end they were killed, just as they feared," the witness said. The bodies were dumped in a mass grave near the Mugera market. In July 1994, units in every RPF battalion were operating jails in the areas they controlled, counting on the "loyal population" to inform on and imprison Hutus they considered Interahamwe. The witness said the RPF considered the "loyal population" to be Tutsi genocide survivors and Tutsi refugees who had grown up in Uganda, Congo and Burundi and had been repatriated to Rwanda. The witness said that government soldiers were arrested and executed in these dungeons, as were Hutu intellectuals, former regime members and all people considered obstacles, bipingamizi—which was anyone who might disagree with the RPF. "Civilian cadres were the ones who identified individuals to be delivered to soldiers," he said. "They did so according to their own interests. All the soldiers had to do was kill." After the genocide, when the International Red Cross and NGOs became aware of the existence of some of the dungeons, the RPF moved the prisoners to other locations, where they were executed.[6] Another ICTR document features testimony from a civilian cadre who said that many of his colleagues in Byumba were routinely denouncing and delivering Hutus over to the Directorate of Military Intelligence.[7]

I was also leaked a top secret, 54-page-long ICTR document from 2005 that described in detail the killing operations carried out by Kagame's forces in Giti, a commune where no genocide against Tutsis was committed. The testimony from a senior DMI official stationed in Giti is grisly. He describes DMI mobile units arriving in Giti and neighboring Rutare in April, rounding up Hutu civilians, and shooting them or hacking them to death with hoes. He said Tutsi volunteers were recruited into the RPF at a fast pace in these areas and that they helped dig mass graves. The DMI agents called these Tutsi civilians the Tiger Force. He added that the Tiger Force later planted banana groves over the graves in order to camouflage the sites.[8]

I met Abdallah Akishuli on a broiling afternoon in 2014 at a train station in a small town in northern France.[9] Part of his face was bruised and swollen, and one of his eyes was bloodshot. A few days earlier, a gang of youths had beaten him and stolen his cash, he told me. He looked vulnerable, boyish, unsettled. I couldn't help but wonder whether the thugs who attacked him were RPF agents who might have been monitoring his activities and discovered he was going to speak to a journalist. Rwanda had a reputation for intimidating, silencing and murdering critics abroad. Abdallah tried to reassure me, but he also worried that the cafés and shops in the center of town weren't private-enough places for us to talk about war crimes. He wanted to go somewhere else but wouldn't say where.

I didn't want to get into his car. I didn't really know him; we'd only spoken twice on the phone and Skype, after another Rwandan source had put us in touch. I convinced myself that so far I'd been good at judging people, and that in our conversations before I'd arrived in France, Abdallah had seemed without guile.

So finally I agreed and got in, and we drove through little villages and their roundabouts, but he couldn't settle on a safe location. When I asked him where he wanted to go, he was vague. Eventually we turned onto a road that twisted through a lush forest of linden and beech trees. The longer we drove, the more rattled I became. Riding with Abdallah to an unknown destination that day caused a crisis of self-doubt and fear.

Eventually, out of this dense wood, we came to a magnificent, moated château surrounded by an enormous baroque garden of fountains and ponds. He parked in the public parking lot, and we got out of the car. I breathed easier. We found a bench and after several minutes he began to relax in the vast and beautiful space. It was soon clear he had a lot to get off his chest and he intended to be thorough. He allowed me to tape him.

Abdallah, a Tutsi, had longed for a country where Tutsis and Hutus could live side by side, enjoying equal opportunities and rights, something he felt was elusive under President Habyarimana. When the genocide broke out in 1994, he had already joined the RPF as a civilian cadre and was in Uganda for training, receiving, like thousands of others, both military and ideological instruction. He understood what the *abakada* were: party organizers from Rwanda, Uganda, Burundi and Congo tasked with mobilizing support for the RPF. Their work fell under the authority of the RPF Secretariat, the party's political governing body.[10] The cadres worked as de facto militia alongside military officers and intelligence officials in a system similar to how civilian cadres operated in Mao's China, the former Soviet Union and Nazi Germany.

In the first few weeks of the genocide, Abdallah was working as a cadre in Byumba and providing assistance to displaced civilians. He said it was in this prefecture that he began to witness the singling out and disappearance of Hutus. In late May, Abdallah was sent to Ndera, a village just a few kilometers northeast of Kigali's airport, which was now behind the battle lines and securely under RPF control. Ndera was a bucolic town of scarlet-chested sunbirds and long-horned cows grazing on lush fields on the edge of dense forest. Abdallah's job, along with more than a dozen other cadres, was to help lodge and feed thousands of displaced civilians who had gathered in Ndera to escape the genocide—by then, a total of thirty to forty thousand homeless people. They mainly came from Remera, Kabaza and Rubirizi, he said, though some had been sheltering at the Amahoro stadium in Kigali, where they'd sought refuge with UN peacekeepers at the beginning of April. These internal refugees—displaced by war yet close to their homes—were eventually housed in abandoned homes, buildings and schools throughout Ndera.

The person Abdallah and the other cadres reported to was a DMI officer named Francis Mutiganda. (Mutiganda would later become the much-feared head of the RPF's External Intelligence operations.) He also directed the soldiers who worked with the DMI detachment to pull out any Hutus who had ended up in the Ndera displaced persons' camp and kill them, Abdallah told me. "DMI killed massively in Ndera." Soldiers from the RPF's headquarters in Kigali arrived to assist in the task. Abdallah watched as DMI agents and soldiers took the Hutu refugees, sometimes twenty at a time, to secluded areas about two to three kilometers from the camp—often homes where no one could hear—and shot them. Their bodies were covered with mattresses and burned before the remains were buried.

If the groups were small enough, DMI agents would tie up their victims with ropes and crush their skulls with hoes. Those victims were buried in graves and their murders were blamed on the Interahamwe militia. "This was not a secret among cadres. Everyone knew what was going on," Abdallah said. "The only criteria for selecting victims was ethnicity: he or she had to be Hutu. The objective was to reduce the number of Hutus in the camp." Sometimes Hutus were picked out by how they looked; sometimes other refugees denounced them, Abdallah said. "If a Tutsi orphan accused a Hutu in the camp of killing his family, DMI would take away the alleged perpetrator along with . . . his children, wife, the grandfather, all his loved ones. They'd all be killed." If a Hutu wanted to protect himself, he might denounce another Hutu in the camp. If a woman asked authorities where her husband had gone, she was taken, with her children and all her relatives, and executed.

Abdallah explained that DMI operatives also enticed Hutu civilians with promises of food, telling them if they got on buses they would be able to cultivate sorghum and rice in another location. "The refugees were hungry and would come running." (Many of the peasants in the camp soon realized that those who went to cultivate crops disappeared, and so they refused to get on the buses.) The RPF also asked young Hutu men to be brave and fight for the liberation of Rwanda. Many Hutu youths came forward, believing that they would be safe if they joined the RPF. They were eliminated too.

Abdallah contends that DMI was able to conceal these massacres because it controlled the zone tightly. If any member of the UN peacekeeping mission arrived or a journalist wished to report from there, he or she was carefully escorted and care was taken to ensure that the outsiders did not have independent contact with refugees. In any case, as Abdallah told me, the world viewed the RPF as "the saviors. And saviors did not kill."

He estimates that, in Ndera, the DMI managed to kill about a hundred people a day over a thirty-day period, eliminating about 10 percent of the displaced population. But it wasn't restraint that limited the death toll to only 10 percent of the population, mostly Hutu. "If only 10 percent was killed,"

Abdallah said, "it wasn't because the RPF felt pity for the others; it was because the DMI detachment was too small to exterminate the rest. This was the maximum number of Hutus the agents could target." In fact, he and the other civilian cadres and the DMI soldiers were scolded by one of the RPF's highest-ranking women, Rose Kabuye, when she visited the camp in June, who complained that the number of Hutus who had been killed was not satisfactory.

Abdallah heard Kabuye tell the RPF team, in Swahili, a language preferred by RPF members who grew up in Uganda: "If you don't want to do it, then lie down and we'll kill you."

"Everybody was aware of these operations," Abdallah told me, "from the lowest soldier to the highest general. What happened in Ndera happened throughout Rwanda."

The sun was beating down on us as Abdallah recounted these stories, and he kept wiping the sweat off his brow. He had much more to say.

One of the more shocking aspects of operations in Ndera, and throughout Rwanda, was how cadres handed over Hutus to the RPF to be executed, he admitted. "There were those civilian cadres who were guided by zeal and who worked of their own free will for DMI. About half of the cadres helped screen Hutus ahead of their execution."

He said there were three categories of civilian cadres: those who tried to stick to providing social assistance to Rwandans in RPF zones and political indoctrination to the civilian population; those who became involved in the war effort and facilitated war crimes by denouncing and delivering Hutus to the murderous death squads; and a third group of extremely zealous individuals who participated directly in the killings.

Abdallah considered himself to be firmly in the first category and told me he was profoundly disillusioned by what he witnessed in Ndera. "I was trained to help people, to bring justice. But once I arrived in the field, I discovered the opposite. I was completely deceived." He was shocked by the level of depravity and the lack of remorse that the soldiers and their superiors displayed, driven by what he called a perverse moral certainty. He said he saw no duel of the soul in any of the killers, none of what Shakespeare called the "blushing, shamefaced spirit that mutinies in a man's bosom"—that thing we call *conscience.*

"Usually, a criminal has a guilty conscience. But with the RPF, it was not like this," Abdallah told me. "These were men wearing a human face but who were in fact not human at all. The people who carried out these crimes were smiling and elegant. They could kill and then come sit next to you and act as if nothing happened. You would never suspect anything because their conscience would be clear. It was beyond comprehension."

Abdallah's account of what happened in Ndera is corroborated, in part, by evidence from a former DMI officer who gave sworn testimony to the ICTR. Under oath, the officer said he was sent to Ndera in late June or early July (about the time Abdallah left) and assisted in screening Hutus there, who were mainly from Nyamirambo, Muhima, Kanombe and the Amahoro stadium.[11] "I pointed out the suspects to be eliminated based on my knowledge and information at hand," the witness said. He described suspects being loaded into a minibus and driven to Camp Kami, where they were executed. "There were fifteen DMI members there who executed these people. The victims were tied up and brought to a place called the cemetery. At night they killed with *agafunis*."[12]

At about the same time Abdallah was in Ndera, Théogène Murwanashyaka was close by, watching once again as a large group of Hutus were summoned to their death. This time it was at Kanombe, close to the airport on the outskirts of the capital. He saw a line of thirty RPA soldiers directing hundreds of unarmed, exhausted Hutu men, women and children to a local primary school. It was broad daylight, and he thought the refugees lugging their mattresses were headed there for shelter. But a short time later, he heard gunfire. "I heard everything. Once again, it was wartime and so killing was happening everywhere. But I was shocked that people with no strength whatsoever to fight were slaughtered like this. They were the living dead, even before they were shot. There was such hatred for Hutus, the RPF was ready to eliminate anyone."

Théo said the killing campaign relied on information provided by civilian cadres.[13] "In most cases, Kagame's army was not familiar with the area [when they moved in]," Théo said. "When soldiers arrived in Byumba, we noticed immediately that civilian cadres were telling us where the civilian population was, who was a Hutu and who was Tutsi. If they were Hutu, they were eliminated."

Alongside the civilian cadres were the political commissars, who ingrati-
ated themselves both in the battalions and in the civilian population. The
political commissars were the ones who called the bogus meetings, luring
civilians and promising them supplies or security. At the time, the RPF's
chief political commissar was Frank Mugambage, a man who went on to
become Rwanda's ambassador to Uganda. Mugambage was also a member
of Kagame's influential High Command Council. Théo remembers a deeply
troubling incident in Kigali where about fifty people—Hutus and Tutsis—
escaped the Interahamwe by hiding in the home of a Hutu minister who'd
served in the Habyarimana government. The minister protected these people,
many of whom were friends of Théo's family. But certain Tutsi members of
this group began providing information to the RPF about their Hutu colleagues, moderates who had gone into hiding when the genocide began.
When the RPF seized control of the area, they rounded up these Hutus, who
numbered about twenty, and killed them.

These Tutsis who denounced their Hutu neighbors were indeed "extremists," Théo said. "In some cases, civilians were more extreme and zealous
than the RPA was. The rank-and-file RPA soldier was trained for battle. The
political commissars and civilian cadres who chose to work with DMI had
other intentions."

From the very beginning of the rebel movement, Théo said, "the RPF had
two objectives: seize power and as much as possible eliminate the Hutu population in their territory. That's what they did. This is not invented. It actually
happened." And with the help of cadres and commandos, the RPF had successfully infiltrated the capital and other areas of Rwanda by 1993. Théo
admitted that his own family hid grenades in their Kigali home before the
genocide because the RPF had asked them to and had convinced them it was
for their own protection. By April 1994, the RPF had some 600 cells throughout the country, 147 of them in Kigali.[14]

Théo said the role of *abakada* and Tutsi civilians in crimes against Hutus
is well known inside Rwanda but is never spoken of. A good number of
Tutsis are vehemently opposed to Kagame but are afraid to talk about the
past because they are not willing to implicate themselves. "Kagame holds
this over their heads," Théo said. "And Hutus have been completely silenced

on the issue." No wonder: Hutus who dare to accuse the RPF of crimes end up in jail, disappear or are charged with genocide.

Pierre, who now lives in exile in North America, was a young Tutsi soldier who was part of a DMI unit. He said that more than twenty years after the genocide he still lives through prolonged periods where his dreams and waking hours are haunted by images of savagery. The scenes that play out in his head are those in which civilian cadres help the DMI kill civilians. "The political cadres sent whoever they wanted to their death. How many Hutus were killed in Kibungo in operations in June 1994? There were soldiers and civilians who enjoyed watching whole families being butchered, and young ladies being abused in public and killed." [15] He recalled, for example, an incident in which "a civilian cadre named Martin grabbed a machete and took a Hutu aside, in front of a soldier named Abbas Musonera, and cut the victim's head off. And they laughed hysterically." Sometimes Tutsis were targeted if they had been married to a Hutu or if their children shared both ethnicities. Pierre said that often the children were put to death too. Those blood-soaked months filled him with a rage that has never left him, directed toward senior commanders and the top members of the RPF Secretariat who he alleges conceived these crimes.

Abdallah said many Tutsi civilian cadres were caught and killed in Hutu-controlled zones of Rwanda before Kagame's forces moved in and took over. But in the northern and eastern prefectures, which quickly came under RPF control, cadres were free to carry out their dirty work with no worry of reprisals. After RPF troops seized Gitarama, Butare and Ruhengeri in June and July, the party recruited new cadres quickly. A significant number of Hutus had already fled to Zaire from Gisenyi by the time the RPF took control in July, fearing the RPF's murderous advance. Many of those who stayed put in their homes eventually were targets for slaughter. Farther north, in Ruhengeri, DMI units aided by civilian cadres massacred Hutus in July and August and buried the victims in mass graves. There were an estimated four thousand *abakada* in Rwanda during the genocide. By the end of 1994, the RPF had increased their numbers to fifteen thousand.[16]

Deus Kagiraneza is the most furtive, mercurial Rwandan I've interviewed in the course of this work. Our encounter, in May 2013, was brief, frustrating and confusing. But he unintentionally let slip some important context to the puzzle of Rwandan history. Kagiraneza is a Tutsi raised in Rwanda, an educated and well-connected former RPF cadre, who became the prefect of Ruhengeri and, later, a parliamentarian. Along the way, he also worked in intelligence.

In 1999, he was sent to the Democratic Republic of Congo, where he became treasurer of Rwanda's Congo desk, a division of Rwanda's External Security Operations (ESO). The ESO was run by External Intelligence and oversaw Rwandan economic activities in the DRC. He would eventually tell a Belgian senate committee probing corruption in the DRC that dealers in minerals and other resources in Rwandan-controlled areas of the country had to go through the Congo desk to do business, and that a secret accounting system existed that enabled Rwandan military officers and political leaders to siphon off and hide vast sums of money.

In 2000, Kagiraneza fled Rwanda after breaking with the regime. After settling in Tournai, a quiet town in western Belgium near the French border, he gave an interview to a Rwandan journalist, Deo Mushaidi, in which he apparently confessed that widespread killings had occurred in his prefecture and throughout Rwanda after the genocide. In the article, Mushaidi reported that Kagiraneza had said: "We had a mission to physically eliminate anyone, especially the Hutu, who did not support the RPF. We accomplished that mission in Ruhengeri where I was the prefect, and all over the country as well. Most of the prefects and administrative authorities were RPA military officers."[17] Mushaidi also quoted Kagiraneza asking for forgiveness. "The current government committed these horrendous massacres and crimes," Kagiraneza allegedly said. "I held an important position within the government and participated, under the orders of my army supervisors, in some of these crimes. This is why I have chosen the road to exile and I am ready to provide more detailed testimonies. I offer my unconditional support to all Rwandan-loving people who are determined to overthrow the criminal and bloodthirsty regime led by General Paul Kagame."

I had a lot of questions for this man.

Kagiraneza had agreed to come to Brussels to meet me at my hotel, but in the end he insisted I come to Tournai. Shortly before our appointment, he called to tell me that his wife had been admitted to the hospital. He didn't offer any details about her condition, but I offered my sympathy and agreed to meet him near the train station at a time that was convenient for him. He did not appear to want to cancel.

I wasn't nervous about meeting him; I was intrigued. A Rwandan dissident I trusted told me that if I convinced Kagiraneza to open up, he'd offer a wealth of information. Still, I'd slept fitfully and by the time my train pulled into the station, my head was throbbing. I'd told him on the phone that he could pick me out by my pale skin and brown hair. He spotted me in the main lobby, before I saw him. He seemed uncomfortable. There was no smile, not even a fake one, and he didn't seem to want to look me in the eyes; he walked a circle around me with his hands in his pockets then suggested we go across the road to a café. We'd just ordered coffee when his phone rang. He answered and said, "Yes, yes, not too long," in French. He told me when he hung up that it had been his wife. I asked how she was, but all he said was that he couldn't be away from her long. Yet his phone rang and rang; she certainly had the energy to keep calling him.

I told him I was seeking information from victims and ex-RPF familiar with operations, and also looking for any documents, official or unofficial, that anyone might want to give me. But he knew all this; I'd already contacted him twice on the phone and in e-mails and was just filling in space to see if I could make him more comfortable. It wasn't working: he seemed both cocky and defensive.

So I dove in, asking him about his time as prefect in Ruhengeri in 1994, and about the admissions he had already made. I was shocked when he replied that he was suing the reporter because the article was a complete fabrication.

"Okay," I said, "but what did happen under your watch in Ruhengeri? Can you tell me about your actual experiences at the time?"

The tape recorder was rolling, with his permission.

"Would you like to know whether I used real bullets or machetes?" he snapped. And he went on to insist that he'd established a peaceful relationship with Hutu peasants and ex-combatants, gaining their trust and persuading them to lay down their weapons: "There wasn't an attack or an ambush during the time I was governor."

His phone kept ringing.

My head was spinning from his turnaround. But before I could gather myself to end the interview, he told me my project was "ambiguous" at best and that it would not lead to truth and reconciliation. In fact, it would do the opposite. If I insisted on exposing the crimes of the RPF, he said, the inevitable question would arise: "Who killed Hutus on the hills of Rwanda? It was Tutsis who knew those that needed to be killed. Because the RPF members from Uganda did not know who to kill." My work, he insisted, would demonize interior Tutsis; they would be suspected of having delivered their Hutu neighbors into the hands of RPF killers. "And so you see, people will believe that these poor unfortunate Hutus were victims of their Tutsi neighbors."

We were looking at each other nervously by now. I decided to move away from the explosive issue of civilian complicity in RPF crimes, and so I asked him about Gersony's findings and the witnesses who claimed that unarmed Hutus had been invited to meetings or held in camps and then executed.

"I was part of the war," he bristled. "People died during the war. It was a war that took no prisoners. We took power with weapons and not by the ballot box." Compared to the Rwandan Patriotic Army, he said, "the former Hutu army was poorly equipped and poorly organized. It was not a fair battle."

I told him I had statements from eyewitnesses that Hutu males were lured into joining the RPA but were, instead, screened, tortured and killed.

He denied this too. "There was no ethnic selection or discrimination. That's false."

What about the cases of Tutsis from Rwanda, Burundi and Congo who were recruited by the Training Wing and later disappeared? I told him I had read they were often accused of spying for the former Habyarimana government and killed.

He said he had no knowledge of such killings but admitted that Tutsis who were not raised in Uganda were discriminated against in the upper echelons of the RPF.

"What were you doing before and during the genocide? What was your role?"

"I was in the army," he said.

"Where? Doing what?"

"At army headquarters, in economic planning."

This would prove to be untrue.

Still, he said, he'd like to see the outline of my book. He was interested in the testimonies I'd collected so far and the conclusions I'd drawn. Would I show him my stuff?

"I'll be in touch," I said.

We shook hands and I ran to the station to catch the next train back to Brussels. I would later learn from other dissidents and refugees that Kagiraneza was suspected of being a double agent working on behalf of the Rwandan government.

Nearly two years later, I would find out that Deus Kagiraneza had been one of Kagame's loyal apparatchiks. According to the ICTR's Special Investigations Unit, whose members interviewed him, Kagiraneza was born in 1960 in Nkumba in the Ruhengeri prefecture and studied at a seminary in Byumba. He was a founding member of the RPF, having joined in 1988. He worked at the Ministry of Finances in Habyarimana's government, but in 1990 he was arrested on charges of collaborating with the enemy, convicted and sent to jail. He was eventually released, and in 1991 he fled to Uganda, where he underwent commando training with the RPF, learning urban fighting and intelligence. He later worked as an instructor at the Training Wing, and screened recruits with the DMI. In his interviews with the UN investigators, he denied the quotes attributed to him by the Rwandan journalist in which he'd said that prefects appointed by the RPF were ordered to have the "maximum number of Hutus killed."

But other witnesses told the Special Investigations Unit that Kagiraneza was known to have trained recruits to kill with the *agafuni*. They said he was also part of a group of officers who interrogated young recruits to establish their loyalty. Recruits who did not pass the interrogation were executed, and witnesses claimed that Kagiraneza participated in some of those executions.[18]

From the ICTR report on the testimony investigators received about Kagiraneza:

In June 1994, Kagiraneza accompanied Colonel Jackson Rwahama during a visit to the DMI section in Kirambo in the commune of Cyeru in Ruhengeri prefecture. Jackson Rwahama stated he was not happy with the work done by the DMI since he had seen Hutus on the road. He gave orders to kill the maximum number of Hutus. Deus Kagiraneza saw our source with the regional president of the MDR (a Hutu political party). He ordered that the regional president of the ruling party, a Hutu, be killed since "no Hutu was any good."

The person he targeted was killed that night.

In other sworn testimony from a separate ICTR document, a witness said one of the primary tasks of RPF intelligence officials was to detect infiltrators among recruits. He claimed that Kagiraneza played a key role in a team of intelligence agents carrying out such detection. He also described how skilled Kagiraneza was at using the *agafuni* to crush skulls and said that he himself had killed recruits with Kagiraneza.[19]

Deus Kagiraneza also played a role in Abdallah's ultimate disillusionment with the RPF and his eventual decision to flee Rwanda. Abdallah had been devastated by the genocide and troubled by the polarization of ethnic identity and sensibility that the RPF promoted. But since the RPF represented the survival of Tutsis, who else was there to turn to?

After the genocide, Abdallah told me that he ceased being a cadre and became first a vendor selling household goods then a taxi driver. He struggled to make a living for his family. But he also said that in 2002 he briefly worked in security for President Kagame ahead of the 2003 elections. Then, in 2005, he learned that his father, who had also been an RPF cadre, had died at the hands of the RPF. His father had disappeared in the first few days after the genocide began, but the family did not know how he died or who had killed him. No one would provide them with answers. Kagiraneza had personally interviewed Abdallah about his father on at least two occasions, during the invasion war. Abdallah said he had described his father as loyal to the cause, outspoken, honest and well-meaning. Realizing that the RPF was suspicious of his father, he said nothing else. Among his fellow cadres, his father was known to speak his mind. He refused to condemn Habyarimana completely since the late president had achieved some measure of progress for Rwanda, in terms of building infrastructure and providing health care. Abdallah alleged that Kagiraneza wrote up an incriminating report classifying his father as a negative influence, and that that report led to his father's incarceration in the immediate aftermath of the genocide, and later to his execution. Abdallah said that he only discovered the full circumstances surrounding his father's death and the deaths of other Tutsi detainees in 2005, after speaking with a former Republican Guard soldier. The soldier, who had been one of Kagame's security guards, told him that his father and other prisoners had been kept by the RPF in Butaro, in northern Rwanda, before they were murdered. The soldier did not say who ordered the killings, but Abdallah believed he knew. Like his father, these Tutsi detainees were wrongly accused of being Habyarimana spies. Kagiraneza had conducted their interrogations and had a reputation for eliminating perceived opponents.

His father's murder at the hands of the RPF was the ultimate act of betrayal, but Abdallah reserves his harshest criticism for the senior members of the RPF Secretariat and the High Command Council, who conceived and planned these crimes, rather than those who worked on the ground. "Everyone knows who the policy makers were," Abdallah said. "It is ridiculous to attribute all responsibility to one man, Paul Kagame. I do not want to call into question Kagame's intellectual capacity, but he did not come up with these ideas by himself. The point is, everyone knew what was going on and no one discouraged it."

But Abdallah's admission that he'd returned to intelligence work to provide security for Kagame had raised a red flag for me. In a subsequent interview I probed more deeply, and he at last revealed something he had been hesitant to share with me when we'd met in France. He'd become embroiled with the DMI in 2002 by force.

One day a local official called Abdallah and asked him to attend a meeting at the city hall. When he arrived, he was immediately taken in a van to DMI headquarters, then to Camp Kami, and finally to a camp at Nasho in the Akagera National Park. There he and about two hundred civilians underwent training, in his case for a period of fifteen months. He had not been told beforehand about the training, nor had the others. Their families did not know where they were. They lived in huts and slept on the ground, and spent their days undergoing military instruction and being trained in spying. Bus drivers, teachers, nurses, doctors, civil servants, journalists and other professionals were trained at Nasho. The prolonged absence of these individuals, followed by their sudden reintegration into their professional spheres, was not questioned; it was a common occurrence. The heads of hospitals, schools, charities and private businesses understood what the RPF does, and how its intelligence system works. "You wear two hats. You have your job, and you are a spy for the RPF," Abdallah said, adding, "Rwandans know what's going on. That's why very few talk in public. They are afraid." Over two decades, thousands of people have received instruction at Nasho, Gabiro, Kami and another camp called Ndego, near Lake Muhazi. Abdallah told me that Ndego was "a training ground for real criminals" where people learned how to kill, kidnap and poison people. "It was also a slaughterhouse where people seen as opponents of the regime were slaughtered." The trainees learned to kill by watching veterans carry out executions. (A former intelligence official, now in exile, confirmed Abdallah's account. Neither Abdallah nor the former intelligence official knew whether Ndego is still being used by the RPF for this kind of training.)

But several sources have told me that the thousands of cadres trained at the secret camps wield significant power in today's Rwanda. The cadres are no longer called *abakada*. They are now known as *intore*, a word meaning "chosen one" in Kinyarwanda, and they work in every profession, at home and abroad. They are trained to spy on Rwandans in all walks of life. Yet nowhere is their presence felt more acutely than at the local level, through a neighborhood surveillance system called Nyumbakumi that uses agents from military, political and civilian spheres to exert control. There are often as many as four *intore* members monitoring every ten, or even fewer, households in Rwanda. These *intore* report to DMI agents and representatives of the RPF Secretariat, and they work jointly with members of a separate military reserve force known as the Inkeragutabara. Moreover, other DMI intelligence staff are present to secretly spy on the *intore* in the Nyumbakumi system.[20] The objective is to instill fear in order to keep civilians in their place, to intimidate and force obedience. People speak in code or say nothing in public. They hide their true feelings, and sometimes they betray one another to protect themselves.

Many Rwandans I've interviewed complain that Rwanda has ceased to be a country. Instead, it is a powerful system of control.

9

SPINNING LIES FROM TRUTH

ONE OF THE CRUELEST LIES PEDDLED BY THE RPF AND REPEATED AD nauseam by Western journalists and academics is the official narrative of Giti during the genocide. Giti is described in most books and mainstream media as the only commune in Rwanda where Hutus did not commit genocide. Its mayor, in particular, has been lauded for warding off Hutu extremism and preventing the massacre of Tutsis. But I've pieced together an account of events in Giti that shows this story to be a startling and effective use of propaganda by the RPF. And it serves as a chilling indicator of the RPF's modus operandi in other areas of Rwanda before, during and after the genocide.

On April 23, 1994, a little more than two weeks into the genocide, a student of mixed Hutu-Tutsi ethnicity named Clément was in his hometown in Giti commune paying a visit with a friend to an elderly neighbor. At 6 p.m., with daylight fading fast, the neighbor told him and his friend, Gaudence, to head home. "It's getting late, children. Go now," she warned. "You never know what could happen after dark."[1]

Giti residents were on edge. On April 10, RPF forces—the 21st and 101st Battalions—had entered the commune and several Hutu clergy at a nearby seminary had been slaughtered. The killings had set the tone for several days of terror. Yet now, two weeks later, an eerie calm had settled in, and some dared to hope that perhaps the war was over.

Clément and Gaudence mounted his bike and rode along red ocher paths through Giti's verdant hillsides. When they reached the main health center, next to the primary school, they saw RPF forces shepherding a large number of people into the school. Gaudence told Clément she was frightened and they should hurry home. When Clément saw how brutally soldiers were shoving people into the courtyard, he agreed, and he pedaled them away as fast as he could. When he got home, his father, a Hutu lawyer and well-known community leader, was missing. The next morning, just as the dawn haze was lifting, Clément and his brother set off to find him. Fearing the worst, they headed directly to the primary school, where they spotted his abandoned bike. It was so early in the morning, no soldiers stood guard on the building. They dreaded to investigate but forced themselves to creep closer. As they entered the compound, they stopped in shock.

"The courtyard was completely littered with corpses. And the classrooms inside were full," Clément told me, drawing in a breath. He and his brother soon found their father among the heap of dead. "His head was split open and his ankle was crushed. Looking at him, I felt a kind of fear I can't describe now. We immediately ran away to a nearby sorghum field."

When he and his brother collected themselves, they went home to tell their Tutsi mother that their father had been murdered. Clément could not let his father rot in the sun or be devoured by dogs. At nightfall, he went back to the school to steal his father's body. With the help of a cousin and a neighbor, he carried him home and buried him in secret so that his soul could rest in peace.

Another neighbor, a young Hutu mother, had by some miracle survived the slaughter at the school. She'd been rounded up on April 23 with her baby strapped to her back. She told Clément that RPF units had seized Hutu civilians from their homes and at roadblocks throughout Giti and brought them to the school, packing them in tightly. Around her were Hutu teachers, officials, politicians and businessmen—anyone seen as having wealth or influence. When night had fallen, soldiers selected the most robust of the Hutu men, gave them weapons—*agafuni* in addition to clubs—and ordered them to kill their own family members and friends, a depraved tactic that Hutu militia also used against Tutsis during the genocide. After these men had killed their loved ones, they begged for a quick death and were given their wish. The young mother was struck on the back of her skull and blacked out. Soldiers must have thought she was no longer alive. When she woke up hours later, she discovered her baby dead beside her.

With the collaboration of their Tutsi neightbors, other prominent Hutus and their families were chased down and killed in the weeks that followed. It took military intelligence units some time to locate one beloved primary school teacher named Sindambiwe. Before they did, RPA soldiers shoved his wife and children into a banana fermentation pit used to make banana beer, and they drowned. A few days later, they found the teacher hiding in the forest among the acacia and eucalyptus trees and shot him dead.

Clément managed to survive. He had inherited what he describes as "classic Tutsi" features from his mother, although in most Rwandans such physical characteristics are fluid and often difficult to distinguish, especially for outsiders. In the first few days of the RPF's invasion of the commune, looking like a Tutsi allowed him to evade capture. But when the bloodbath got more intense and widespread, Clément owed his life to his Tutsi godfather, whose son was an RPF soldier who played a key role in singling out Giti residents for elimination. The godfather's son saw Clément being caught and kicked to the ground by an RPF lieutenant named Jean Jacques Mupenzi. Clément thought Mupenzi was going to shoot him dead on the spot, but the soldier came to his rescue, insisting that Clément "was one of our children."

The mayor of Giti, Edouard Sebushumba, was Hutu, and went into hiding as soon as word spread that Tutsi soldiers had arrived in the area. Like his constituents who believed "*les Inkotanyi vont nous dépecer*" ("the Rwandan Patriotic Front are going to butcher us"), the mayor feared the worst. He hid for nearly a month in a shack owned by a poor old lady. When word got out as to where he was, the RPF immediately went to her home, where they found him with his hair and beard grown so long he was barely recognizable.[2]

By then, though, the RPF was interested in making a deal with him. They told Sebushumba not to be afraid, that he should go back to his house and that the RPF would protect him from here on in. In return, the RPF would declare to the world that Sebushumba was the only mayor in Rwanda who ensured that no genocide against Tutsis had taken place in his commune.

And so it came to pass that the mayor of Giti became famous for warding off Hutu extremism and preventing the massacre of Tutsis in his commune. In most accounts of the genocide, Giti is still described as the only commune in Rwanda where Hutus did not commit genocide. What better camouflage for what happened to Giti's Hutus than a story of the triumph of good over evil?

Sebushumba has stayed silent about what really happened in Giti, and for his silence he was rewarded, first with his life and then with a political career that would eventually land him a seat in the Rwandan parliament, a post he held until 2008. But Sebushumba was not a "moderate Hutu"—the term usually applied to Hutus who opposed the killing of Tutsis during the genocide. He was an exemplary Hutu—in the service of the Rwandan Patriotic Front. As the only mayor who "prevented genocide," he is still regarded as a hero in Rwanda.

Investigators for the International Criminal Tribunal for Rwanda did find out what had really gone on in Giti and its neighboring commune of Rutare. A summary document from the ICTR's Special Investigations Unit confirmed that DMI "used the commune of Giti as a killing area and mass gravesite. Most of the victims were transported by trucks and killed by traditional weapons, agafuni and firearms."[3] They said the commune was subjected to RPF massacres during three different periods, the first barely two days after the shooting down of the presidential plane on April 6.

The investigative unit established that, in April and May, "local civilians assisted RPA soldiers by giving them lists of persons presumed to be Interahamwe," even though no Tutsi had been killed in the commune, so presumably no Hutu extremists were on the ground there. "These persons would be gathered in houses, shops and executed by the RPA using guns and grenades. The commercial center located in the middle of the commune of Giti was one of the massacre sites."[4] From mid-June, when the RPF's Military Police arrived in Giti, and onward, Hutus the RPF had rounded up in different areas of the country were brought into the commune to be killed.[5]

In a subsequent ICTR document, a former DMI officer clarified in shocking detail the macabre methods used to exterminate unarmed Hutus in the area.[6] The 55-page confidential document describes a set of operations, from April 17 to 25, in which a contingent of a hundred DMI operatives led by Jackson Rwahama, the deputy head of the DMI and a key operational commander, rounded up entire Hutu families then slaughtered them with grenades, guns and hoes.

"Eliminating the maximum number of Hutu intellectuals was a priority because these people posed an immediate and future threat of exposing the truth regarding RPF activities. And the death of these intellectuals would weaken the potential for political parties in the short or long term," said the officer, who directly participated in some of the operations. The witness said DMI staged attacks in which Tutsi soldiers pretended to be Interahamwe and killed entire families.

In one incident, Colonel Rwahama and Major Jack Nziza, a key intelligence enforcer, intercepted Hutu civilians on their way to a displacement camp and had them brought to a series of houses on a nearby hill surrounded by a banana plantation and a forest. With Kalashnikov-wielding soldiers standing guard outside, DMI troops threw grenades into the houses, killing between three hundred and four hundred people, according to the witness, who expressed remorse for his role in the violence. "It was horrible to see. Corpses were completely burned. There were no survivors."[7]

In Giti, the DMI contingent rounded up prisoners—mostly men—and slaughtered them in the house of a local politician. The witness remembered the victims' skulls being smashed by hoes and "brain matter all over the floor." The DMI continued to kill waves of displaced Hutus streaming into Giti from other areas, separating them from Tutsi families, who joined in the grim task of digging graves.[8] DMI officers held meetings to persuade people hiding in the bush to come home, and murdered them when they did. The RPF eventually ran out of spots to bury victims and began loading refugees onto trucks at night to transport them to Gabiro to be killed. Giti became a clearinghouse for murder.[9]

What was it like to be trapped in the madness of such killing?

Simbi was a child soldier in 1994, only sixteen years old when he became part of a rotating unit in Giti, Rutare and Kinyami. His hands are small and his skin is soft, his voice and manner quiet and steady. We spent two days together in 2014, during which he poured out excruciating details of his past.[10]

"When I saw what was happening on the ground in 1994, I was scared because it was the first time I'd seen crimes against humanity committed in an exaggerated way. Afterward that fear transformed into anger. The crimes rose to a level that my conscience could not manage. I eventually decided to no longer work with these people I considered animals. For me, what this regime has done goes beyond criminal or genocidal. It goes beyond the human imagination. I honestly cannot find the words to qualify it."

Simbi told me that he and the other soldiers "covered the heads of victims with plastic bags to smother them. Some victims were dropped into a big pit, where they were surrounded. Then they were gunned down. It was *work* that was done daily. It's difficult to estimate how many victims there were. It was certainly in the thousands."

Giti was the first killing mission for this soldier, who joined Kagame's army just before the genocide because he believed he could help liberate Rwanda. He quickly discovered otherwise. "The language from my commander, [who is] now Rwanda's inspector general of police,* was that the Hutu population brought there [to Giti] was the enemy. The victims were mostly women and children, because a lot of men who were stronger had escaped to the mountains. In fact, the majority were women, children and old people."

Another DMI member who was in Giti said Hutus were subjected to abject cruelty under the direction of Jackson Rwahama. The officer recalled scenes of agony in which hundreds of peasants were piled on top of each other in a large open grave, some dying slowly, others already dead. He said he watched the flickering of eyes and twitching of bodies until life was extinguished—collectively and completely.

On occasion the slaughter became a game. At a school between Giti and Rutare, the DMI unit discussed whether to let a group of heavily pregnant women go free. After much back and forth, it was decided they would be allowed to walk away. The women collected their belongings and started to leave the school, the officer explained. "Before the women even walked fifty meters, soldiers started shooting them in the back. They killed them." [11]

Clément, the student who lost his father, said the massacres continued in earnest from April 23 through to June and extended beyond the commune of Giti. In one incident in early May, he and a dozen other youths were hiding in a banana grove on top of a hill overlooking the Nyabugogo River, which flows into Lake Muhazi. From their close vantage point, Clément and his friends witnessed RPF soldiers surround a few thousand Hutu refugees, then separate the women from the group. The women were escorted to a camp of Tutsi survivors in nearby Rutare. The refugees who remained were young and

---

* The witness was referring to Emmanuel Gasana Rurayi, who is still Rwanda's inspector general of police.

old men, boys and male babies. The soldiers directed the refugees to take off their shirts and made the strongest Hutus tie the arms of the others behind their backs using their own clothing. The Hutu men were then ordered to hack them to death with hoes. Then they themselves were killed.

"We saw everything that morning. If I'd had a camera, I would have filmed it," Clément said. "Why would we stand by and watch such a sordid scene, you ask? The RPF had killed so many people. At that point we wanted to see what they were going to do next. After this massacre, we said our time was going to come. We believed we were all going to die."

The negation of the abominable crimes committed by the RPF in Giti and other areas of Rwanda distorted the historical record and left an open wound for countless Hutus such as Clément. It was also a reminder of how effective the RPF was at creating a counternarrative in order to conceal its own crimes, and how journalists and academics unknowingly contributed to the RPF propaganda's dark purpose.

In 1994, the organization that defined how the West viewed the Rwandan genocide was called African Rights, a London-based NGO led by Somali lawyer Rakiya Omaar and British academic Alex de Waal. A book they wrote together, *Death, Despair and Defiance*, was a huge compendium of Hutu-on-Tutsi violence that was published in September 1994, just weeks after the Rwandan genocide ended. For analysts and observers desperate to understand how the genocide had happened, its 750 pages offered a list of perpetrators and a compelling narrative of how Hutu ideologues had conceived their genocidal project against the Tutsi years in advance. First off the mark, the book set history in motion and had a substantial impact on the legal proceedings of the ICTR. For a time, the tribunal considered *Death, Despair and Defiance* the bible of the genocide. Over the years, African Rights became enormously prescriptive and influential; it scolded the international community about who had been morally right during the war, who should be arrested and why. It staunchly defended the RPF against reports that its troops had engaged in violence, and shamed other human rights investigators and journalists who called attention to RPF abuses.

But recently the organization has run into some trouble. Luc Reydams, an academic from Notre Dame University, has done groundbreaking research, deconstructing the NGO's murky operations and methods, and providing compelling evidence that its account of the genocide was produced with the "full and active support of the RPF." His article "NGO Justice: African Rights as Pseudo Prosecutor of the Rwandan Genocide," published in *Human Rights Quarterly* in 2016, reported that African Rights eventually ended up on the RPF payroll, working closely with Rwandan intelligence operatives and even moving to a building that housed the Directorate of Military Intelligence, although by that time Alex de Waal had left the organization.

Omaar rejected the accusations. She told me, "Luc Reydams has not written a well-researched, academic piece of work. This is a politically motivated, politicized settling of accounts in a much larger context. He produces absolutely no evidence whatsoever in his article that *Death, Despair and Defiance* was produced in any shape or form with the RPF." She did admit, however, that she received US$100,000 from the RPF government for work that African Rights did for the tenth anniversary commemoration of the genocide. In retrospect, she said, that was "a mistake." When I pressed her on why she dismissed or failed to acknowledge the massacres of Hutu civilians by the RPF in the first two editions of her book and in her reports many years later on the Gacaca proceedings, she insisted that "the people I had access to [in Rwanda] were Tutsi survivors of the genocide. At that time, it seemed that they were the targets of a well-organized genocide."

In his interview with Reydams, Alex de Waal brazenly took credit for creating a narrative of the genocide—namely, that the Hutu government had planned the elimination of Tutsis years in advance. But a few weeks before Reydams's article was published, de Waal, who had left the NGO and was now an academic at Tufts University, admitted in an essay in the *Boston Review* that he had been wrong about the Hutu conspiracy to commit genocide.

But the narrative was powerful at the time, and remains powerful. Even when international observers noticed what was happening, they often chose to minimize or dismiss RPF atrocities. For instance, Human Rights Watch had discovered that the RPF had waged violence in Giti, and "swept through [the commune] like fire."[12] But the killings merited only a sentence in its own enormous reference report on the genocide, *Leave None to Tell the Story*. The lies are still shading and confounding the truth.

10

SCENES FROM A
COUNTERINSURGENCY

IN LATE 1996, WITH THE GENOCIDE OVER AND THE COUNTRY UNDER HIS
control, Kagame put an ambitious politico-military plan into action. He
sent his troops and DMI mobile units into eastern Zaire to uproot more
than a million Hutu refugees who had fled Rwanda following the genocide
and were living in camps just inside the border. Using the formidable levers
of RPF propaganda, he sold Western governments and international media
on the rationale behind this campaign—to protect innocent Tutsis by hunting down armed Hutu *génocidaires* who were hiding in the cover of those
refugee camps—and it worked. Congo was where I first personally encountered the results of Kagame's counterinsurgency, which led to an endless
war in the Great Lakes region that has cost the lives of millions of Congolese
and made Kagame and his most trusted senior commanders rich.[1] But most
immediately, the 1996–97 invasion of Zaire forced hundreds of thousands
of Rwandan refugees back home to face a new round of ethnic cleansing.
Unlike the genocide, which was widely condemned by the international
community even as they allowed it to proceed, the counterinsurgency campaign against Hutus went on for two years with little outcry from the world.

Rwanda's northwestern regions, Gisenyi and Ruhengeri, bore the brunt of
the new wave of killings. Their rolling hills, lush vegetation and fertile volcanic soil are the breadbasket of Rwanda. But they also were considered by
Tutsis to be the birthplace of Hutu extremism. When Juvénal Habyarimana
came to power in 1973, he was seen as having fostered patronage networks

for the Hutu elites in the northwest, where he'd been born. Members of the Hutu extremist party, CDR, in addition to hard-liners from Habyarimana's ruling MRND, were mostly—but not exclusively—from northern Rwanda. These individuals were blamed for much of the anti-Tutsi sentiment that fueled the genocide against Tutsis.[2]

Many Tutsis, at this point, still saw the RPF as their protector, which was not surprising. In the aftermath of the genocide, Tutsis sought revenge and order, but there was seemingly no end to the fountain of revenge, justified by the simple notion: "They had it coming."[3]

The eighteenth-century German philosopher Hegel said tragedy occurs not when good and evil collide, but when opposing sides believe they are right and take that belief to its logical conclusion. In the Rwandan tragedy, the two forces with their inexorable objectives were the RPF and Hutus who were ready to fight to hold on to power. At the heart of the struggle were the usual victims: Hutu peasants and their Tutsi neighbors.

Paul, a middle-aged Hutu from Gisenyi, which borders the Virunga Mountains, said that after the genocide the presence of Hutu insurgents was a threat to the regime and to civilians in general, both Tutsi and Hutu. "We saw the insurgents in our area in March 1997, sometimes very early in the morning. They were imposing, and well armed. They had been active in the camps in Zaire. When the RPF began killing peasants in our commune, many young males who would otherwise not agree to fight decided to join these rebels. They said, 'Instead of being killed by the RPF, we'll join the rebels and at least have a chance of surviving.'" Villagers desperately wanted stability but were caught in the madness. The vast majority of peasants did not harbor Hutu insurgents or provide support to them, but some Hutu families did, and everyone was punished for it. "We held meetings and discussed what to do," Paul said. "Many of us suggested calling in the army every time we saw insurgents in our communities. Yet we were afraid of the authorities; we lived in fear."[4]

Also, the Hutu population was increasingly humiliated at RPF-run public education meetings where the entire ethnic group was scolded for harboring genocidal ideology. While hundreds of thousands of Hutus from the regions sought shelter in refugee camps in Zaire, the Hutus who stayed on in their homeland had to share living space with Tutsis who had moved into northwestern Rwanda from Masisi, in the northern Kivu province of Zaire, after the genocide. These Tutsi incomers were mostly from families who had been expelled from Rwanda in the 1960s and had settled in eastern Congo for decades.

Meanwhile, all around them, the authorities were arresting many Hutus whom Paul and his neighbors believed to be innocent of any wrongdoing. "We knew who the criminals were, who had killed Tutsis during the genocide and who were innocent," he said. "Many Hutus did not commit crimes and were rounded up and put in jails anyhow, without being charged, and subjected to deplorable conditions." Paul believed that in many cases Hutu peasants were killed so that the new Tutsi regime could confiscate their property.

Many senior Hutu officers in the defeated government army told authorities they were war-weary and unwilling to support a Hutu insurgency. The RPF invited these men to join its military, gained their trust and eventually killed most of them and their families. "They got tricked into trusting them," Paul said, "then they were murdered one by one." The systematic elimination of Hutu soldiers, many of them of apparent goodwill, followed the slaughter and disappearance of a vast number of young Hutu men who had been recruited by the RPF in the aftermath of 1994.

The high-profile killing of François-Xavier Uwimana, a colonel who had left the Hutu military, was a prime example of the RPF taking revenge on an innocent man. Uwimana had opposed the Hutu extemists and saved Tutsis during the genocide by helping them to cross the Zairean border. He eventually fled to Zaire with his family, but after the RPF had assumed power, he returned and approached the new regime with open arms. The RPF accepted his support. Yet in January 1997, he and his older children were murdered in the courtyard of his home by a group of RPF soldiers. His wife and new baby were inside the house and survived, but his wife was so traumatized by the murders that she could not take care of herself afterward. She and her young child had to be looked after by Catholic clergy.[5]

An alarming number of ex-FAR soldiers who came back from Zaire and Tanzania were murdered.[6] Others who were killed in that same month of January 1997 included Major Laurent Bizabarimana, his family and neighbors, who were slain on January 18 while celebrating his return; Corporal

Jean de Dieu Mbatuyimana, shot dead at Muhoza military camp on January 20; and Colonel Stanislas Hizimana and his wife and two children, killed on January 21. The RPF arrested Colonel Augustin Nzabanita and Lieutenant Nsabimana, who were then found hanged in their cells at Gisenyi prison on January 23; Major Lambert Rugambage ended up at the morgue in Kibungo on January 29, apparently beaten to death.

In Ruhengeri, farther north, tens of thousands of Hutu peasants were forcefully rounded up at least twice and brought to the local stadium, where they were threatened by government and military officials. Tutsis who had just resettled from the Congo to Ruhengeri and who had mistakenly been brought to the stadium were picked out of the crowd and told to go home while their Hutu neighbors were ordered to stay. A government minister named Jacques Bihozagara issued thinly veiled threats against the crowd, while soldiers brandishing machine guns circled the stadium, offering up their own sinister message. Jérôme, a resident of Ruhengeri who was brought to the stadium, said a colonel told the crowd that "eventually we're going to plant tobacco plantations where you live. They will be big." Which suggested to every Hutu who heard him that they would be killed and their land would be seized. Another military official whom Jérôme did not recognize perversely evoked the Bible. "Like in Solomon, no soldier wears a sword for nothing. You think we're here to protect you?"[7]

"It rained and we kept sitting there. It got dark and we kept sitting there, listening, swallowed by our fear," Jérôme remembered. Soldiers, some indifferent and others snickering, watched them closely. If a soldier did not like the look on someone's face or someone dared to meet his eye, he would pick the offender out of the crowd and that person would disappear. Many were taken to jail and were never seen again. Mostly the soldiers singled out men, but some women were taken too. Jérôme said, "If it was your time to die, you died. That was it. We knew what was happening. No one asked any questions."

It was after 8 p.m. when people were allowed to leave the stadium. Many of them had up to fifty kilometers to travel to get home, and as they set out, soldiers pointedly reminded them that the roads would be dangerous. Jérôme said the whole exercise "was all about scaring and humiliating Hutus."

The beginning of 1997 was harrowing for the family of Rwandan-Canadian Guillaume Murere, who was living in Gatineau, Quebec, at the time. In his hometown of Kabaya in Ruhengeri, his parents and siblings were in deep mourning over the slaughter of his sister Claire and her five children, who were victims of an RPA attack at a refugee camp in Congo as they were fetching water. Their deaths plunged Guillaume's mother into abject despair and mental disarray. She died shortly thereafter, in early March.[8]

Guillaume's mother was the sister-in-law of the RPF chairman, Alex Kanyarengwe, a founder of the RPF and one of the rare Hutus who had been brought into Kagame's inner circle. Close relatives and friends gathered at her home to take part in a vigil the night before her funeral. Kanyarengwe paid his respects and at about 11 p.m. left with his military escort to return to Kigali. But many of the closest family members stayed overnight. At seven o'clock the next morning, when they were outside having porridge around the fire, a contingent of soldiers arrived and surrounded the young men. Given what was happening all over the sector, the family knew what was coming. A niece pleaded with the soldiers at least not to target Guillaume's elderly father, a man with few years left whose wife had just passed away, and they spared him. But the soldiers shot the other men in the yard and in the banana plantation immediately adjacent to the house. Some thirty people were killed, including Guillaume's brothers, his nephew and several cousins. Guillaume, who was working as an engineer for Hydro-Québec at the time, received a panicked call from a cousin in Kigali telling him the news. Guillaume said, "It was unbearable."

Word spread fast of the killings. Jérôme, a family friend who lived nearby, went to the scene to help with the burials.[9] He said the victims had been shot in the head and were unrecognizable. Kanyarengwe had been notified, and when he got back to the house that morning, Jérôme said, he was apoplectic with outrage. "What has happened?" he yelled. "People say the RPF is killing civilians. Now I see with my own eyes what they are doing!" He summoned a local contingent of soldiers and upbraided them for what had happened. "You can't say that these people were troublemakers," he shouted. "They had nothing to do with insurgents! They were gathered for a funeral. Look at their heads! They were shot at point-blank range." It might have been news to Kanyarengwe, but by this time most peasants in the commune knew that the counterinsurgency campaign was being used to cover a greater strategic objective. An officer with the Gendarmerie confirmed that scores of civilians were targeted by the army in Musanze, an area that was free of insurgents. Still, the army conducted door-to-door searches and killings, and pounded villages with helicopter gunships. "It was well organized and really terrible," said a former officer who was in the region at the time. Hundreds of civilians fled, but the RPF tracked them down and killed them.[10]

There seemed to be nowhere to hide. Rwandans who hoped they'd be spared because they lived near RPF military bases, where insurgents rarely dared to go, were no better off. "We knew this was not about hunting down insurgents. It was about hunting down the population," said Neza, an elderly woman who lost many family members in a devastating three-pronged operation carried out adjacent to Mukamira, the RPF's military headquarters in the west.[11]

I interviewed Neza at a location outside Rwanda where she was receiving medical care for an illness, after which she returned home. She and her family were from Rambura, in Karago, considered the heartland of the former Hutu regime. Her family's hilltop home was two hundred meters from Mukamira, which was the base out of which the counterinsurgency campaign was run.

"What soldiers would do is calmly order us to go to a meeting, pointing their guns at us," she told me. "Women and children were told to attend. And we'd ask: why call a meeting after dark when we are getting ready to feed our children? But the soldiers would insist: 'Don't worry; it won't take long.' We knew what they were doing. Those of us who were not surrounded by soldiers, who could get away at that moment, ran and hid in the banana plantations. Others could not."

In February 1997, her extended family and close neighbors were called to an evening gathering. Neza herself heard the soldiers knock on her door but would not open it when the soldiers ordered her to go. (At that stage, soldiers were not breaking into the homes on her hill to force people to obey, she said.) Later that night she heard gunshots and grenades go off in the distance. No one dared to go out in the dark to find out what was happening for fear of being killed. By morning, she and her neighbors discovered thirty-two people dead, seven of them children under five years of age. Some of the victims were relatives who lived on her hill.

On a Saturday several months later, in November 1997, soldiers showed up on Neza's hill in the early evening, knocking on doors and stopping people in the fields. "They hadn't killed enough people, so they came back for more," Neza said. "It was the second part of the operation, as far as my family and neighbors were concerned." She was in a cornfield when three Tutsi soldiers told her to go to a meeting. "Why are you always convening meetings at this hour, when we need to feed our families?" she asked. But they all understood what was actually going on.

"Go!" said the soldiers.

"I'll be there in a minute. I need to get a bucket for my corn," she said, and she managed to slip into the dense plantation around her. Another of her children saw what was happening and escaped quickly into the bushes. But her husband, their son and her nephew, who had just finished high school, were surrounded by soldiers and forced to go with the military. "They were caught," she lamented.

When it got dark, gunfire and explosions rang out in the vicinity of the barracks. She was overwhelmed with dread: she knew the RPF was slaughtering her family. There were seventeen victims that night, among them Neza's husband, son and nephew. Nine of those killed were children. She, like other neighbors, sought refuge on a nearby hill. But the nightmare wasn't over yet. She said, "Three days later the soldiers came back."

It was morning. Neza had gone back to her hill to bring some milk to her frail 95-year-old father, who had refused to leave their hut. She changed his clothes and warned him he would have to come with her; it was too dangerous for him to stay. But he dug in his heels. "I am too old for them to be interested in me. I'm not moving." She kissed him goodbye and left.

But when she got back to her friend's home on the neighboring hill, she began to worry. And she'd forgotten the dried corn she'd meant to fetch from home. She wanted to go back and check on her father, and get the corn, but she was too frightened. Within an hour she heard shots ring out from the area where her hut was located. Once again the worst was happening and she could do nothing about it. A farmhand told her that the soldiers had broken down the door of her hut, barged in, and shot and killed her elderly father, then went next door and killed the 60-year-old neighbor woman. The soldiers then pillaged both homes.

She waited three full days before she risked going home to bury her father, fearful that the military might be waiting around to kill the victims' remaining loved ones. In addition to losing her husband and her father, Neza lost five of her nine children during and after the genocide.

What happened to Neza's family was neither random nor an isolated case of ethnic reprisal. The cleansing that was central to the RPF's brutal counter-insurgency campaign was being conducted hill by hill.

And all these killings stoked the fervor of the Hutu insurgents the RPF had told the world they were fighting. By July 1997, two northwestern communes in particular were rife with Hutu rebels. In Rwerere, Hutu forces chased out the RPF as the population fled to the Virunga Mountains. In Rubavu, insurgents attacked a jail where Hutu detainees were being held, released the prisoners and then killed those who would not join their forces.[12] Instead of channeling its anger against the Hutu rebels, the government turned even more violently against the civilian population throughout western Rwanda. "The RPF sought revenge," Paul said. "They were wild and crazy. They were animals."

On the morning of Friday, August 8, 1997, security forces killed an estimated four hundred people at Mahoko market. Brigitte Tuyishime, a young Hutu teacher, was there with her children and her sister.[13] Like many other people in the area, she had begun spending her days at the market or near the town hall or at the hospital in order to avoid being caught alone at home when RPF security forces carried out raids. "It was genocide," she said. "They were not attacking Tutsis. They were killing unarmed Hutus."

That morning she and her family ran to a neighbor's home. They found others already sheltering there, including frightened Tutsi children. They all hid under several beds for hours until security forces came, in search of several Tutsis they'd heard were hiding there. The woman who owned the house said that, indeed, she had some Tutsi children with her, but that no insurgents were present in the house. The soldiers ordered them all to go back to the market. When Brigitte and her children got there, they found the market littered with corpses and surrounded by armored vehicles. She saw businesspeople, peasants and teachers she recognized lying in pools of blood. Tutsi residents were escorted away in military vehicles, apparently being taken to safe areas in Gisenyi town. She and her children were allowed to leave. They hurried home, trembling. The government tried to convince the population that the people they had killed had been harboring insurgents. But Brigitte believed they were targeting the Hutus capable of helping other Hutus successfully put their lives back together.

Amnesty International was one of the few international agencies to document the Mahoko market killings in detail. In a report released in September 1997, its researchers confirmed that RPF security forces killed several hundred civilians at the market, and also slaughtered several thousand civilians throughout the region.[14] "It is dark here," Amnesty quoted residents as saying. "We are waiting to die. We breathe a sigh of relief when 24 hours go by, then we worry about the next 24 hours. It is like a 24-hour contract. We go to sleep knowing from one day to the next that we may not be here."

By October, Paul and other able-bodied Hutu men had fled to the mountains to avoid the violent raids, and he had sent his wife and children to Kigali to stay with friends where it was safer. Many people who fled their homes were not so lucky, and were caught and killed by security forces. Not all women and children had the means to flee, nor did they have the stamina to keep running. Thousands sought refuge in caves in the commune of Kanama, long a hiding place for civilians fleeing previous waves of violence, deep and dark caverns of volcanic rock where they could hide from Kagame's soldiers.[15] Paul's 42-year-old sister and her five young children took refuge there, along with many other family members and friends. In the last few days of October, the RPF decided to move in on the caves.[16]

Serge was a young Tutsi soldier who was part of the DMI team that attacked the civilians in the caves, an operation he said was ordered by the directorate's chief, Karenzi Karake. Several brigades arrived on the scene, where thousands of civilians—not insurgents—were hiding. Serge told me that on October 23 the DMI team cordoned off the area, and military units began throwing grenades into the caves' entrances. They followed with machine-gun fire before sealing off the openings, preventing any possibility for escape. Several thousands of people died there.[17]

Serge, now in exile, said the cave operations—in addition to the many raids in which the RPF killed unarmed Hutus—were all part of a larger scheme. "There was a plan during the counterinsurgency to eliminate the civilian population in the north . . . Yes there were insurgents trying to overthrow the government. But the war against these fighters was used as a pretext to reduce the Hutu population. There was no doubt about it."

Another former RPF officer, who was stationed with the Gendarmerie in western Rwanda during the counterinsurgency, was categorical. "If the RPF did not commit genocide in 1994—and I believe our troops did—it certainly carried it out during the counterinsurgency. It was appalling from every standpoint. No human being could witness what went on and not be sickened by it." The officer left Rwanda in 1999, as soon as he was able to flee safely.

Amnesty did extensive interviews with villagers who had lost their loved ones and concluded that the RPF killed between five thousand and eight thousand civilians in the caves.[18] But Amnesty could not get access to the site. In early December the army was still cordoning off the area and would not allow independent investigators to pass. On December 8, the RPF allowed human rights observers and journalists to tour the area while armed soldiers guarded the cave entrances, which were blocked with stones and rocks. Several journalists and observers reported smelling rotting corpses and seeing bullets on the ground. Authorities claimed the dead were some insurgents who had been using the caves as a hideout.

Despite overwhelming evidence that Kagame's forces had killed thousands of civilians in cold blood, the United States government resorted to its historical habit of swallowing RPF propaganda and defending the killers. The US ambassador for war crimes at the time, David Scheffer, issued an appallingly inaccurate report, which I later obtained from a congressional staffer.[19] After visiting the site on December 15, Scheffer wrote that the entrances were blocked and the army was "keeping vigil." "RPA soldiers did not know how many armed insurgents may remain there. The last firefight occurred three weeks ago as insurgents fired from the unblocked cave opening. I saw evidence of bullet holes in the tree trunks rising from the large cave opening. The RPA claims there have been no attempts at surrender by those who may remain alive in the caves." While Amnesty was trying to turn the lights on to reveal the RPF's brutality during the counterinsurgency, Scheffer's report kept them turned off, leaving only darkness and more violence.

Scheffer minimized the number of dead as reported by Amnesty. "The smell of death, however, was not as overpowering as I have experienced at graves exhumations where [there] are hundreds of bodies. If there were thousands of dead bodies in the caves, the smell of death would have been much more powerful and the flies more numerous." He went on: "I doubt the RPA could have, or would have desired, to enter the caves in order to commit such large-scale killings. It would have been very difficult to kill large numbers of civilians inside the caves."

Though Amnesty had come to its conclusions based on the testimony of actual sources in Gisenyi—the grieving families who lost their loved ones—Scheffer accused the organization of relying on one person now living in Belgium. But there is no indication in his report that Scheffer interviewed Hutu peasants himself; he cites only RPF authorities. "The Amnesty International allegation of 5,000 to 8,000 civilians massacred, which apparently is based [on the evidence of a person] in Belgium who claims to have some Rwandan sources, may be without evidentiary foundations. The government of Rwanda strongly denies the allegation, which it regards as ludicrous."

Yet Scheffer managed to muster moral outrage over another attack, no less painful but smaller in terms of victims. On December 10, 1997, the Mudende refugee camp in Rwanda, which housed Tutsi refugees who had fled from the violence in neighboring Congo, was horrifically assaulted. Attackers used machetes, grenades, nail-studded clubs and guns to kill hundreds of Tutsis, before setting their huts on fire. The Rwandan government, the United States and Amnesty International concurred that Hutu rebels were behind the attack, although Amnesty questioned why Rwandan security forces had not moved the refugees to a safer zone, since the area was highly volatile and the camp had already been attacked by armed groups in August.

In his report on this attack, Scheffer wrote, "In a manner characteristic of the genocide of 1994, the attack on Mudende camp was genocidal in character, resulting in the deaths of at least 327 Congolese Tutsis and perhaps some of the insurgents and the severe wounding of 267 Tutsis. One hundred and fifty Tutsi women may have been abducted by the insurgents."

The *New York Times* ran an urgent story on the attack, whose headline was MACHETE RETURNS TO RWANDA, REKINDLING A GENOCIDAL WAR. The lead paragraph of the article was poignant:

> The little girl's head had been split by a machete. A long ragged suture ran from her left eye across her ruined skull. Her breath fluttered shallow and light, and her frail body seemed to cling to the world of the living with no more than a butterfly's strength.

The article said that Hutu guerrillas had attacked the camp, "leaving nothing but burning tents and leaflets preaching genocide in their wake."[20]

But several former intelligence officers and soldiers from the RPF painted a different picture of the attack on the refugee camp, claiming that the incident was a false flag, floated by the RPF. (A false flag is when one side in a conflict carries out an attack on its own people and blames it on its enemy in order to achieve political leverage.) Just as during the genocide, when RPF technicians infiltrated the Interahamwe and killed Tutsis at roadblocks to help spur the violence, the RPF's clandestine forces had attacked Tutsis at Mudende.

"Everyone knew that the RPF staged that attack. It was common knowledge in intelligence circles," one officer said. He'd heard that a prominent RPF member at the time, Aloyse Inyumba, had condemned the incident, internally, and worried how the government would keep the matter a secret. Inyumba had said some of the refugees who were killed had relatives in the army, and that these soldiers were already aware the RPF was behind the massacre. She argued that they would not be able to contain their anger and stay silent. Another High Command soldier I interviewed called the Mudende attack a "brilliant and cruel display of military theater" on the part of the RPF. He said an associate of his was involved in the operation and had revealed to him how it went down.

Staging an attack on the camp achieved several key objectives. On a purely practical and mercenary level, senior army commanders managed to steal the refugees' cows, which in a poor country such as Rwanda were valuable. The attack also spread fear among Tutsis and created sympathy for their cause, while demonizing Hutus and fueling suspicion about the possibility of their returning to commit genocide. The slaughter also triggered an inter-national outcry, which further justified the RPF's brutal counterinsurgency campaign against Hutus. And finally, the Mudende attack persuaded the United States to continue training RPF soldiers and supplying Rwanda with military materiel.

Amnesty had already criticized the US and South Africa for providing military aid and training to Rwandan security forces. Its statement said:

> The US army, in particular, has been involved in a training program for the RPA. Despite being one of Rwanda's closest political and military allies—capable of exerting pressure for positive changes in the human rights situation—the US government is not known to have publicly condemned or demanded an end to persistent human rights violations in Rwanda. The international community has allowed death to become a banality.

Rwanda's state-sponsored violence during the counterinsurgency reached its apotheosis at the end of 1997. The methods used were vintage RPF, drawn from years of rebel war in Uganda where its fighters had helped Yoweri Museveni overthrow the governments of Idi Amin and Milton Obote. The RPF honed and polished these techniques—infiltration, staging attacks, spreading terror and killing political opponents—in Rwanda before and during the genocide. The RPF's use of terrorism, in particular, was strategic. As the American scholar Michael Stohl has argued in his research on state terror-ism, terrorists are primarily interested in the audience, not the victim. How the audience reacts is as important as the act of terror and its casualties.

Rushashi, a commune in Kigali North, was a bold and early test of how the RPF played to its intended audience, unleashing fear and instilling a culture of silence.[21] On Sunday, July 7, 1996, Rushashi and its neighboring commune, Tare, were flooded with RPF troops who set up roadblocks and placed vehicles strategically throughout villages. Vincent Munyandamutsa, the Hutu mayor of Rushashi, was on his way home early that evening when he was stopped on his motorbike by intelligence agents and fatally stabbed in the face and chest. This man had been honored with a human rights award for his exemplary actions during the genocide and had initially cooperated with the RPF after it seized power in July 1994. He was a highly respected

figure in Kigali North and adored by family and friends. He had helped persuade Rwandan refugees to return from Zaire and had conducted rural campaigns to encourage people to turn over their weapons.

His goodwill toward the RPF turned sour, though, as villagers began to
disappear and whole families were murdered in his commune in 1994 and
1995. Once he began to see the true face of the new regime, he could barely
sleep at night, said a close family friend. He also railed at the number of people
being thrown in jail without charge. He told authorities he would not comply
with putting people into crowded dungeons where they would perish.[22] He
had been known to release civilians he believed were unfairly imprisoned,
invoking the wrath of DMI commanders in the area. By 1996, he had confided
to friends that he believed his days were numbered. "I think they're going to
kill me. It could be any day now." The night he was stabbed, the RPF killed
seventeen other civilians in carefully planned ambushes in the area.[23]

The RPF's official line was that Hutu rebels were responsible for these
coordinated, surgical killings. Residents knew better. It was the RPF soldiers
who had put up roadblocks all over the commune; how could insurgents have
slipped through?

A villager who lost a loved one in these coordinated attacks told me in an
interview, "The RPF did not want any Hutu leaders. They wanted an illiterate
population, people they could control and use at will. Hutus who did well,
economically or intellectually, had to be eliminated so that authorities could
rule as they wished."[24]

In Belgium in April 1997, the exiled human rights activist Joseph Matata
meticulously compiled and then published a list of dozens of Hutu judges,
lawyers and other legal staff who had been arrested or assassinated while
attempting to perform their duties in post-genocide Rwanda.[25] The list was
alarming by any measure, and remains so today. Matata did not mince his
words, charging that Rwanda's judiciary had been ethnically cleansed by a
"gangrened regime" run by a group of extremist Tutsis bent on institutional-
izing the regime's impunity from the law. As a result, civilians had nowhere
to turn for protection. There was no legal recourse for a population under
attack by a terrorist state.

What kind of long-term solution could be wrought from such ethnic cleansing, coupled as it was with a propaganda campaign to fan fears of insurgents and false-flag operations carried out by the RPF? The only thing these tactics accomplished was to widen the historical ethnic divisions among Rwandans and exacerbate the wounds caused by the genocide. The counterinsurgency campaign fueled the suspicions Hutus held about what would happen when Tutsis once again dominated Rwanda, which in turn created more of a threat to Tutsi peasants from Hutus who either were hard-liners or felt that they had no choice but to join the Hutu rebels. Post-genocide reconciliation was an impossible dream, exploded by the regime's relentless heightening of contempt and fear of the other. And as the international community largely kept quiet about these atrocities being committed in the name of the counter-insurgency, Hutus and Tutsis were left to suffer in silence. A devastating silence. And outsiders who, out of human solidarity, tried to break that silence were eventually targeted too.

In the first five weeks of 1997, more than a dozen foreigners were killed in orchestrated operations conducted by Kagame's intelligence network. Four UN observers were killed on January 11; three Spaniards working for Doctors of the World, an NGO, were slain on January 18; a Canadian priest was shot dead as he offered Communion in Ruhengeri on February 2; and five UN human rights staffers were massacred in Karengera on February 4.[26] These were not random acts caused by the heightened violence in the region. A former intelligence official with direct knowledge of these assassinations said that the operations that targeted foreigners in Rwanda during the counter-insurgency were planned and coordinated by the DMI and the Gendarmerie's Special Intelligence division.

The Spanish aid workers—a nurse, a doctor and a journalist working for the newspaper El País—were silenced because they had been shown mass graves of people allegedly killed by the RPA, according to the Spanish lawyer Jordi Palou-Loverdos, who represented the families of victims.[27] The aid workers had been in western Rwanda for only a few months, treating the many injured peasants. Eventually a few of these peasants showed them the graves. The reporter, Luis Valtuena, brought a camera. The three were already being followed by DMI agents, but probably had no sense of the consequences about to hit them when they became witnesses to crimes so explosive they could damage the Rwandan regime's carefully cultivated reputation.

According to an intelligence officer present, on January 17, Kayumba Nyamwasa, who, as head of the Gendarmerie, was based in northwestern Rwanda and working closely with the DMI, held a meeting to discuss how to "eliminate the problem" of white people talking with survivors about the massacres in Ruhengeri. A Gendarmerie officer told me the RPF openly claimed that the Spaniards were collaborating with Hutu insurgents by giving them army uniforms. Even at the time, he doubted the veracity of this charge.[28]

The next night, the three Spaniards, along with another foreign national—a US citizen named Nitin Mahdav who was also a member of the Doctors of the World team—were attacked in their NGO residence in Ruhengeri. Mahdav, who had just arrived in western Rwanda a few days earlier, was the only one to survive, though he was seriously injured.

Mahdav, who now works for USAID, told me in an interview in 2016 that his recollection of the attack is sketchy—understandable given the trauma he endured.[29] He said they all heard shots fired outside the house. Then a group of armed men, who he assumed were Hutu insurgents, broke in. The men demanded their passports and then three of them confiscated the foreigners' belongings and took off, leaving one man behind. He held the aid workers hostage until the others returned several hours later. Then they all started shooting, killing the three and seriously wounding Mahdav in the leg. (Eventually his leg had to be amputated.)

I asked Mahdav if his Spanish colleagues had talked about being shown the mass graves. He hesitated at first, then said, "It's vaguely ringing a bell, but I can't say that I remember." When I pressed him on whether he believed Hutu insurgents were responsible for the killings, he would not say. "I don't think about it. I have no recollection who told me they were Interahamwe." I asked if he was afraid to give a full account of what happened that night. He said, "I suppose I would have been scared had I been in Rwanda. The thought of them sending a death squad to kill me in my parents' house in suburban Pittsburgh crossed my mind, but I'm sure that's highly unlikely."

The two deadly attacks that same month on UN staff prompted a full-scale investigation by the UN's Human Rights Field Operation in Rwanda. In June 1997, the UN produced a report that included thirty-seven annexes of photos and other evidence. The report was written by William O'Neil, head of field operations, and Javier Hernandez Valencia, from the Office of the UN High Commissioner for Human Rights. UN staffer Marcel Zinsou, who was living a hundred meters from the Spanish aid workers' residence in Ruhengeri when it was attacked, also filed a report. Despite numerous requests by Spanish authorities followed by a court order to produce this evidence, the UN refused to divulge any information about its investigations. Both documents remain in confidential keeping at the UN Archives and Records Management Section in Geneva.[30] But Spain wanted justice for these deaths, and for the four other Spanish citizens—Catholic priests from the Society of Mary—who had also been murdered, allegedly by Rwandan soldiers, at a refugee camp in Bukavu, Congo, in 1996, as well as for a Spanish priest named Joaquim Vallmajo, who had been killed by the RPF in Byumba in April 1994.

In 2008, invoking the principle of universal jurisdiction, the investigating magistrate on the Rwandan inquiry, Judge Fernando Andreu Merelles, issued arrest warrants for forty of Kagame's senior commanders on charges of genocide, crimes against humanity, terrorism and other serious offenses. The warrants related to the murders of the Spaniards, but also to the mass killings of Hutus by Kagame's Tutsi army in Rwanda during the genocide and in Congo in the late 1990s. Merelles and the Spanish victims' lawyer, Palou-Loverdos, produced a 185-page indictment based on detailed testimony from RPF officers and soldiers who had defected and were now living in exile under varying degrees of witness protection. The arrest warrants shocked Western nations who had poured billions from their foreign aid budgets into post-genocide Rwanda. But the indictment failed to persuade authorities in Europe, North America or Africa to actually extradite any of Kagame's top aides to Madrid. Generals Kayonga, Karake and Cesar Kayizari all continued to travel as they pleased, even to London to receive expensive medical treatment when needed. And despite the wealth of evidence the Spanish inquiry had amassed against Kagame himself, as head of state, the president enjoyed total immunity. He would continue to speak at Ivy League institutions in the United States and to be feted at the United Nations.

On Sunday, February 2, 1997, two weeks after the Spanish aid workers had been killed, Father Guy Pinard, a 61-year-old priest from Shawinigan, Quebec, was also murdered.[31] Pinard had spent thirty-five years in Rwanda and had openly condemned the rampant human rights abuses committed by Kagame's forces in Ruhengeri, where his parish was located. A Rwandan who was close to the priest, and who witnessed his murder, told me, "He was a serious, frank man. He didn't mince words. He defended the weak. He never tolerated lies. During the war and even after the RPF took power, he condemned the disappearances, assassinations, arbitrary arrests that were occurring. He would denounce crimes openly during his sermons. He spoke of everything, even in front of RPF members sitting in the church. He would say he preferred to face death than remain silent in the face of atrocities."[32]

Father Pinard was giving Communion to a congregation in Ruhengeri when a man known as Dieudonné, a Tutsi with close ties to the RPF and the brother of an army lieutenant, joined the line. After taking Communion, the man moved off, then took a pistol out of his trench coat and shot Pinard in the back.

The witness, who was just a few feet away from Pinard when he was killed, said, "I didn't realize what was happening at first when he fired the shot, but one parishioner tried to apprehend the assassin as he fired another shot at the ceiling. The church was full and panic ensued. The crowd began to scatter. People were falling over each other. Women and children were yelling. We thought the church was surrounded by the RPF." In the chaos, the shooter escaped.

"The priest did not speak after he was shot. He did not yell. Not a word came out of his mouth. He fell to the floor and died immediately. His blood flowed. It was horrible." The witness was interrogated and beaten by authorities immediately after the killing. Within weeks he'd fled to Kenya, where he gave a detailed statement to the Canadian High Commission in Nairobi.[33] But he said that, unlike with the Spanish authorities, nothing happened as a result. "I cannot understand how an embassy that purports to represent the Canadian people can receive a testimony about the assassination of one of their citizens and doesn't even want to follow up. No one called me for an interview or even responded."

The *Globe and Mail*'s Africa correspondent, Geoffrey York, and I told Father Pinard's story in a feature published in the newspaper in November 2014.[34] The priest's colleagues and family told us that the Canadian authorities did not seem interested in investigating the crime. Roger Tessier, a priest with the missionary society known as White Fathers, to which Pinard belonged, said the RCMP did come to see him in Nairobi after the murder, but he had no sense that they followed up. Richard Dandenault, another priest who was a friend of Pinard's and now lives in Sherbrooke, Quebec, said there was no real follow-up.[35]

Louise Roy, Father Pinard's sister-in-law, said the priest knew that his life was in danger but refused to leave Rwanda. "He was very outspoken and the Rwandan government was afraid of him talking," she said. "I don't recall the Canadian government ever calling us back to say that any investigation had been done, or that it had found out anything. The Canadian government never did much about this. I don't think it was that important to them."

Father Pinard's murder wasn't the first time a Canadian priest was targeted by people or forces loyal to Kagame. Father Claude Simard, who had spent nearly three decades in Rwanda, helped protect Tutsis during the genocide and documented massacres carried out by Hutu militia and other extremists. After the genocide, Father Simard was appalled to discover that the RPF was committing similar atrocities against Hutus in Butare, and started to make tape recordings of his observations. But he was not content merely to observe. He met with the Rwandan interior minister, Seth Sendashonga, and asked him to tell the Rwandan military to stop its reprisal attacks on his parishioners. The RPF's military intelligence were already aware of Simard's recordings. On October 17, 1994, shortly after his meeting with the interior minister, the priest was beaten to death with a hammer, gagged and left in a pool of blood.

Two separate reports by the UN peacekeeping force still in Rwanda, at that point led by the Canadian general Guy Tousignant, implicated Kagame's forces in the murder. Father Simard had been afraid of being killed and had expressed his fears in a letter to a Canadian friend.[36] One of the reports indicated that the letter and cassettes were taken on the night of his murder.[37]

A former senior intelligence official who worked for Kagame told us that the killing of Father Simard was organized by the DMI's counterintelligence department and the Special Intelligence section of the Gendarmerie. "They were scared of one thing—the information they suspected he had. Simard was a witness willing to reveal what he saw. He was a key figure, among others. He was not the only one: many people disappeared," the former official said.

One of the UN investigations was conducted by Major Tim Isberg, a Canadian UN military observer in Rwanda. Despite the evidence he had collected which showed that Kagame's regime had killed a Canadian citizen, he said Canadian authorities never approached him about his findings. "It's more than disappointing," Isberg told me. "It's another part of the Father Simard tragedy, because it's a tragic situation if Canadian officials don't take interest. Canadian officials certainly had a responsibility from a Foreign Affairs perspective to investigate a murder of a Canadian citizen on foreign territory."

Canada has given roughly $550 million in aid to Rwanda since 1994, including $30 million in 2016. Why does it keep sending money to a government that is strongly suspected of murdering two Canadian citizens? It seemed that the RPF could now commit crimes out in the open and still receive billions of dollars in aid. And Kagame could continue to receive human rights awards despite these murders, the Spanish indictment and Amnesty's reports—buoyed by propaganda and protected by powerful friends in the West. What were these Western allies supporting? From the point of view of the RPF's victims, it all seemed to be in praise of blood, an endorsement of mass murder.

Among Kagame's greatest suppporters in the West is Bill Clinton, who was the US president when the genocide began. Clinton has hailed Kagame as "one of the greatest leaders of our time." The Clinton Foundation has awarded Kagame its Global Citizen prize, saying "from crisis, President Kagame has forged a strong, unified, and growing nation with the potential to become a model for the rest of Africa and the world."

Four years after the genocide, during a trip to Kigali, Clinton apologized to Rwandans, saying the United States should have done more to limit what had happened in Rwanda in 1994. More? The US did nothing to stop the carnage and, in fact, worked hard to "stay out of Rwanda" altogether. In her book *A Problem from Hell: America and the Age of Genocide*, Samantha Power showed that the United States led a successful effort to remove most of the peacekeepers from Rwanda and worked aggressively to block the subsequent authorization of UN reinforcements. Washington refused to use its technology to jam Hutu radio broadcasts that incited murder of Tutsis. Most tellingly, US officials refused to use the word *genocide* to describe what was going on, for fear the country would be morally obliged to act.

Clinton would feign ignorance over what was really happening, but US officials were in fact following events closely. The United States was monitoring activities in the region with its highly classified Kennen Keyhole-class satellite—a sophisticated digital camera orbiting the earth—and other reconnaissance technology.[38] It also had access to remote sensing images from the Landsat TM mosaic, which can reveal mass graves. In 1994, the United States would have been well aware of killings in both Hutu-controlled zones and those seized by Kagame's forces. The Pentagon would have been able to detect the DMI's mass graves throughout Byumba and Kibungo in April and May, and would have been aware of Kagame's bulldozers and the RPF's outdoor crematoriums at Gabiro, on the edge of Akagera National Park.

The former UK prime minister Tony Blair has been described as Kagame's cheerleader-in-chief, and has been crucial to turning on the taps of aid and then keeping the flow of money going. When Blair was in power from 1997 to 2007, Great Britain became the second-biggest bilateral donor to Rwanda, after the United States. On the twentieth anniversary of the genocide in 2014, the *Economist* noted that Britain's Department for International Development (DFID) alone had poured half a billion pounds into the impoverished nation.

After leaving office, Blair created a private charity largely bankrolled by millionaire businessman Lord Sainsbury of Turville, called the African Governance Initiative (AGI)—ostensibly set up to help drive Rwanda's development and deliver public services. The AGI is known to have embedded itself in Rwandan government institutions, working in the offices of the president and the prime minister, as well as the Rwandan Development Board and Ministry of Public Service. (The charity is so firmly partisan on behalf of the regime that it's been accused of undermining the interests of British foreign policy.)[39]

By not intervening during the genocide or during the countersinsurgency, Western governments sent a strong message to Rwandan Hutus that their suffering did not count. And Kagame noticed. Along with its president, the United States, the most powerful nation on earth, openly sided with Rwandan security forces, providing cover for their atrocities and increasing its military assistance. The counterinsurgency in Rwanda ultimately proved to be a period of dramatic social change that would sow the seeds of tyranny in Rwanda for years to come. The RPF's official narrative of the genocide stipulated that only Hutus perpetrated violence, that Tutsis were either victims or saviors. It thus became morally acceptable to criminalize an entire ethnic group and dismiss a plethora of inhumane acts committed against its members. Restoring "order" post-genocide really meant creating a world in which Hutus were rounded up and jailed without judicial recourse, a world in which every Hutu family was suspected of harboring *génocidaire* insurgents, a world in which Hutus who escaped to neighboring Congo were guilty in the eyes of the international community. If Hutu blood was shed in the wake of the Tutsi genocide, it meant Hutus got what they deserved. Like the remorseless goddess Nemesis, the RPF dealt a heavy dose of revenge, not only for what Hutus did in 1994, but for what their parents and grandparents had done decades earlier.

11

AN ILLEGAL DEAL

WHILE PAUL KAGAME AND THE RPF WERE CLEARLY WILLING TO GO TO any lengths to manipulate the truth of their victory in Rwanda and obscure their crimes, they were also playing to an international audience who still wanted to believe in them. People in Western governments knew or at least strongly suspected that Kagame's commandos had killed Habyarimana and the others on the presidential plane in the act that triggered the genocide. Robert Gersony, hired to investigate in August 1994, had passed on compelling evidence of Kagame's death squads to the United Nations before that terrible year was even out. It was known in NGO and Western government circles that Kagame's troops had killed thousands of Hutus in Kibeho in 1995, and unleashed war in Congo in 1996, all the while conducting a campaign of slaughter against refugees in Zaire. The counterinsurgency campaign, along with the high-profile murders of the three Spanish citizens in 1997, had set off a judicial investigation in Spain, targeting the RPF. But the attitude to the Kagame regime barely wavered: the international community believed it needed to step up to support Kagame's leadership not only as a way to pay its dues for not intervening in the genocide, but also because the consensus was that he and his regime were the key to creating stability in the region. But how much more destabilizing could one man be? The region was still awash in blood.

The group of rebels who had come to power in the genocide had now established a dictatorship. Rwanda was a single-party state, dangerous to its citizens and the wider region, and financially backed by the West. It possessed a veneer of moral superiority that made it apparently invincible as it went to any lengths to quash challenges to its authority and the official story of the genocide. Still, in 1999, the United Nations tribunal dedicated to prosecuting war crimes in Rwanda set up a clandestine unit to investigate crimes committed in 1994 by Kagame's army—the Special Investigations Unit, whose top secret report was eventually leaked to me.

The unit was created in 1999 by the ICTR's deputy prosecutor, Bernard Muna, on the instruction of its first chief prosecutor, Louise Arbour. As its three core investigators explained in the summary report of their findings, dated October 2003, "the team was to work in the greatest secrecy. At the time, only the hierarchy of the division of the investigations knew of the existence of the operations."[1]

The team sought to gather all information the Office of the Prosecutor had in its possession on alleged offenses carried out by the Rwandan Patriotic Army. The ICTR's Evidence Unit provided it with copies of documents seized in a stunning raid in Kenya in July 1997 that had captured Rwandan fugitives Jean Kambanda, the country's former prime minister; Pauline Nyiramasuhuko, the former minister of family and women's affairs; and two military commanders, Gratien Kabiligi and Aloys Ntabakuze—all sought for the genocide against Tutsis. Before the team members started looking for witnesses, they also analyzed reports by human rights organizations such as Amnesty, The International Federation for Human Rights (FIDH) and Human Rights Watch, and from Rwandan organizations such as Collectif des Ligues et Association de Défense des Droits de l'Homme au Rwanda (CLADHO) and ARDHO.

In 2000, Arbour was replaced by Carla Del Ponte, a woman who had already made a distinctive mark in the annals of international justice. The former Swiss investigating magistrate had risen to fame for taking a strip out of the Sicilian mob. She was credited with breaking a Mafia money-laundering operation, pursuing former Soviet bloc officials suspected of stowing illegal funds in Switzerland, and delivering up evidence to Pakistan of money laundering by Benazir Bhutto. Surely a woman with such an impressive résumé could successfully take on Rwandan war criminals, both Hutu and Tutsi? For many of Kagame's critics, she appeared to be the best hope to ensure that the ICTR operated with a modicum of judicial conscience.

That said, Del Ponte appeared to have made a colossal error in judgment by going directly to Paul Kagame in December 2000 to inform him that she was launching investigations into RPF crimes. A few days later she made things worse by holding a press conference to announce that she could have an indictment against the RPF ready within a year.[2] The team had been in The Hague, going through ICTR documents and compiling lists of potential witnesses, and had just got back to Kigali. They were startled that Del Ponte had taken such steps, given that their best avenue to success was to operate discreetly. "I learned not to be surprised with anything she might do," a lawyer who worked with the court told me, shaking his head. In contrast, his advice had been "to go underground, stop being political, stop being high profile, get your house in order and get organized."

By 2001, the team had realized that the best way to obtain evidence against the RPF was to get testimonies from inside the organization, but for reasons of safety, they could not investigate on Rwandan territory, where the greatest evidence lay. They had no choice but to interview Rwandans in exile in several countries, tapping the circles of political dissidents and deserters from the RPA. The investigators wrote in their summary report:

> Thanks to them, we know the political organization of the RPF and the military organization of the RPA; the positions of the troops before April 6, 1994, the movement of the troops during the war of 1994, and the military hierarchy, battalion by battalion. We collected confessions of soldiers and officers admitting their participation in killings and massacres of civilians, before the war, during the war, and after the victory of the RPF.

At first, the biggest challenge the unit faced was the reticence and mistrust of their witnesses. Most of them considered the ICTR to be biased in favor of the RPF and did not believe it would ultimately be willing to prosecute Kagame and members of his regime. The witnesses were afraid for their safety and that of their relatives in Rwanda. Still, by May 2002 the team had succeeded in recruiting a hundred sources, forty-one of whom gave sworn statements. The team also had compiled a list of 518 potential witnesses across four continents: 174 in Africa (including Rwanda), 226 in Europe, 117 in North America and one in Asia.

But a troubling pattern of intimidation and murder of these sources was beginning to emerge. On August 13, 2002, a senior investigator from the unit informed the court's chief of prosecutions, Silvana Arbia, that he believed Kagame's government had infiltrated the Special Investigations Unit and was being "informed of every step made in the investigations." Rwandan witnesses were risking their lives to expose crimes committed by the regime. Who at the tribunal was the mole? And how, logistically speaking, were the names of witnesses and their testimonies being leaked to the RPF when statements given to the Special Investigations Unit were kept under lock and key in a reinforced cabinet, then transferred to a vault. Investigators were the only individuals who had access to these documents.

Douglas Marks Moore, now a judge in Britain, was an experienced trial attorney who became the unit's senior counsel. He remains a staunch supporter of the integrity of his team. "My investigators were tight," he told me in his small office at Woolwich Court, adjacent to Belmarsh prison in London, which houses some of the nation's most dangerous criminals. He insists that the three primary investigators were trustworthy and knew how to protect sources and evidence because of their extensive experience in criminal and police investigations.[3]

"They were not only good, they were the best we had," he said. "The problem was that witnesses kept disappearing." Though by then most of the witnesses against Kagame had fled Rwanda for neighboring countries such as Uganda and Kenya, he said that many of them were being "extracted, tortured and killed. There was no doubt about it." One credible witness was abducted in July 2002 on the streets of Kampala and was never seen or heard from again. Another witness who was ready to testify was kidnapped in Nairobi in December 2002. The unit found out that he'd been brought back to Rwanda, tortured and placed under house surveillance in Kigali.[4]

That same year, Joseph Sebarenzi, the former president of Rwanda's national assembly who had fled to the United States, informed the UN's refugee agency, Amnesty International and Human Rights Watch of the spate of kidnappings of dissidents and requested their help. The British ambassador to Kigali at the time also raised the issue with Rwanda's prosecutor general, Gerald Gahima, in hopes Gahima might be willing to address the issue. The SIU requested additional funds from the court to increase witness protection, although the measure appeared to have little effect. According to Marks Moore, they continued to lose witnesses. And, since the gaffe of her press conference and advance warning to Paul Kagame, her detractors at the tribunal weren't sure that Carla Del Ponte had the ability to deliver the justice she had promised.

Like the tenures of those who preceded her, Del Ponte's tenure as ICTR chief prosecutor, from 1999 until 2003, was riven with contradiction.

Sources who worked for the ICTR at that time told me a nuanced story of how Del Ponte slowed and even suspended investigations against Kagame's commanders only because she was afraid that Kigali would obstruct the main genocide prosecutions. As chief prosecutor, she could not afford to risk losing the Rwandan government's cooperation in the transfer of witnesses from Rwanda to Arusha, Tanzania, where the UN tribunal was headquartered and holding its trials.

Douglas Marks Moore said Del Ponte had no choice in the matter. "She did drag, but I understood why she put the special investigations on the back burner. She didn't want to spook the government of Kagame because she needed the cooperation of his government for the general investigation against Hutu *génocidaires*. The tribunal was principally set up to prosecute atrocities against Tutsis, to prosecute the former Hutu government. I got the impression that Carla wanted to proceed with indictments against the RPF but that [to proceed against them at an early stage] would have been the end of the show."

The problem was that the "targets" the Special Investigations Unit was considering for possible indictments were members of Kagame's inner circle, including the president of the RPA military court, the chief of the Congo desk and the chief of defense staff. "When you start getting into these people, your big picture will close," Marks Moore said, referring to the ICTR's main objective of prosecuting Hutu *génocidaires*. Another lawyer I interviewed said the "big picture" meant getting Kagame to cooperate in a bid to foster stability in the aftermath of tragedy.

Not everyone who worked with Del Ponte was as kind as Marks Moore in assessing her approach. A lawyer who worked at the Office of the Prosecutor during those heady months said she was indiscreet, sought media attention and was ultimately unable to manage an investigation so complex. "Prosecuting the RPF was like going after the Mafia," he said. "You know who the players are and you know what the crimes are. The question is, can you get them linked to evidence that confirms your belief?"[5] Del Ponte had successfully gone after ruthless European Mafia figures who had intimidated and murdered witnesses and killed journalists and judges. But the lawyer observed that Kagame's political and military command structure outsmarted the tribunal at every turn: "We needed to be smarter than they were. And we were not. The Office of the Prosecutor was not smarter than Paul Kagame."

Del Ponte's own actions occasionally made the pursuit of justice even harder. In mid-2002 she took the unprecedented decision to suspend the activities of the Special Investigations Unit. She told the team they needed to digest the information they had accumulated. While they were doing that, for safety reasons, she ordered them to move to Arusha. The effects of that decision were devastating, especially in the eyes of witnesses. (Del Ponte refused to grant me an interview, so I have not been able to ask her about the reasoning behind this decision.)

By that point the team had painstakingly developed its network of contacts and carefully woven a web of trust among former RPA soldiers in exile. It was an extraordinary feat given the dangers these witnesses faced from Kagame's intelligence network. Now their boss had ordered them not only to suspend the investigation but to suspend contact with their informants and witnesses. Which meant that they were also unable to assist witnesses in trouble—all the more painful because, as investigators said in their report, they knew the witnesses' "troubles stemmed from their contacts with our team." Essentially, Del Ponte had hung the witnesses out to dry and eroded any hope they had that the risks they were taking in testifying would lead to justice.

Théogène Murwanashyaka was one of the early witnesses who provided investigators with key testimony in meetings at the Sheraton Hotel and other locations in Kampala, Uganda. He told me that the core team of investigators was professional and reassuring.[6] But when the SIU was suspended, he once again feared that the regime was weighing down the ICTR, that Kagame was all-powerful and untouchable. "I knew how the Rwandan government used its enormous lobbying, money and influence to penetrate institutions and people in power. And I knew Rwandan agents were in Uganda. It was a dangerous, uncertain period. You have to remember, too, that this was the first time a group of individuals that had broken with the regime were testifying against it. No one knew what was going to happen."

During the suspension, the investigators were authorized to consult the archives of the UN High Commissioner for Human Rights. They also got access to documents from Operation Turquoise and the UN's peacekeeping mission, UNAMIR (though the investigators wrote in the summary report that they were "disappointed" with the UNAMIR files and had the "clear impression that this documentation had been beforehand audited").

In 2003, Del Ponte rescinded her suspension of the SIU, and even widened its scope, authorizing the opening of official investigations into crimes committed by the RPF in three different areas of Rwanda: Giti, Kabgayi and Butare. She also authorized files to be opened on the Directorate of Military Intelligence and on two high-level RPF deserters suspected of committing crimes. And finally she ordered that a file be opened into the attack on the presidential plane. In the summary report, Kagame was also listed as a potential target for indictment.

None of the three core investigators was naive or unrealistic.* As Marks Moore pointed out, two had decades of experience in probing police crimes in their respective countries, and the third was a crime analyst who went on to work in The Hague. In their summary report, they evoked the possibility of reprisals by Kigali if indictments were issued against RPF commanders. The investigators predicted that Rwanda would stop cooperating with the ICTR and shut down the court's office in Kigali. That would effectively mean a halt to the main genocide cases, which was patently unacceptable to the United Nations Security Council. The investigators also raised the problem of indicting two of Kagame's dissidents, against whom they had collected a fair amount of evidence. If legal proceedings were initiated against these dissidents while active members of the regime remained unindicted, Rwandan opposition figures and human rights activists would even more firmly believe

---

* For security and professional reasons, I have chosen not to name the core investigators I contacted, or other investigators I talked to who periodically worked for the SIU. None of the investigators released confidential documents to me.

that the ICTR was controlled by Kigali. Their best option, they suggested, would be to transfer the special investigations file to a third party, one that could guarantee judicial independence. The investigators did not elaborate on what kind of third-party court they envisaged. But they noted that this scenario "had the advantage of putting an end to the impunity of the Rwandan Patriotic Army, which is an essential condition for genuine reconciliation in Rwanda."[7] What is extraordinary about their proposal to transfer their work to a third party is how it shows they already knew that the ICTR was unable to prosecute Kagame and members of his regime, given how powerful and untouchable he had become. And at the time they were writing this summary report, they didn't yet know that the Americans had already decided to remove Del Ponte and shut down any possibility of such a prosecution.[8]

Yet the investigators continued the fight. In 2004, under Del Ponte's successor, Hassan Jallow, investigators established tighter cases for prosecuting the senior RPF officials responsible for the Byumba stadium massacre and Patrick Nyumvumba, the head of the RPA's Training Wing, who'd organized mobile death squads. But negotiations were going on behind their backs. The factor that finally shut down the work of the Special Investigations Unit was Paul Kagame's skillful hijacking of the court itself.

In Carla Del Ponte's memoir, *Madame Prosecutor*, she recounts how in May 2003 she was called to Washington for a meeting with the US ambassador for war crimes, Pierre Prosper, who she writes warned her that if she went ahead with her plans to indict Kagame and members of his government and military, she would be fired as chief prosecutor of the UN tribunal. Del Ponte told him she didn't work for the United States, she worked for the United Nations. A few months later, she was removed from her position.[9]

I called Pierre Prosper and asked him whether this was true. He said, "I was surprised by the account. I must also say that it is false. This is not why she was removed from her positions. There was a push from everyone [Europeans, the UN, Africans] to get rid of her." He cited Del Ponte's "public posture," the way she conducted herself and her tense relations with UN member states as reasons for her removal from the ICTR, although she did remain prosecutor at the UN Tribunal for the Former Yugoslavia.

Del Ponte also wrote that she long suspected the Americans had done a deal with the Rwandan regime. And she was right. A May 2003 memo sent by the US embassy in Kigali to Rwanda's general prosecutor, Gerald Gahima, explains what Ambassador Prosper had succeeded in doing. The memo, signed by the US ambassador in Rwanda, Margaret McMillion, and included below, was addressed to Gahima: "Ambassador Prosper's office asks that you confirm your approval of this document."

The deal outlined in the document concerned the special investigations against RPF perpetrators and stipulated the following:

- The Office of the Prosecutor (OTP) has a list of sites where massacres may have been committed in 1994 by members of the Rwandan Patriotic Army that the OTP will share with the Government of Rwanda.
- The Government of Rwanda should have the first opportunity to prosecute such cases.
- The OTP will not seek an indictment or otherwise bring a case before the ICTR unless it is determined that the Government of Rwanda investigation or prosecution was not genuine.
- Both parties agree to identify two to three sites that will be investigated by the Government of Rwanda. The Rwandan government will conclude these investigations by the end of 2004.
- The OTP will share any related evidence, as appropriate, with the government of Rwanda.

In black and white, the ICTR had become a surrogate of Washington and, by extension, Kagame. It had granted Kagame legal immunity from war crimes and terrorism. It allowed the killers to investigate themselves. Western officials had removed Carla Del Ponte, who no matter what her critics had to say was attempting to edge Rwanda toward accountability instead of impunity.

Prosper is now a private lawyer and represents the Rwandan government in commercial litigation. He insisted the deal he proposed did not grant Kagame immunity. "Where's the immunity? The deal was to see whether or not there was a path where there could be some domestic prosecutions that were acceptable to the ICTR. There is nothing illegal about that. I don't understand how the deal was de facto applied. The deal was not that no one

Embassy of the United States of America

Kigali, Rwanda
21 May 2003

RECU le
018 03
2 1 MAI 2003

Mr. Gerald Gahima
General Prosecutor to the Supreme Court
Kigali

Dear Mr. Gahima,

Attached as request is a copy of the "Summary of Conclusions between the Government of Rwanda and the International Criminal Tribunal for Rwanda".

Ambassador Prosper's office asks that you confirm your approval of this document. I look forward to hearing from you.

Sincerely yours,

Margaret K. McMillion
Ambassador

- The OTP will submit all initial requests for access to archives in writing directly to the Prosecutor General.

4. Special Investigations

- Both parties reaffirm their commitment to accountability for serious violations of international humanitarian law.

- The GOR confirms it has prosecuted some of its military personnel in the past for crimes and will share information regarding the number of such cases related to serious violations of international humanitarian law committed in 1994.

- The ICTR and Rwanda have concurrent jurisdiction to prosecute serious violations of international humanitarian law that may have been committed in 1994. The ICTR has primacy of jurisdiction.

- The OTP has a list of sites where massacres may have been committed in 1994 by members of the Rwandese Patriotic Army (RPA), which the OTP will share with the GOR.

- Both parties agree that the GOR should have the first opportunity to prosecute such cases.

- Both parties agree to identify two (2) to three (3) sites which will be investigated by the GOR. The GOR will conclude these investigations by the end of 2004.

- The OTP will share any related evidence, as appropriate, with the GOR.

- The OTP will have an opportunity to review the trials once they have been concluded by the GOR. If a GOR investigation determines that no prosecution is warranted, the OTP will have an opportunity to review the investigation once it has been concluded.

- The OTP will not seek an indictment or otherwise bring a case before the ICTR unless it is determined that the GOR investigation or prosecution was not genuine.

- The U.S. Government, the OTP and the GOR agree to meet again to hear the concerns of Rwanda regarding the ICTR.

be prosecuted." He said the idea was to let Rwanda prosecute crimes and the ICTR review the cases; if the ICTR was not satisfied it could retain jurisdiction. He also said no one told him what to do. "I came up with this idea . . . the issue of complementarity [transferring jurisdiction from a UN tribunal to a domestic court], giving the state the first bite of the apple." He also said Del Ponte initially agreed with the idea, then checked with a UN legal advisor and later said she would not endorse it.

What authority did the US ambassador for war crimes have for reaching such a deal with the Rwandan regime, a decision that betrayed its victims and the whistle-blowers who had risked their lives to provide evidence of its crimes? None, say two lawyers who worked at the Office of the Prosecutor.

"It is illegal on all fronts. Pierre Prosper had no business making this deal. It's a scandalous document," said the first, a prosecutor familiar with the file.[10]

"Of course it's not legal. But it's more fundamental than that," said the other lawyer. "The individuals who engaged in the agreement were not legally authorized to do so. Pierre Prosper could not negotiate with one of the parties in a criminal lawsuit whose jurisdiction lay with the United Nations, and come up with an agreement that would grant immunity or limited immunity to any of the potential subjects of the investigative mandate of the institution. You can't do it. He was running rogue. But he was running rogue because nobody in Washington gave a shit."[11]

The notion that "nobody in Washington gave a shit" and that a rogue ambassador could unilaterally rig the UN war crimes tribunal in Kagame's favor does not stand close scrutiny. It fails to take into account the overwhelming efforts made by other US officials to downplay and conceal Rwanda's abuse of power.

The explanation that Prosper exercised undue authority or acted alone is an abject denial of American agency. As the ambassador for war crimes, Prosper worked for the US State Department, which advises the president and leads the country in foreign policy issues. The US political and defense establishments backed Kagame after the genocide and green-lit his invasion of Zaire, even when it was clear his troops were hacking, burning and shooting Hutu refugees in Congolese forests. By 2003, in any case, Rwanda had become skilled at infiltrating international institutions and influencing governments worldwide. Kagame and his senior commanders had also become rich from looting conflict minerals from Congo. The RPF's senior and military echelon had become experts in mass, spree and serial killing. And there seemed to be no equalizing force willing to stop their dark crusade.

The meltdown at the ICTR had all the elements of a politically charged thriller—a story of high intrigue and cynicism that ended in betrayal. The UN tribunal officially closed down in 2015 without having prosecuted both sides, even though some ICTR lawyers and investigators believed they could prove that the RPF too had committed genocide. Douglas Marks Moore told me, "I saw it quite specifically as two genocides. There was a mini genocide and a larger one. How you can just prosecute one side? I think it's unwise, bluntly. I'm a man from Northern Ireland, so I've been brought up with cultures that are split irreconcilably." Then he added a chilling thought: "I would be amazed if a genocide did not repeat in Rwanda."

In the end, the ICTR indicted ninety-five individuals and convicted sixty-one, all of whom were linked to the former Hutu regime in Rwanda.

THE CONSEQUENCES OF BETRAYAL

ONE OF THE INVESTIGATIONS CAUGHT UP IN THE MESS AT THE ICTR concerned a massacre at a seminary in Gitarama commune on the evening of June 5, 1994, at the height of the genocide.

A six-year-old named Anaïs wanted to steal a few more moments of playtime in the calm circle of candlelight in the kitchen of the refuge she and her Tutsi family had found at the Josephite seminary in the town of Gakurazo. The previous weeks had been terrifying. Her Tutsi father had disappeared and was presumed dead; she and her siblings and her mother had barely managed to fend off marauding gangs of Hutu militia. They were grateful to have been taken in by the Catholic clergy at the seminary. Kagame's army had rolled into Gitarama in early June, and they assumed it was going to be safer now for Tutsis.

Her mother had told her it was time to get ready for bed, but her mother and younger brother had gone outside, so there she was, still playing with the other children in the kitchen. Her older brother, Richard, was being cuddled on the lap of a Catholic bishop in the nearby dining room. But she was a responsible little girl, and as it got darker outside she decided it was time to fetch Richard and go to bed. She was on the stairs between the kitchen and the dining room when she heard gunfire, and then her brother's piercing cries. As the machine guns blasted, she wanted to run to him, but a woman in the stairwell held her back.[1] Richard's cries still invade her thoughts. "I could hear him screaming 'Mama,' over and over," she said. "All I remember feeling is that I had to go in there and get him, but I couldn't."

When I met Anaïs in 2013, she was twenty-five, a beautiful and confident university student living in Europe. She had her whole life ahead of her, yet she was still racked with guilt, believing, as a child would, that she could have saved her brother's life. "Even when I talk about it now, I still feel like, 'Why didn't I just go in there and get him?'" she said, unable to control the flow of tears.

Anaïs's mother, Espérance Mukashema, also met with me. She said Kagame's soldiers had ordered several bishops and priests to attend a meeting in the novitiate's dining hall. She and her two sons—Richard and her baby, Robert—had all been in the dining room, where Richard had been laughing and talking with the priests before he climbed into the lap of a bishop named Innocent Gasabwoya. When Robert, only three, became fussy, she decided to take him outside for some fresh air. She offered to take Richard with her, but the bishop said he'd look after him. "The bishop said, 'No, it's okay, we're playing. Leave him with me.' I had no idea at the time what was ahead in the next few moments. So I went outside."[2]

As soon as she was outdoors, a Tutsi soldier rushed toward her. "He said, 'Madame, you must go in and get that child fast.' I had no idea why, but just as he said that, I saw a group of soldiers with guns run into the dining hall. And in a few seconds they started to kill people, one by one. My son yelled: 'Mama, help me.' I heard his voice and I could not help him. My son was shot in the back. It cut him in two."

Frozen in disbelief and pain, Espérance could not speak. Nor could she flee. The RPA soldiers, who had surrounded the premises, ordered everyone to stay calm.

Anaïs was barefoot as she crossed the dining room, slick with blood and covered with bodies, to get to their bedroom on the other side of the compound. All her mother could say to her daughter was, "Go back to your room now."

"Hours later I still felt like I had my brother's blood on my feet."

The Gakurazo massacre was an unusual crime for the RPF, in that its soldiers shot people in front of witnesses. A young Hutu priest named Emmanuel Dukuzemungu survived the attack even though he was in the line of fire in the dining hall. In an interview, he said that he and several religious colleagues had been rounded up in the surrounding areas, held by the RPF for three days in the nearby town of Ruhango, then transferred to the religious retreat in Gakurazo where Anaïs and her family were sheltering. When they arrived, the RPF commanders were polite and smiling but firm as they ordered all of them into the dining room. Among the clergy was the archbishop of Kigali, Vincent Nsengiyumva, a prominent Hutu.[3]

No one initially suspected anything wicked was about to happen. The RPF officials introduced themselves and explained that they would ensure the "protection and security of all Rwandan citizens." Then a tall young RPA officer with light skin stood up. "I can't understand people who do not want Rwandans to be unified. We will fight them," he warned, which sent a chill through the dining room. The commanders made sure that the most prominent religious figures had places to sit, then requested that the three young Tutsi servant girls who were with them leave the dining room. But the girls refused to go, wishing to stay with the priests. Emmanuel remembered Richard, too, sitting with a priest nearby.

When the RPF officials left, the door opened and four soldiers brandishing machine guns charged in and opened fire on the clergy, all sitting down squarely in front of them.

"We could never have expected it," Emmanuel said. "They began shooting at us. It was absolutely terrifying. The girls were beside the soldiers, and one of them put her hands in the air and begged: 'Please stop!'"

Vicar Jean Marie Vianney Rwabilinda managed to drop to his knees and ask for grace. But it was too late. Amid the deafening roar of fire, Emmanuel ducked then crawled along the wall toward the kitchen. When he got there, he discovered several nuns huddled together, overcome with fear. He pushed past them and hid in the adjacent stables. He sat there in the dark, among the cattle, shaking uncontrollably, unable to speak, not knowing what to do next. The soldiers were looking for others, perhaps for him. He could hear them coming his way. They had flashlights. One of them came into the stable and asked him if he was a priest. Emmanuel admitted he was, fearing he was going to be shot dead, but instead the soldier calmly explained that the shooting was the result of a few troops running amok after their Tutsi family members had been killed in Kabgayi. Emmanuel wondered whether the light was so dim the soldier didn't recognize him as one of the priests who had been targeted. Gathering his courage, he told the soldier he wanted to see if there were any survivors, and the soldier led him back to the dining room, herding the nuns from the kitchen along with him too. It was a scene of sheer horror. The nuns covered their faces with their veils and began to wail, along with the servant girls. "Everyone was dead," Emmanuel said, "soaking in their blood."

The bodies of Archbishop Nsengiyumva and vicars Jean Marie Vianney Rwabilinda and Fidèle Gahonzire were on the floor, legs splayed and heads torn apart. Abbot Sylvestre Ndaberetse was shot dead near the door as he attempted to escape. Father François Mulingo and Vicar Alfred Kayibanda lay facedown amid the gore. Bishop Gasabwoya had fallen but still held little Richard in his arms; they were together in their final moments of life, and now in death. Six other clergy members and a twenty-year-old Hutu refugee named Stanislas, who had been taken in by the priests, were also now lifeless on the floor. Bishop Thaddée Nsengiyumva (no relation to the Archbishop of Kigali) was still sitting in his chair, dead but looking oddly peaceful. "His cheek was leaning on his hand, as though he was asleep," Emmanuel said.

There were no injured to attend to, and he and the women didn't stay long with the dead. Afraid of being alone, he thought he might lie down on the floor in the nuns' dormitory. While he was gathering a blanket and pillow from the linen closet, he looked up and froze as a soldier came toward him. "It was one of the soldiers that fired on us. It was a shock. He was about twenty-five years old, blackish skin, tattoos on his forehead and his yellow beret. We looked at each other. I was paralyzed by fear. I tried to keep it together, stay calm. He asked me for a blanket and I gave it to him."

The RPF promised to investigate what they called this "intolerable act" of vengeance, and they did carry out an investigation, but it was focused on who might reveal that the story of vengeance was a sham and that they had targeted these prominent Hutu clergy for death. When they realized in the following weeks that Emmanuel had witnessed and survived the massacre in the dining room, they went after him. But he had already fled across Rwanda's border into Burundi. He eventually made it to France.

Espérance, with her daughter and surviving son, would also eventually leave the country, after a scary time in which she had to play along with the murderers of her child by saying that the incident had been an act of revenge. She began meeting with SIU investigators in 2001 in Uganda, and continued to give testimony after seeking and gaining asylum for herself and her children in Holland in 2003. The core team called her Mama for her determination to seek justice for her son's murder.[4] As Théo Murwanashyaka's sister, she knew and could recognize many officers in Kagame's army. She testified that it was Brigadier Innocent Kabandana who had brought the Rwandan bishops and priests to the novitiate. Kabandana was the political commissar for Colonel Fred Ibingira's murderous 157th Brigade (and would later serve as a military attaché at the Rwandan embassy in Washington). She also named Major Wilson Gumisiriza (currently a brigadier general in the Rwandan military), Lieutenant Wilson Ukwishaka and Sergeant John Butera. Though Anaïs had been only six, she also gave a witness statement to the ICTR investigators. When she and her daughter gave their statements, Espérance had no idea—nor did the investigators seem to know—that the ICTR's new prosecutor, Hassan Jallow, appeared to have already accepted a deal with the United States not to prosecute any RPF crimes.

ICTR investigators also interviewed Emmanuel. They believed these three witnesses were so credible that they could dismiss the RPF claim that the killings at the seminary were an act of vengeance committed in the heat of the moment. But they needed more witnesses and more corroboration to lay charges. By the end of 2003, the Special Investigations Unit had compiled a list of suspects, but hadn't yet amassed enough evidence that they felt they would be successful at trial.[5]

In any case, from May 2003, when the deal with the Rwandan government was brokered by Pierre Prosper, the ICTR's Office of the Prosecutor was expected to "share any related evidence, as appropriate, with the Government of Rwanda." There is no indication that witness statements collected in good faith by the SIU investigators were passed on to the Rwandan government. But there is reason to believe that information in the dossier on the murder of the Catholic clergy—possibly in the form of internal memos—was communicated by Jallow's office, because potential witnesses in Rwanda who had been mentioned in ICTR documents were eventually approached by RPF military officials and questioned about what they planned to say about the murders.

And there is no doubt that information flowed to the government of Rwanda along unofficial paths, since there were people who were friendly to

Rwanda's interests working for the court. An investigator told me that Louise Arbour had raised a red flag when the ICTR hired a Ugandan named Richard Karegyesa. When Kagame was head of military intelligence in Uganda, Karegyesa was in charge of criminal prosecutions at Uganda's High Court. The two men were known to be professionally close. Karegyesa eventually was promoted to the position of chief of prosecutions at the Office of the Prosecutor at the ICTR, working directly under Hassan Jallow. In 2013, another source at the ICTR told me, "The only reason he's been there until now is that Rwanda insists that one of theirs be in that office to keep an eye on Jallow and keep him on his toes, make sure that Jallow doesn't do a turnaround. The Rwandans must have their own guy in there. So what are we talking about? [The infiltration of the court] is a lot more entrenched than you think. It's not child's play. When people say they don't want to talk [to us], we know why."[6] After the court officially closed in December 2015, Karegyesa was given an influential position overseeing the ICTR's remaining cases through a new UN body called the "residual mechanism."

Pointedly, my source said, "Who is the head of office of the residual mechanism? Richard Karegyesa. Deliberate. It's been done and designed in such a way that there will be no RPF trials. Let's call a spade a spade. It's an incredible story . . . They are never ever going to look at those RPF crimes and they have taken all the steps [to make sure] that it will never come to light."

In 2008, investigators with the Special Investigations Unit came to visit Espérance for the last time in Holland, bringing disappointing news: the United Nations had decided to transfer the prosecution of the men who murdered her son to Rwanda. "I could not believe it," she told me. "I was furious and said no, no, that can't be possible! Kagame organized this crime. I told them the UN couldn't transfer the case to Kigali; it would put us all in danger."

The investigators apologized but said there was nothing they could do. The one Espérance most trusted later called her to say he was mortified when he discovered that the ICTR was handing over the file to Richard's killers. "This is terrible. It is wrong and really hurts," the investigator told her.

Espérance was in anguish, exiled in Holland as Rwanda staged a trial to show it could prosecute its own soldiers. During the trial, key witnesses—two of the Tutsi girls who had been present in the dining room—were allegedly asked to provide false statements. One did, but the other could not and fainted in the courtroom.

Two captains were convicted of murder—not war crimes—and sentenced to eight years, which was reduced to five years on appeal. Their senior commanders were acquitted. An ICTR official said the indictment that Rwanda's prosecutor drew up was a fiction, that the whole story of the Gakurazo massacre was changed, and that the soldiers convicted were sacrificial lambs. Those responsible remained free.

Human Rights Watch called the trial a political whitewash and a miscarriage of justice. In August 2009, its director, Kenneth Roth, wrote a tough letter to Jallow, urging him to recall the case and re-prosecute according to international fair trial standards.[7] He reminded Jallow that Human Rights Watch investigators had given the ICTR the names of the senior RPF officers who they believed ordered and executed the killings. He also pointed out that "armed soldiers were outside the refectory [dining hall] with guns pointed in through the open windows. The shooting began and continued until a whistle blew, at which time it immediately stopped. No other shots were heard after that time." Roth added:

> We request that you execute your mandate to prosecute persons responsible for serious violations of international humanitarian law and that you act on credible evidence of serious crimes committed by senior RPF commanders which we believe your office has gathered. The reported killing of 30,000 people by RPF soldiers, as documented by the United Nations High Commission for Refugees, is by any standard sufficiently serious to merit prosecution.

Espérance also fired off a letter to Jallow requesting the ICTR take over the dossier again. "I read the judgment," she wrote. "It was full of lies."

In September 2009, the Office of the Prosecutor's senior trial attorney, William Egbe, sent Espérance an official response on behalf of Jallow: "The Prosecutor is satisfied that the trial in Rwanda was carried out with due process and in accordance with international standards of fair trial. He has accordingly closed the case file. The Prosecutor regrets that he is unable to be of further assistance to you but wishes to renew to you his sympathy for the loss of your son."

However grotesque, the massacre at the seminary was just one of many systematic killing sprees in Gitarama, where RPA troops, along with DMI staff and their cadres, targeted Hutus commune by commune, hill by hill. There was a reason Hutus fled in the hundreds of thousands to Zaire or ran for cover to the French-secured Zone Turquoise, and it wasn't because the majority of them were guilty of genocide, as the Western press reported. They knew the Rwandan Patriotic Army was out to kill them.[8]

After the genocide, a highly respected Rwandan priest, human rights activist and journalist named André Sibomana began working with local clergy to secretly compile lists of victims who had disappeared after the 157th Brigade and mobile DMI death squads swept through the prefecture beginning in June 1994. Sibomana also went into Gitarama's dank jail—built to hold five hundred inmates but seething with more than seven thousand people—where he asked prisoners to help him compile the names of those murdered. In the end he was able to identify some eighteen thousand civilians, including women and children, who were killed under the RPF occupation of Gitarama from June 1994 onward.[9] The breathtaking 400-page document he created consisted mostly of handwritten names of victims, and included letters of testimony to Rwanda's interior minister at the time, Seth Sendashonga. Some of that testimony names the perpetrators of the crimes, along with the civilian cadres and Tutsi survivors who helped them. One handwritten document lists specific mass grave sites. Another is a letter from a young Rwandan man from Gitarama with medical expertise, who tells how he was enlisted to provide medical aid to Kagame's troops and was transferred to a military hospital near Kigali. He wrote that he'd received reports that the RPF seized people from all over Kigali and brought them to a location near the Saint Agathe orphanage, where DMI soldiers tied them up and struck their skulls with hoes, hammers and clubs. "After that there was the difficult work of burning corpses, using wood and gas brought in on tanker trucks from Uganda, and finally burying the ashes," he wrote. He added that a friend of his from primary school counted an estimated six thousand people arrested in the Kigali neighborhood of Kacyiru over a period of five days.

In August the young man was transferred to Gabiro, where he vaccinated RPF soldiers and provided basic care. "During the eight months I stayed at Gabiro," he wrote, "I would see intense smoke at dusk coming from the adjacent camp, and daily movements of tractor trailers." He went on to write that some soldiers working at the camp tried to escape and others suffered from depression. He himself wanted to leave but was afraid of being caught and killed. He claimed that similar mass killings and burials of Hutus were being carried out at Masaka, the DMI headquarters in Kigali.

The former prime minister of Rwanda, Faustin Twagiramungu, gave me the original document—a bursting mound of barely containable papers, some dog-eared, held together in a gray binder—at a hotel in Sherbrooke, Quebec. I kept the original for several months, poring over it, and then made a photocopy before I returned it to Twagiramungu. Some survivors who provided the names of their murdered loved ones or neighbors had added their fingerprints as proof of authenticity.[10] "It is the best form of Rwandan testimony that exists," Twagiramungu had assured me during our meeting. Some of the victims listed were killed where they stood in the hills of Gitarama; others, he said, were "packed into trucks and taken away to forests in Nyungwe and Butare and never came back. Some were thrown into rivers. We can't resuscitate these people. They are gone. But we had to know why."

After he fled Rwanda in 1995, Twagiramungu showed the document to Belgian authorities in a bid to launch a civil case against the Rwandan government using universal jurisdiction. But Belgium did not respond to his request. He also showed the document to an ICTR investigator named Michel Stassin. "They cannot pretend they did not know what happened," Twagiramungu told me. When I contacted Stassin, he confirmed to me that he had indeed received the evidence and had no explanation for the lack of follow-up.

As interior minister, Seth Sendashonga had tried to shame the RPF government into taking action on these crimes and stopping the ongoing cleansing and reprisals. Because of his criticism, he was eventually forced out of government, along with Faustin Twagiramungu. Both men were allowed to leave the country in 1995. With the help of fellow Rwandan dissidents in exile, Sendashonga transferred all the names of victims so painstakingly gathered in the handwritten document onto a computer file.

In 1996, he and Twagiramungu gave that electronic file to the ICTR, along with three packages of documents, all addressed to the UN's special rapporteur, Réné Degni-Segui, who was the court's highest official at that time. Degni-Segui sent Twagiramungu a response on July 8, 1996, noting that his office had received the evidence and would keep the former prime minister informed of "the conclusions of investigators." The ICTR never got back to Twagiramungu. (In an interview from his home in Abidjan, Degni-Segui told me he remembered receiving the file from Twagiramungu but said there was a "trafficking problem" at the tribunal at the time and many files "disappeared.")

Meanwhile, Sendashonga held a press conference in Nairobi in which he brandished the evidence before media and human rights organizations. Yet his efforts received scant coverage, with the notable exception of the French newspaper *Libération*'s Stephen Smith. Sendashonga was assassinated in Nairobi by Rwandan agents in 1998. And Father Sibomana, a beloved figure who had saved the lives of Tutsis during the genocide, died in Rwanda in 1998 after authorities refused to allow him to leave the country to seek medical treatment.

Even after all these years, Twagiramungu says the injustice still shocks him. "The international community has not listened to us. They have listened to the killers. I've asked myself what is the meaning of power in Africa. Why have killers been applauded by the international community and by peasants who are afraid to speak up in their own country?"

It also shocks him that Paul Kagame is lauded for saving Rwanda and halting the genocide when, as he points out, "you do not stop genocide by committing another genocide. What is genocide? It is decimating people who are not like you. What do you call the crimes committed against these people by the RPF?" He holds up the mammoth document, shaking his head in disbelief.

ICTR investigators from the Special Investigations Unit eventually opened a file on the killings in Gitarama with a view to prosecuting the responsible Tutsi commanders. They listed targets for indictment and described some of the killings, based on testimony from RPF informants. In one account from Musambira, in the heart of Gitarama, intelligence staff from Kagame's army poured burning plastic on Hutus they'd detained, scorching them so that they would denounce others. One group of intelligence agents killed 350 people, suffocating them with plastic bags. RPF agents also tied victims' limbs together, and strangled them with ropes. As the document pointed out, "The aim of this operation was the same for all: eliminate the Hutu." [11]

Twagiramungu told me that in September 1994 he asked Paul Kagame to pay a visit to Gitarama, which was where Kagame's father had come from. Kagame agreed and organized a trip with the then education minister, Pierre Rwigema. When Kagame returned to Kigali, he told Twagiramungu that he'd received a warm welcome but that something unsettling had happened. Kagame said he had noticed some big mounds of earth and had asked villagers about them. They'd told him that there were people buried there.

People killed by the Interahamwe? Kagama had asked.

No, said the peasants, they were killed by Kagame's own people.

"He admitted that his boys killed these people," Twagiramungu told me. "I followed up on it. At around two o'clock the next morning, RPF people went there to dig and take the bodies. I have no idea where the bodies were brought. They were probably burned. They made the evidence disappear."

The former prime minister lost hope long ago that justice could be fairly rendered in the current political climate, but he has continued, from exile and at risk to himself, to urge civic discourse and ethnic reconciliation in Rwanda. But he also hopes the task of building a democratic Rwanda will be taken up by a younger generation, for whom the scars of 1994 may not run so deep.

13

THE ASSASSINATION
OF HABYARIMANA

IN FEBRUARY 1996, JIM LYONS, A FORMER FBI AGENT WHO WAS A specialist in counterterrorism, was asked by the US State Department to become a chief investigator at the ICTR. When he arrived in Kigali, he was initially tasked with finding witnesses to crimes in Kibuye and Butare communes, with a view to obtaining statements implicating Hutu mayors, commune officials, Interahamwe and local businessmen in the killing of Tutsis. Within a few weeks his mandate had increased in scope and became three-fold: the ICTR now sought to investigate and prosecute Colonel Théoneste Bagosora, who was seen as the leading Hutu military power behind the genocide; to probe killings by the Hutu Presidential Guard; and to investigate and prosecute the individuals, believed to be Hutu hard-liners, responsible for shooting down Habyarimana's plane, which had also killed the president of Burundi, Cyprien Ntaryamira, and several French crew members.

Lyons's National Investigative Team, as it was then known, soon grew from three to twenty investigators from the United States, Holland, Canada, Germany, Senegal, Mali and other nations. One of the leading members was Michael Hourigan, a former police detective who had become a Crown prosecutor in his native Australia.

In 1996, Hourigan obtained information that shortly after the crash, a UNAMIR soldier had overheard a broadcast over an RPF network saying that the "target" had been hit. A soldier in the armed forces of Rwanda reportedly heard a similar message. These small clues changed the course of Hourigan's efforts.

In early 1997, three potential witnesses—former and current members of the Rwandan Patriotic Front—came forward with evidence. Two of the witnesses knew of each other's cooperation. The third informant was believed to have no knowledge that the other two had come forward. "Two had participated in the downing of the plane. The other had direct knowledge of the operation," Lyons told me. Their testimony was extremely detailed. The informants named individuals involved in the planning and execution of the attack. They told investigators that Kagame and his senior commanders had formed a commando-type group whose aim was to shoot down the presidential aircraft as it approached Kigali airport.

This crucial testimony—combined with earlier reports about the RPF broadcasts on shortwave radio on the night of the crash—led investigators to believe there was solid evidence that Kagame was behind the downing of the plane. "What better way for Kagame to become a hero than to start the genocide himself by shooting down the plane and then marching into Kigali with his army and saving everybody," Lyons said, adding that Kagame already was "the fair-haired boy of the US government and the Brits, trained by the CIA and MI6."

In late February 1997, Lyons was at the US embassy in Kigali with Hourigan when the Australian lawyer placed a call on an encrypted phone to the ICTR's chief prosecutor, Louise Arbour, in The Hague. They were being extremely careful with the information they'd acquired, and the names of the informants. "We knew that Kagame was tapping all the phones of the tribunal," Lyons said. Hourigan briefed Arbour on the status of the investigation. "I only heard half the conversation, but when Michael got off the phone he said Judge Arbour was very excited about this and she wanted him to come to The Hague to brief her in person."

In a sworn affidavit he subsequently submitted to the ICTR, Hourigan wrote: "I informed Judge Arbour in considerable detail about the information implicating President Kagame. She was excited by the breakthrough and advised me that the information corroborated some other information she had just learned from Alison Des Forges the week before." [1]

Hourigan flew to The Hague, only to be astonished at what happened at the meeting. "Arbour told him to shut down the investigation, that the ICTR had no mandate to investigate the plane crash; it had no jurisdiction," Lyons said.

Hourigan insisted that the plane crash—the event that set off the genocide—was a terrorist attack and indeed within the ICTR's mandate. Article 4 in the ICTR Statute specifically called for the body to investigate acts of terrorism. "She was pretty rough with him in her attitude," Lyons said. "But she didn't make that decision by herself. Someone gave her the orders to shut it down."

In Hourigan's own written account of their first phone conversation, he said, "At no time did she suggest that our investigations were improper. On the contrary, I would describe her mood as upbeat and excited that at last we were making significant progress into the events surrounding the plane crash."

Hourigan left the ICTR in 1997, shortly after being told to shut down the investigation, and died of a heart attack in 2013. But in an interview he gave in 2008 to Phil Taylor, host of CIUT Radio in Toronto, he had this to say:

That Rwandan story is such a can of worms. You've got massive numbers of civilians being killed. You've got the UN being incompetent and malfeasant and not discharging its duties properly and people being slaughtered on its watch. You've got various nations, superpowers, standing back, like [they're surveying] a chessboard, trying to move to places on that chessboard because they want to get access to resources in Congo. You've got, at the same time, a genuine world community who just doesn't understand what's going on, can't understand why this bloodbath is happening, trying to force all these various players to do things.

And so, I realize now when I look back on it, it was sort of World Politics 101 for me. When I went to Rwanda, I went there really starry-eyed and thought, "Look, we've been given a job to do: We'll tell the truth." And I can tell you with the greatest confidence and great disappointment that, after my two years there, I've totally lost any love affair with the UN.

We didn't discover the truth; we were actively thwarted and worked against. And now, years later, they've probably spent probably close on $300 million; they've only prosecuted people they've been told to prosecute. You know, some of the main offenders responsible for some of the biggest crimes have been left untouched. And all the while now, the European and North American powers are plundering that region's resources, with millions still dying in Congo.[2]

Arbour, who served as a judge on Canada's Supreme Court for several years after she left the ICTR and is now the UN's special representative for international migration, long insisted the court had no mandate to investigate the plane crash that killed the two African presidents and unleashed the genocide. She declined my request to be interviewed on her tenure at the ICTR and her exchanges with Hourigan. Yet in recent interviews she's conceded that the Rwandan government's hostility made it difficult—even dangerous—for the tribunal to investigate crimes by the RPF. "The office of the prosecutor was sitting right in the middle of the country, where allegedly some of the leadership elements had to be investigated," Arbour told the *Globe and Mail* in 2016. "That's not, frankly, very doable."

She added, "We worked in a very fragile environment. I had a lot of concerns about the safety, the security of our witnesses. I don't think we had anywhere near the kind of human resources, capacity, know-how, to do that work while we were sitting in that country."[3]

In 1999, when the tribunal created the Special Investigations Unit, investigators collected testimony from informants outside Rwanda on the plane attack, even though there was no official mandate to do so, because their informants insisted on talking about it. They simply wouldn't let it go. It was too important in terms of history.

Investigators believed that both sides had their own reasons for carrying out the assassination. They could not exclude the theory that Hutu extremists carried out the attack on Habyarimana's plane, with the help of France, as a means to justify a genocide against Tutsis. They pointed to the fact that the pro-Hutu, extremist newspaper *Kangura* and the radio station RTLM predicted that catastrophe would engulf Rwanda. They had evidence that French military intelligence officers were in Rwanda before the genocide and unconfirmed reports that two of those French soldiers may have been assisting elements from the Hutu army in Masaka, the hilly location in Kigali from which the missiles were thought to have been fired.

Members of the former Hutu government, along with extremist elements and several researchers, had advanced the theory that the RPF had carried out the attack with the help of the Belgian soldiers deployed to UNAMIR. Their argument was that the death of Habyarimana benefited the RPF and that the RPF already possessed the missiles, while the Rwandan army at the time did not have such missiles, nor were its soldiers trained to handle them.

What the investigators were told by their own informants, supported by other evidence, was that the RPF were indeed responsible for the assassination.[4] Kagame, who was the head of the Rwandan Patriotic Army, held three meetings to prepare the attack and several high-level officers attended those meetings.[5] Kayumba Nyamwasa, then head of the DMI, was overheard by one of the informants, at one of these meetings, stating: "If one does not shoot at Habyarimana's plane, that will not be useful to anything."

The investigators confirmed the existence of the team in charge of the missiles, and that the team members were trained in Uganda and knew how to use surface-to-air missiles (SAM). In its report on the plane crash, the SIU named Captain Joseph Kayumba as the head of the missile team and wrote that several sources confirmed that, before the attack, the team had control of at least two missiles.

The informants offered two, slightly different, versions of the transport of the missiles. The first was that the missiles were brought in a white van or cream-colored car from Mulindi (the RPF's military headquarters in northern Rwanda) to the CND headquarters in Kigali and then to a house in Masaka. The vehicle was found burned a few days after the attack. The second version was that the missiles were transported directly from Mulindi to Masaka in a blue van. The investigators regarded the first version as more plausible and better corroborated.

In their report, the investigators went on to name possible targets for indictments:

1) Frank Nziza: "He was the head of the team that shot down the plane," the investigators wrote. "He confessed to the source that he is the one who fired the two missiles on the plane."

2) Mutayega Nyakarundi, the member of the missile team who ensured the security of the missiles at Mulindi. He handed over the two missiles to Frank Nziza and Didier Mazimpaka to be transported to Kigali, sources said.

3) Didier Mazimpaka, who sources said brought the missiles from Mulindi to Masaka.

4) Bosco Ndayisaba, who hid the missiles in a family home in Masaka.

5) Kayumba Nyamwasa, who took part in the three planning meetings for the plane attack and was overheard expressing his opinion about it.

6) Charles Kayonga, who was involved in the operations as head of the 3rd Battalion based at CND headquarters.

7) Jack Nziza, Sam Kaka, a colonel named Ndugute and James Kabarebe, who were present and also involved in the preparatory meetings.

8) Paul Kagame, who chaired the three meetings.

The ICTR collected other testimony that indicated the RPF deliberately ignited the genocide. In 2002, a sergeant from the RPF's Charlie battalion said a group of soldiers were trained in a place called Nyamicucu, near the Ugandan border: "The training consisted of the handling of firearms, how to kill with knives, ropes, hoes and how to fight in populated areas (house to house fighting)." In December the soldiers were moved to Mulindi, the RPF's military headquarters.

The sergeant said, "On April 6 1994 at 19:00 hours the order was received by (Charles) Kayonga—commanding officer of the third battalion—to be on 'Standby One'. This meant to be in full battle dress and ready for an attack. All the companies moved into the trenches surrounding the CND. At approximately 20:30 hours, I saw the president's plane crash. We stayed in the trenches all night and the next day at 14:00 hours were ordered to stop the advance of the FAR (Rwandan Armed Forces) and the Interahamwe. We were also ordered by Kayonga and Karamba to kill all Hutus. The Interahamwe had started the killings."

How were the RPF leaders able to ready themselves for the outbreak of bloodshed if they didn't know what that night would bring?

In 1994, French judge Jean-Louis Bruguière gained international prominence for having tracked down and captured Carlos the Jackal, one of the world's most wanted terrorists. Four years after the presidential plane was shot down, Bruguière was asked by the families of the French pilot, copilot and engineer on the flight to find out who was responsible for their deaths, and he agreed to open an investigation.

Bruguière and his investigators collected testimonies from RPF defectors and Western officials. His probe concluded that Kagame had tasked a team of commandos with bringing the anti-aircraft missiles from Mulindi to the CND and then on to the house in Masaka, the district from which the rockets were fired on April 6.[6] The evidence implicated a two-man firing squad: Eric Hakizimana fired the first rocket, which missed the target, and Frank Nziza fired the second, which hit the jet and caused it to explode in flight. (Three years earlier, in 2003, ICTR investigators had also identified Frank Nziza as head of the missile team that shot down the plane).

Filip Reyntjens, one of the most respected researchers on Rwanda, testified to Judge Bruguière that members of Uganda's military intelligence had admitted to him that the missiles used in the attack were given by Uganda to the RPF as part of a larger consignment of weapons from the Soviet Union.[7] Reyntjens even procured the serial numbers of the missiles and passed them on to the inquiry.[8] In later years, Reyntjens became even more certain the RPF had shot down the plane after he sought to get a receipt for the missile transfer to the RPF. A Ugandan student of his with contacts in the military agreed to go to the barracks in Mbarara, where the missiles had been stored before being transferred, to get hold of the receipt. Once inside the army barracks, the student found the receipt but was caught by the Ugandan authorities and prosecuted for high treason, punishable by death.[9] (Reyntjens paid for the young man's attorney. The case was ultimately dismissed when one of the main witnesses against the student, a senior Ugandan commander, died before the trial.)

In November 2006, Bruguière went public with his results, boldly accusing Kagame of killing Habyarimana and triggering the Rwandan genocide. While he could not issue an arrest warrant for a sitting head of state, he urged the ICTR to prosecute the president. And he did issue arrest warrants for several RPF officials, including James Kabarebe, Kayumba Nyamwasa, Charles Kayonga, Eric Hakizimana and Frank Nziza.[10] Kagame responded by breaking off diplomatic relations with France and accusing the French government of complicity in the genocide.

In 2007, Bruguière left his job as an investigating magistrate to enter politics, while the inquiry was still gathering evidence for the French public prosecutor. Bruguière was replaced by judges Marc Trévidic and Natalie Poux. By then, Nicolas Sarkozy was in power and wanted to improve relations with Paul Kagame. At the time, France's foreign minister was Bernard Kouchner, the founder of the international NGO Médecins Sans Frontières (Doctors Without Borders) and a staunch supporter of Kagame. Kouchner wanted the French arrest warrants against Rwandan officials annulled, and he wasn't shy about saying so, publicly.[11]

A classified cable from the US embassy in Paris, released by WikiLeaks, provides evidence of possible intervention from Kouchner's office when he was foreign minister. The cable discussed the arrest and transfer to Paris of Rose Kabuye, one of nine RPF officials charged by Judge Bruguière on the basis of her "complicity in assassinations by a terrorist enterprise." French officials had suggested to Kigali that Kabuye offer herself up to arrest, while she was traveling in Europe, in order to get access to the French investigation. Once she was detained, she and her defense lawyers would obtain access to thousands of pages of crucial testimony that had not been published in Bruguière's 2006 report.[12]

The cable reports that Kouchner's chief Africa adviser, Charlotte Montel, admitted to a US embassy official that the French had played a role in steering judicial proceedings: "Montel conceded that several GOF (government of France) officials had quietly suggested to the Rwandans that one of the nine [accused] agree to be arrested, which would allow the Rwandans to see what kind of case the French had against the nine."[13] In late 2008, Kabuye, then Kagame's chief of protocol, was arrested in Germany and was willingly transferred to France for questioning.[14] The judge interviewed Kabuye and then released her. In a subsequent interview with the media, Kouchner said, "[I]n getting access to the dossier, she will be able to, with her lawyers, dispel these enormous misunderstandings, I infinitely hope. We must restore normal ties with those who endured the genocide, with the Rwanda that is renewing."[15]

Meanwhile, the new French judges ratcheted up their probe. They hired ballistics and acoustic experts to provide an on-site, scientific study of clues surrounding the rocket launch. The experts did simulation tests, examined the possible trajectory of the missiles and gathered testimony from witnesses who heard and saw blasts on the night of April 6. But independent observers expecting rigor from that examination found the scientific methodology of the French examination, released to the media in 2012, questionable.[16] The investigators tested 25H booster rockets instead of the SA-16 missiles used in the actual attack. And the tests were not conducted at any of the possible locations where Hutu elements or RPF forces might have been based prior to the genocide. Instead, investigators carried out the tests in northern France, where soil and noise levels were different.[17]

In a 338-page ballistics report, the investigators concluded that the missiles were most likely fired from a location in Kanombe, an area that included the military barracks where former Hutu forces were based. The report did not say who fired the rockets, but it ruled out Masaka as a launch site, contradicting Bruguière's findings. In response, Kagame's allies said it was time to lay the issue to rest since the RPF appeared to be exonerated.

But the French inquiry was not over yet. Judge Trévidic continued to receive testimony, most notably from high-level RPF defectors such as Major Jean Marie Micombero and Theogene Rudasingwa, the former head of the RPF Secretariat, which was in charge of the political wing of the movement. Rudasingwa said Kagame had told him that he had ordered the assassination of Habyarimana and that his commandos had carried it out. In his account, Micombero, a former judge of the RPA's military court and the secretary-general of the Ministry of Defense, named those who planned, coordinated and provided logistics for the attack.[18]

Micombero, now a dissident in exile in Belgium, tried to arrange to bring a new witness to the inquiry: a young man named Emile Gafirita, who had joined Kagame's High Command as a child soldier in the early 1990s. He was one of Kagame's presidential bodyguards and had been involved in special operations during the genocide. In 2009, he broke with the regime and fled to Uganda. "He is a veritable hard drive of knowledge," Micombero told me in an interview in Belgium in July 2014. By that time, Micombero had helped Gafirita move from Kampala—where he had been at serious risk of kidnapping by RPF agents—to Nairobi, Kenya, and was trying to get him to Paris. Micombero was also translating his testimony from Kinyarwanda into French to submit as evidence.

On the night of November 13, 2014, I got a panicked call from Micombero.[19] "They got him," he said, his voice shaky and low. "The RPF kidnapped Emile tonight." The details of the young man's disappearance were sketchy at first, but in the next few days I would discover what happened and why.

Almost immediately after Trévidic had written Gafirita's name in the file of witnesses to be heard, a lawyer defending the RPF senior commanders accused in the case passed on that information to his clients in Kigali. Gafirita had been effectively delivered over to his abductors. I called the lawyer in question, Leon Lev Forster, to ask whether he had indeed passed on the young man's name, and he admitted he had the right to inform his clients in Rwanda. Forster said, "You're asking me whether I informed my clients, but every normal lawyer informs his clients of the evolution of a case . . . It is perfectly legitimate that clients be informed of the reasons a case is reopened. But we didn't know when this witness was going to be heard or where he was."[20]

I contacted Filip Reyntjens, who was outraged that Trévidic had revealed Gafirita's name before the young man arrived in France. "The judge could have been more careful," Reyntjens said, and only entered his name into the proceedings after he was safely in Paris, instead of leaving him "completely on his own in Nairobi, where he was expected to be prey for Rwandan operatives."

After the kidnapping, sources I interviewed said that Gafirita was seen at Kami barracks on the outskirts of Kigali. It is not known whether he is still alive.

There would soon be another victim of the Trévidic inquiry.

The events of Chryso Ntirugiribambe's life would disturb even the coldest heart.[21]

He was considered a Hutu but was actually ethnically mixed, born to a Hutu father and a Tutsi mother. He'd always loved children and wanted to become a teacher, but his family pushed him to pursue a better-paid career. He wasn't interested in politics or business, so he went to military school, graduated with distinction and eventually became a captain in Rwanda's Gendarmerie. His loved ones say he was horrified as the genocide unfolded and that he succeeded, with other gendarmes, in saving many Tutsis at Kigali's Sainte Famille church during attacks there by Interahamwe.[22] After the war was over, he approached the RPF and requested to join their ranks, in hopes of reconciling Rwandans. But he quickly realized his life was in danger since the RPF was killing "reporters" like him (the term used by the RPF to describe Hutu soldiers who switched to their side). He decided to escape on foot to Zaire with his family, but lost track of his wife and baby daughter during the grueling trek. When he found them, years later, his wife was suffering from serious health problems. He desperately wanted to rebuild their lives together, and eventually found a job at the ICTR as an investigator, working on high-level cases with Canadian defense lawyers such as Christopher Black and John Philpot.

After his job at the ICTR ended, he joined family in Nairobi. Two of his five children were living in Toronto and he applied to the UN refugee agency for asylum in Canada, hoping to reunite his family. But in 2012 tragedy struck when his wife died of liver complications. By 2014, he was still heartbroken in Nairobi, working to support his family, when members of the opposition group Rwanda National Congress (RNC) quietly reached out to him to see if he could secure safe lodging for Gafirita. It was supposed to be a quick, confidential and one-time-only job.[23] Chryso did not know who Gafirita was and did not wish to get involved in Rwandan opposition politics. Yet he reluctantly agreed to help because he was told that the young man's testimony was important to the French inquiry. Chryso's friends and family insist he had very little contact with Gafirita directly and never saw him again after he had got him settled in the Kenyan capital. But after Gafirita was kidnapped, Chryso started to receive text messages from Gafirita's phone, now in the hands of his kidnappers, warning him that he was "next in line." Chryso told a family friend he was terrified.

On June 23, 2015, nearly six months after Gafirita disappeared, a group of armed men abducted Chryso at gunpoint and shoved him into a car. Kenyan police acknowledged the kidnapping and told me in an interview that "the Rwandan embassy would be able to give out more information on the matter."

Like the young man he had helped, Chryso was apparently taken to Kami and tortured.[24] After the kidnapping, the UNHCR rushed his children out of Nairobi and brought them to Canada to join their siblings. In 2016, Chryso's eldest daughter, Chrystella Ntirugiribambe, officially appealed to the Canadian chapter of the International Committee of the Red Cross to try to locate their father in detention, if he is still alive. Red Cross officials have told her that they have not been able to find him in any of the Rwandan prisons they monitor.

Knowing something and being able to prove it in a court of law are two different things. Initially it was an open secret among RPF soldiers that Kagame had ordered the shooting down of the presidential plane. (Kagame himself bragged to the BBC that he had every right to assassinate Habyarimana. In 2006 he told the BBC: "I don't care that Habyarimana died in the field. I was fighting that government, the government that made me a refugee for all those years, for which I had a right to fight.")[25] But it didn't take long before it became politically injudicious for the RPF to admit it had shot down the plane, given the scope and scale of the bloodletting it triggered.

As time went on, anyone outside the country who had detailed information about the plane crash became a target of Rwandan intelligence agents. One of them was a young man named Eric Léandre Ndayire.[26] Léandre was from Masaka, the site from which the missiles were allegedly fired, and was a well-known RPF civilian cadre who became a technician involved in clandestine operations. His family was close to Théogène Murwanashyaka's father, who owned a pasture close to Léandre's home. After the genocide, Léandre became a useful informant for the DMI and initially the RPF considered him to be loyal to the cause. Amid the painful ruins of the country, Théo and Léandre became close friends, and eventually Léandre confessed to Théo that he had been closely involved in the assassination of the former president.

Théo said that Colonel Charles Kayonga, commander of the CND battalion in Kigali, knew where Léandre's family lived and had approached him, saying he wanted to use his sister's house, near an agricultural co-op, for a job. Léandre told Théo that Kayonga did not tell him what the job was, but asked that his sister, Bélancille, temporarily move out of her house for security reasons. When an RPF officer made a request of any kind, Tutsi civilians acquiesced and did not ask questions. Léandre, a devoted cadre, made the necessary arrangements to move his sister to Nyamirambo, west of the capital.

After his sister's home was evacuated, the plan became clearer. Two RPF reconnaissance teams inspected two homes in Masaka—his sister's and one that belonged to the father of Bosco Ndayisaba, who is cited in both the ICTR and Bruguière reports as a member of the missile team. Léandre told Théo that his sister's home was the one ultimately chosen to hide the missiles used in the attack on the president's plane.

"Léandre accompanied the group that placed the missiles at the house and was with the team in Masaka when the missiles were fired. He was directly involved in the operation," Théo said. Léandre told him that another civilian, Christophe Kayitare, was stationed by the RPF at the control tower at the airport to signal the arrival of President Habyarimana's plane, communicating over two-way radio with the missile team in Masaka. As the Falcon 50 aircraft approached the airport, the first missile was fired but missed. The second missile tore into the fuselage, hit the engine and brought down the jet, killing everyone onboard.

Léandre said that after the war, Christophe Kayitare was killed so that he could not be a witness, but he himself was considered more of an insider and was therefore protected. Then he fled to Uganda with a wave of defectors, including Théo. By 2005, Léandre was living in Kampala and wanted to testify to the French authorities investigating the plane crash with a view to getting to Europe. Théo had already established his credibility as a witness with the ICTR SIU team and the Spanish authorities who were investigating war crimes by Kagame's regime. With Théo's help, Léandre provided detailed intelligence on the plane attack in a series of e-mails to Jules Robin, who informants were told worked for the Bruguière inquiry.[27]

Théo sent the messages from his e-mail account, explaining that the eyewitness testimony came from a person who had directly assisted in the commando operations, and then he named individuals he said were part of the missile team. (In the exchanges Léandre was identified by his first name, as Eric Ndayire, because he believed Théo's e-mails could be hacked by Kigali and his nickname would make him instantly recognizable.) Robin demanded more details and, for the most part, Théo and Léandre provided them. But Théo warned Robin that they both were in danger in Kampala and that they needed protection immediately—ideally, permission to come to France. Eventually, Robin appeared satisfied with the testimony and replied that Théo and Eric could travel.

But before they could make arrangements, Robin inexplicably cut off contact. Théo eventually got through to him to demand an explanation. The man told him that Léandre's testimony was indeed important but that he'd lost some of their correspondence. He asked Théo if he could resend the e-mail messages.

Théo was furious. He knew it was costly and legally complicated to bring witnesses to Europe and provide them with security, and he suspected that the French had a limited budget for RPF witnesses and that he and his friend were not going to be among them.[28] Yet, as Théo pointed out, "Léandre was one of the rare people who, apart from those individuals still inside Rwanda working for the government, was an eyewitness to the attack."

In 2006, when Bruguière held his press conference on his initial findings and issued arrest warrants for Kagame's top military aides, Théo said it was a surreal experience: "I saw the evidence that Léandre had provided to the inquiry. It was in black and white before my eyes, but they never mentioned his name." In the meantime, Léandre was increasingly worried for his safety. He went to the French embassy in Kampala and insisted on giving his testimony to officials there. He contacted an international human rights group in Uganda in the hope it would help him, but he had no luck. When it was clear that he couldn't get out of Uganda, he became increasingly indiscreet and desperate.

In 2007, Théo had been granted asylum in Spain as a key witness for the Spanish indictment against the RPF, most notably for his testimony on the Byumba stadium massacre. Théo tried to get Léandre brought to Madrid as a witness, but he ran out of time. In November 2007, Léandre disappeared from Kampala. His wife and children were so distraught, his wife risked returning to Rwanda to look for her husband. She encountered a DMI agent who promptly told her that she should not bother to search for him: he'd been kidnapped, brought over the border and killed.

If that were the end of Léandre's story, it would be disturbing and sad enough. But it wasn't. Théo and I could not understand why the French had abandoned this young man who had provided crucial, eyewitness testimony. Even if a decade had passed, his life still mattered, especially to Théo. We wanted answers. But it was impossible to get an official explanation from Paris. The inquiry's investigators had changed, the judges had changed, and the person who had led the probe under Bruguière was not willing to comment. I tried to reach Jules Robin, but could not find him because he had never actually existed.

It turned out that "Jules Robin" was a pseudonym French investigators had used in dealings with former RPF informants. When I informed Théo that he had been corresponding with a phantom, he was speechless at first, and then incensed. Why would such an important judicial inquiry undertaken by a permanent member of the UN Security Council resort to such dubious methods?

I got clarification, to some degree, from a former French military officer who has closely followed the inquiry. Colonel Michel Robardey had been with the French Gendarmerie stationed in Rwanda from 1990 until 1993, and assisted in facilitating the negotiations for the Arusha peace accord. Since the genocide, he has regularly researched and written about the investigation into Habyarimana's assassination. He is now retired but retains close connections with the French military and political establishment.

Robardey told me that French investigators had decided to use a pseudonym in dealing with informants because they were worried that Kagame's military intelligence had infiltrated their probe. In 2004, the broad conclusions of Bruguière's inquiry had been leaked to the French press.[29] After the leak, there was a heightened level of suspicion and new precautions were put in place. "They were afraid of DMI penetration, and how it would endanger the investigation," Robardey told me.

Their fears were well-founded. Two high-profile witnesses, Abdul Ruzibiza and Emmanuel Ruzigana, eventually buckled. Days after Bruguière released the arrest warrants in 2006, Ruzigana, who had been a DMI technician, retracted his testimony in Norway, where he lived in exile.[30] He said he had no idea who had actually shot down the plane and was not aware of the existence of an RPF commando team. Ruzigana also said the inquiry had distorted his testimony.[31]

By 2008, Ruzibiza had also gone back on his testimony and announced to an elated Rwandan national media that he too had been manipulated by the French.[32] But two years later, as he lay on his deathbed in Norway suffering from liver cancer, he told a journalist from the French magazine *Marianne* that his initial testimony had been true but that he had been threatened by the RPF into issuing a retraction.[33] Ruzibiza insisted that the individuals he'd named as being responsible for shooting down the plane were indeed guilty. He said he had recanted because he had been afraid for his life and that of his family.

Robardey said, "I can confirm to you that the testimony Léandre gave, through Théogène Murwanashyaka, was true and very important." But Léandre didn't get to tell the world, only a nameless investigator hiding under a pseudonym. Léandre's death at the hands of the RPF, Robardey added, was "tragic and highly regrettable."

Léandre was neither the first nor the last person who died trying to expose the truth about who set off the genocide.

During Habyarimana's rule, Théoneste Lizinde was a controversial and much-feared individual who had worked for the government's Central Intelligence Bureau until he was arrested on charges of plotting a coup. Lizinde, one of the rare Hutus to defect to the RPF, was rescued by Kagame's rebels in January 1991, during a prison break in Ruhengeri. It is alleged that Lizinde, who had deep knowledge of military, human and counter intelligence, played a key role in helping Kagame select Masaka as the site from which to launch the missiles that brought down the plane. Kagame's former bodyguard, Aloys Ruyenzi, stated before the Bruguière inquiry that he was present at a March 31, 1994, meeting attended by Kagame, Nyamwasa, Kabarebe and others when Lizinde pulled out a map that showed the selected site. Ruyenzi gave the same testimony to me, to BBC Television and to the journalists Charles Onana and Barrie Collins.

But Lizinde's son, whom I spoke to in Belgium, has a different recollection of events.[34] Félix Flavien Lizinde said he did not believe his father helped plan the assassination of Habyarimana, or that he knew when the attack was going to take place—because if he had known, he would have immediately evacuated his family to a safer location. (All of Lizinde's family, with the exception of Félix, were in a Hutu-controlled zone when the slaughter began and were killed by génocidaires.) Félix said that on April 6 Kagame asked his father to leave the CND in central Kigali to go to a meeting at Mulindi, near the Ugandan border. When Lizinde arrived, Kagame was not there. Lizinde was still waiting for Kagame in Mulindi when he heard the news of the plane crash.

And yet Félix admitted that his father knew who organized and executed the attack, and that his detailed knowledge of events made him a principal target for Kagame's operatives once he'd defected and fled to Kenya. In

October 1996, Lizinde was found on the outskirts of Nairobi, shot dead. His son says the RPF killed his father, first and foremost, because he had proof Kagame was behind the assassination of Habyarimana. The Rwandan regime also wanted Lizinde eliminated because he was compiling evidence, along with the now-dissident Seth Sendashonga, of Kagame's extrajudicial killings, which they intended to submit to the ICTR.

The families of those killed in the presidential plane attack still clung to hope that the French authorities might ultimately provide closure, if not justice. In 2016, Trévidic was replaced by the investigating magistrate, Jean Marc Herbaut, who soon heard testimony from Kagame's biggest enemy: Kayumba Nyamwasa, who had been the head of RPF intelligence (DMI) before the genocide but fell out with his boss in 2010, allegedly over money and power disagreements, and fled the country. Living in exile in South Africa, Nyamwasa wanted to explain, once and for all, the event that unleashed the most ferocious killing spree in African history. Nyamwasa told the inquiry that Kagame was indeed responsible for the assassination, but claimed—astonishingly—not to have been involved himself. "I never participated in the planning of the crime. I did not participate in the execution of the crime. I did not condone the crime. I was not in a position to stop the crime," he wrote in a sworn twelve-page deposition Geoffrey York and I obtained for the *Globe and Mail*.[35]

In his statement, Nyamwasa gave a detailed account of hearing Kagame and two other aides describe how they'd orchestrated the attack. He said he was summoned to rebel headquarters at Mulindi at 10 p.m. on April 6 and saw Kagame and the aides listening to radio reports of the assassination.

"We kept listening to the announcements and comments for about five minutes, until Paul Kagame reduced the volume of the transistor portable radio and told us that President Habyarimana's aircraft had been shot down by our own troops. He explained that he had kept it secret within a small group under his direct command to avoid any leakage." Nyamwasa said that Kagame and the commanders told him that the missiles had been smuggled to Kigali under a load of firewood on a truck.

"It is only Paul Kagame who had interest in Habyarimana's death," Nyamwasa insisted. "His motivation was to grab power and he used his close bodyguards to achieve his objectives. He never believed in negotiations and does not believe in political settlements even now."

The French inquiry has been hampered by errors in judgment and political interference. Yet it remains the only hope for establishing who bears moral responsibility for unleashing the worst crimes in contemporary African history.

14

BECOMING A TARGET

MY DRIVE TO UNDERSTAND THE DYNAMICS OF RPF CRIMES—IN particular what Kagame's troops did in 1994—involved years of searching for and finding clues, and deriving meaning from them. Even the smallest detail could lead to the discovery of a pattern. In many cases, the information had been right in front of me all along. The powerful myths and misinformation surrounding Kagame's Rwanda were such that I often felt as if I needed a magnifying glass to see the obvious.

I began to explore how Rwanda's most powerful men had influenced and infiltrated the ICTR, the UN itself and other international institutions in 2009, with the help of a Canadian peacekeeper named Tim Reid, who had worked in the region.[1] One of Kagame's most notorious spy chiefs, Karenzi Karake, had become the deputy commander of the UN and African Union peacekeeping mission UNAMID, in Sudan in 2007. The UN had renewed Karake's mandate in 2008 despite the fact that the Spanish judge Fernando Andreu Merelles had indicted Karake and thirty-nine other senior RPF commanders for genocide and other war crimes committed in Rwanda and Congo during the 1990s.[2]

I soon discovered that someone else had risen to an even more powerful position in UN peacekeeping under the media's radar. UN bureaucrats had quietly appointed Patrick Nyamvumba, a Rwandan general who was close to Kagame, as UNAMID commander. When I checked, Nyamvumba was not among the forty men Merelles had targeted. But while reading the English translation of the Spanish indictment, I came across his name, misspelled, on page 117. One of the protected witnesses, TAP 043, alleged that

Nyamvumba had been involved in massacres in Murambi, Kizimo and areas surrounding Kigali in 1994. And I remembered I had run across his name in excerpts of a book called *Rwanda: The Secret History*, written by a former RPF soldier named Abdul Ruzibiza (the man I wrote about in the last chapter, who recanted his testimony to the French inquiry, and then gave a deathbed interview to a French journalist insisting that he'd been telling the truth in the first place).

The book was out of print and Ruzibiza, a former RPF soldier, was soon to die in exile in Norway. But before he perished, he had also testified at the International Criminal Court for Rwanda and to the Spanish court, and his book was tabled as evidence at both tribunals. In it, Ruzibiza alleged that Nyamvumba had directed a battalion that invited Hutus to community meetings in order to massacre them and free up their land for returning Tutsi refugees. The bodies were allegedly dumped in mass graves and incinerated. Unfortunately, there were few details of those operations in the book and the Spanish indictment, and there was no direct testimony from eyewitnesses. I needed something more concrete and compelling if I was going to do a news story. I soon found out that Spanish investigators were preparing a second indictment and that Nyamvumba was expected to be on the list. A Spanish lawyer told me he had warned the UN Department of Peacekeeping Operations about the findings on Nyamvumba, but it seemed to have made no difference.[3]

I spent a good part of 2011 looking into Nyamvumba's past. I confirmed that he had been on the ground in Kibeho, Rwanda, in 1995, when Kagame's troops had opened fire on displaced Hutus, a brazen attack that killed thousands. He had also been the commander in Kisangani in 1999 when the Rwandans were fighting the Ugandans over valuable resources in Congo. The battles between Rwandan and Ugandan forces caused considerable loss of civilian life. It seemed that Nyamvumba had left a trail of blood wherever he went. And yet here he was now, being praised by Washington and by UN secretary-general Ban Ki-moon for his exemplary protection of civilians in Darfur. In April 2012, I requested an interview with UN peacekeeping officials on how Nyamvumba—and Karake before him—was vetted. My request was delayed well past June 2013, when Nyamvumba finished his mandate. The United Nations appeared to have great confidence in Rwandan generals:

Nyamvumba was gone, but it had just named Jean Bosco Kazura as commander of the UN's peacekeeping force in Mali.

By then I was working full-time on Rwanda, collecting a critical mass of research with a view to writing a book. I'd met Rwandans in exile in their homes, in restaurants and in hotel lobbies. In addition to my interviews from 1997 in Congo, I'd clocked hundreds of hours of testimony by phone and on Skype. I had begun to investigate Rwanda's counterinsurgency campaign, and needed more sources on RPF atrocities against Hutu civilians in western Rwanda during the period after the first Congo invasion. I'd also made contact with Rwandan refugees living in Uganda, both in Kampala and in camps in Nakivale.

On top of all of that, I was seeking a richer, more anecdotal narrative of Nyamvumba's operations, and several sources in Europe were ready to speak to me about their experiences in northern or eastern Rwanda. I headed to Belgium, the UK and France for a series of interviews in May 2013. My one-on-one encounters went well. But a small meeting I organized in a conference room at the Ibis hotel in central Brussels to speak with key sources on the RPF's war from 1990 to 1993 became a free-for-all. A few individuals I'd never heard of and who were not invited showed up. One of them identified himself as Hutu, a former filmmaker who said his name was Seif. He claimed he'd been arrested by the RPF and tortured in jail. He would not say why or how he managed to escape Rwanda. He questioned the use of the word *genocide* to describe what had happened in Rwanda in 1994, and asked me to state my opinion on the matter. I told him that I believed that a genocide had indeed occurred. Though I pressed him for details, his account of his experience in jail remained full of holes. It was nearly midnight when the meeting wrapped up, and everyone else was eager to get home. But Seif loitered in the hotel lobby and approached me before I got into the elevator to say that he had important documents to give me. He asked if we could go somewhere private—my room perhaps? I was not inclined to invite strange men into my hotel room at night and said no. Instead, I gave him my e-mail address. I later discovered through a trusted source that Seif was an RPF agent who worked for Kagame's security detail when Kagame was in Brussels. What might have happened if I'd invited him to my room that night? I was rattled for the rest of my stay in Brussels, and vowed to be much more careful, but I had no choice but to go ahead with scheduled interviews.

The following week I headed to France, near the border with Luxembourg, where I had an interview planned with a former High Command soldier who had worked in intelligence for Kagame but who later fled to Uganda and was now living with his wife and children in a small blue-collar town in Lorraine. I interviewed him over the course of two days and found him forthcoming and sincere. When we were finished, his wife kindly drove me to the bus station. I got on a bus heading to Metz, the biggest city in the region. Just before the bus pulled out, a man who looked African got on. He glanced at me as he boarded then sat in the seat behind me. I didn't think much about his presence during the hour-long ride to Metz, where I was due to catch a high-speed train for Paris. At the station, I needed to stamp my train ticket, go to the bathroom and get a coffee. I looked at the clock; the train would be leaving shortly. When I emerged from the public washroom, the man was there, lurking so that I would see him. Our eyes met. I headed to an espresso machine and he came to stand behind me. He was a slight man, and not very tall, but he made me nervous. I took one gulp of my espresso, dumped the cup and lugged my suitcase up the stairs to the platform, my computer bag slung over a shoulder. There were many people on the platform, and I felt a degree of safety in the crowd.

As I headed toward my assigned car at the far end of the train, I looked back and he was following me. I picked up the pace, struggling with my bag. I looked back again and he was closer. My thoughts were racing. Would he grab me, pull out a pistol or a knife? Would he dare do such a thing with all these people around? I scanned the platform looking for security. I should have yelled, but I was totally out of breath. I was close to my car now, and turned to find him only a few meters away. I hoisted my bag up the steps and got onto the train, panting. I watched him through the window in the door. He'd stopped on the platform. He continued to stare, but he was not getting on. I placed my luggage in the baggage compartment and found my seat. He was still standing there. I sat down and tried to calm myself. I kept watching him.

Within a few minutes, two security officers approached him and began to ask him questions. Had they seen him trail me? Possibly. Yet neither of them came on board to ask me questions. The train began to move out of the station. I couldn't figure out who might have tipped off the Rwandan intelligence service that I was in a small town near the Luxembourg border. I refused to believe that the former High Command officer I'd interviewed for two whole days was collaborating with Kigali agents. (He remains to this day a Rwandan dissident.) But somehow Kagame's extensive intelligence apparatus had found out I was going to see him, maybe by hacking into my e-mail. It occurred to me that it might be too dangerous to continue this work.

Yet by the time I arrived at the Gare de l'Est in Paris, I'd convinced myself that these were isolated incidents. To me, the stories and information I had collected in Belgium, France and the UK were more important than these apparent risks. I just needed to keep my head down and resume the search for the truth.

When I returned from Europe in the summer of 2013, I wrote a feature for *Le Monde Diplomatique*, a monthly online newspaper, on the growing threats against Hutu and Tutsi refugees in Uganda.[4] After it appeared, I began to get calls at home at all hours of the day and night from unknown numbers or ones registered in Uganda. When I'd answer, the callers would hang up without saying a word. I'd hit Redial and no one would pick up. I also received a call from a person claiming to be a refugee activist who had been kidnapped in Uganda and brought to a house in Kigali—a place of torture and death. He told me he'd escaped and had returned to Uganda, where he was now in hiding. He suggested I secretly go with him to Rwanda, where he could assist me in investigating crimes on the ground. The person he claimed to be was known to other activists I trusted. I taped our conversations and played them for Manzi Mutuyimana, a refugee who had worked in the Nakivale camp and was now living in Chicago. Manzi did not recognize the man's voice and said he was not the refugee he knew and had worked with. He was an impostor.

I documented all the calls and the numbers that were not blocked. My husband, worried, asked me why I was carrying on when it felt as though our house was under siege. I began disconnecting the phone at night.

By late 2013, I had collected more than a dozen detailed accounts from former RPF soldiers and officers, civilians, a human rights activist and a UN court investigator of grotesque crimes committed against unarmed Hutus by Nyamvumba and Kazura during and after the genocide. The most chilling stories—of mass graves, death wagons and open-air crematoriums—came from Nyamvumba's close former colleagues, who had intimate knowledge of these operations. Within the first few hours after the presidential plane was shot down, an elaborate killing enterprise he directed had begun, employing personnel from three divisions of the army—the Training Wing, the Directorate of Military Intelligence and bodyguards from Kagame's High Command—to create mobile units that moved into the rear of Kagame's main battalions. As soon as a battalion had seized an area, these units would chase Hutus and kill them, filling up the fields, swamps and rivers with blood. The mobile units would also lure unarmed Hutus to meetings, enticing them with offers of food and other necessities, then butcher them. As time went on, the killing teams sought greater efficiency. As I've outlined earlier in the book, Hutus were falsely promised safety and loaded onto trucks and brought to Akagera National Park, only to be killed and then burned at Gabiro, the military training barracks on the edge of the park. Witnesses estimated that hundreds of thousands of Hutu civilians were killed in these schemes.

The Gabiro barracks had been seized from Hutu military forces by the RPF within the first few weeks of the genocide. The barracks became home to the RPF's Training Wing, which trained new recruits for battle. Nyamvumba was head of the Training Wing, and used Gabiro as his base. According to his former colleagues, Jean Bosco Kazura was one of Nyamvumba's deputies, and Nyamvumba reported directly to Kagame himself.

I had pieced this story together with great caution. But it was so explosive, so nightmarish and so different from the usual narrative of the genocide that no mainstream media outlet was willing to believe it, much less publish it. I took a big breath and sent the feature to Jeremy Hammond, an investigative journalist who is a recipient of the Project Censored Award. He decided to post it on his website, *Foreign Policy Journal*, on December 10, 2013.[5]

Five days later, on Sunday, December 15, my husband and I attended our children's Christmas piano concert in downtown Montreal. Afterward, the four of us went to a steakhouse to celebrate. I didn't think to check the answering machine when we got home that night. The next morning, after dropping off the girls at school, I saw there were a few messages.

I pressed Play and heard a muffled female voice that was low and strange, and sounded African to my ears. She simulated the sounds of an explosion and gunfire, then said in French, "C'est pile le rouge, c'est comme ça!" (*It's red, that's what it is*). She switched to English: "It's in the air." She let go with more imitations of explosions and gunfire: "Boom! Pouff! Boom!"

I more than understood the implication, and was unsettled and angry. But then she uttered the name of my younger daughter, who was just six years old, and I stopped breathing. Shaking, I called my husband and played the message for him. Stunned, he urged me to phone the police. The police officer who took my call asked me who left the message. I told her I didn't know: the person hadn't left a name and had called from an unknown number. I told the policewoman about the article I'd just published and said I suspected the caller was someone working for the Rwandan government. The officer asked me to file a full report as soon as possible.

I notified the school and we set up tight procedures for dropping my daughter off and picking her up. My husband and I rethought how we handled our older daughter's movements as well. I alerted the Canadian Security Intelligence Service (CSIS), the Royal Canadian Mounted Police (RCMP), the Department of Foreign Affairs, and federal and provincial members of Parliament. A Montreal detective, who described the phone message left on my answering machine as "chilling," was assigned to my case. The police periodically monitored my home, and promised to dispatch a car immediately if any of us dialed 911. My husband beefed up our alarm system, installing panic buttons on the ground and top floors, and we told our daughters never to answer the door if someone knocked or rang the bell. We didn't explain why, exactly, but they understood I had concerns relating to my work.

By late December, I was physically and emotionally unwell. My jaw had locked. It hurt to talk and I had trouble opening my mouth and chewing. The dentist thought I might be grinding my teeth at night, and prescribed painkillers and Valium to help me relax. Then my right foot started to swell, and soon I could not flex or bend it. Christmas was a washout and I felt I had not only put my daughters in harm's way, I'd let them down on what should have been a joyous holiday. By now I was limping, my back rigid and misaligned.

By New Year's Day, I could barely move. That was the day I learned that Rwandan dissident Patrick Karegeya, Kagame's former spy chief, had been strangled in South Africa.

My husband drove me to Emergency at the nearest hospital. I had a battery of blood tests and X-rays and it turned out I was suffering from some sort of inflammatory response. A month later I got a full diagnosis. I had developed an autoimmune disorder, in which the body turns against its own healthy cells. I had deteriorated so quickly it was hard to accept. I started taking methotrexate in weekly oral doses, along with a few other drugs to reduce inflammation. Methotrexate is a chemotherapy, prescribed for lupus and rheumatoid arthritis, that often triggers nausea. In my case, the nausea was debilitating the day after ingesting the pills, so I began taking it weekly by injections I gave myself in the flesh of my stomach. That was the only way I could tolerate the drug.

By December 2013, when I received the phone message evoking violence against my younger daughter, I was living in a prison of my own making, carved out of Rwanda's violent past and shaped by a gang of deceiving, thieving thugs. I was bewildered and intimidated. My stress levels could not have been higher. It was hard for me to tell the difference between anxiety—which is a normal response to a threat—and actual fear. Something had to give, and it had turned out to be my body.

I was not powerless in the face of these threats, though. Not all my coping strategies had collapsed. Canadian authorities reacted quickly to my complaints. The detective assigned to my case looked over my phone bills and made queries with phone companies. Because of the international nature of my case, he suggested CSIS officials meet me to discuss my research and activities. I began meeting two CSIS agents in Montreal hotel rooms. The location of the scheduled meetings was never communicated by cell phones, which I was told are easy to tap. I would only find out the location minutes before the meeting. One of the agents would open the door while standing behind it so that no one in the hallway would see, and I'd walk into the hotel room. Such measures were disconcerting at first, and reinforced my fear that I was being tracked by the Rwandans. But these agents were highly professional. Their main task was to gather information from me. They revealed little about what they knew, but they did say they were making progress in understanding how Rwanda operated abroad and what methods it used in Canada. They warned me that Rwandan agents were skilled in hacking into e-mails and monitoring phone calls and possibly Skype. "They have been well trained. Be very careful."

I remember one of the CSIS agents asking me pointedly, "What are you going to do?" I was definitely at a crossroads. I could immediately stop my research. If I did so, I'd sleep better, get healthier sooner, defuse the tension at home and put an end to the threats against me and my family. Or else, taking every precaution imaginable, I could keep moving forward.

In the midst of this dilemma, in the spring of 2014, I began working on a story with the *Globe and Mail*'s Africa correspondent, Geoffrey York. York had already been collecting testimony from Rwandan dissidents in South Africa whose lives had been threatened by Rwandan operatives. He'd also secured an interview with someone who'd been recruited to assassinate one of Kagame's enemies, General Kayumba Nyamwasa, now living in exile in South Africa. I'd also recently gained the trust of a former RPF officer in Belgium who was ready to go public with the most compelling evidence to date of a murder-for-hire operation by the Rwandan government. Major Robert Higiro had been demobilized in 2010 after mildly criticizing two Rwandan commanders. He fled the country but was later tracked down and pressured to help organize the assassination of Nyamwasa and another enemy of Kagame's, his former spy chief Patrick Karegeya. The head of Rwandan intelligence at the time, Dan Munyuza, promised Higiro that if he carried out the task, he'd be rewarded financially and considered a national hero. But Higiro knew that whether he agreed to the job or refused it, his life was in danger. He decided to play along, but to warn Nyamwasa and Karegeya of the plot. Higiro went to South Africa and began to tape the conversations between himself and Munyuza to use as evidence against the Rwandan government.

Munyuza offered Higiro and those who helped him one million dollars, to be paid in installments, to get access to Nyamwasa's bodyguards by bribing them or to organize a hit squad that could murder the two dissidents. Eventually the negotiations broke down when Munyuza would not provide up-front money. At that point Higiro fled South Africa to Kenya then Belgium. After Karegeya was strangled to death at a luxury hotel in Johannesburg on New

Year's Eve 2013, Higiro decided to come forward to me with his tapes. After months of discussion, I went to Brussels in April 2014 to meet Higiro in person and copy the tapes. Geoffrey York and I had the recordings translated by two separate, independent interpreters, one of whom was an academic and another who did work for the courts. We verified Munyuza's voice on the recordings with three former officers in exile. The *Globe and Mail*'s story, entitled RWANDA'S HUNTED, was published on May 2, 2014. It laid bare Kigali's campaign of silencing critics with violence and raised "new questions about the world's moral stand on Rwanda."[6]

The *Globe* story's evidence was so tight that the Rwandan government was not able to refute it. The US House Foreign Affairs Committee eventually held a hearing on the issue and invited Higiro to testify. At the hearing, Higiro listed the names of at least thirteen prominent Rwandans who had been murdered or had disappeared. US Congressman Christopher Smith said the *Globe*'s findings were credible, and called for an international probe into Rwandan hit teams in foreign countries. The United States decided that Higiro was at risk living in Belgium, which is home to a sizable population of Rwandans, and eventually offered him asylum.[7]

At the same time, I had begun to receive a number of confidential documents from the International Criminal Tribunal for Rwanda, from sources who had worked there. Eventually Clarise Habimana sent me the SIU's top secret report on their investigation of crimes committed by Kagame's army, a catalog of horrors whose information I've already described. And more witnesses were approaching me than ever before. My most trusted sources, Théo and an officer I've promised not to name who had worked in military intelligence, helped me vet these witnesses and I began to plan a trip to Holland, Belgium and France to do more interviews.

My relationship with my husband had become increasingly strained as my reporting intensified. And yet he continued to encourage me. In May 2014 he had the front-page assassination plot story framed so our daughters could give it to me for Mother's Day. After my diagnosis, he spent every minute he was not working on planning a family dream: designing and installing a patio and an in-ground pool in our backyard. By early June the pool was heated and ready to enjoy, swimming the best therapy for my aching joints. By summer I was in the pool with the girls every day. He had installed an underwater lighting system that changed color. At night, after the girls went to bed, I would bask in the warm water, my nerves settling as I watched the ripples change from blue to green to pink.

In July 2014, I packed my bags and left for Europe. I went to The Hague to conduct two lengthy interviews then took a train to Brussels, arriving early in the evening on Sunday, July 13. I emerged from the subway on foot, pulling my luggage, and headed toward Place Sainte-Catherine. The weather was mild and for once I wasn't in a hurry. As I walked up the sidewalk toward the Novotel where I had a room booked, I saw two black Mercedes parked in front of the entrance, with security personnel standing nearby. It was a mid-range hotel, not a likely place for a celebrity or dignitary to stay. The security men looked squarely at me as I walked up to the entrance, and I proceeded through the automatic doors to the reception desk, feeling conspicuous. The clerk watched me closely as I walked toward him. When I introduced myself, he said, "We've been waiting for you, Ms Rever."

I wasn't sure what to make of that, and mulled it as I checked in. When I turned to head for the elevator, a white-haired man in a dark suit approached me and introduced himself as the coordinator of Belgium's state security protection unit. He was there with bodyguards, he explained, to offer me government protection during my stay in the country.

"May I ask why?" I dreaded his response yet knew what he was going to say.

"We have reason to believe that the Rwandan embassy in Brussels constitutes a threat to your security," he said, adding that I could refuse Belgian protection but he recommended I accept it. He said a risk analysis indicated that the threat against me was "severe," a level 3 risk, which meant that an attack was possible and even probable, but that authorities had not been able to determine when and where it might occur.

He spoke clearly and I understood the words he said. But I had difficulty fathoming what a severe threat actually meant. Was I at risk of assault? Could I be shot in the street? Could someone abduct me from my hotel room?

As I stared at him, trying to take this in, he pulled out a contract for me to sign. I read it over, registering the word *severe* in the first paragraph, and signed at the bottom. For most of my stay, I would be accompanied by two armed bodyguards and travel in an armored vehicle. He explained that normally four bodyguards and two armored vehicles would be mandated for a level 3 threat but they wanted to avoid attracting too much attention in the middle of Brussels.

The state security official then introduced me to one of the bodyguards, who would stay in the room next to mine and inspect my room every time I entered it. He was tall, and wore a black jacket, crisp jeans and a serious expression. He handed me his card and asked for a complete rundown of all my scheduled interviews, who I was seeing, where and when.

Nicholas (his real first name) accompanied me to my hotel room. He opened the door, checked the bathroom, the closet, scanned the entire room, then gave me his cell number and told me he'd be right next door. After he left, I took off my shoes and lay on the bed. I was reeling. Somehow, I had never imagined it would come to this. The Belgians believed that the Rwandan government, which I'd proved used its embassies to kidnap and kill Rwandan refugees around the world, now wanted to murder me.

I couldn't bring myself to call my husband that night. I was too scared to tell him this news, too scared for my own life, and feeling deeply confused. Yet I did not want to go home. I had important interviews to do, and on some level I was grateful that someone had decided to help me continue my work. Did the Canadian Security Intelligence Service request this protection from Belgium? They were the only people, apart from my husband, who knew my itinerary. But what would Canada know about threats coming from the Rwandan embassy in Brussels?

Belgian and Canadian security never told me why the Belgians stepped in to protect me. But a Rwandan dissident gave me a clue as to what might have been behind the round-the-clock surveillance. After Patrick Karegeya was strangled at the Michelangelo Hotel in Johannesburg, tensions between South Africa and Rwanda shot up. In March 2014, there was another attempt to assassinate Kayumba Nyamwasa, also in South Africa, which prompted the expulsion of three Rwandan diplomats from the country. One of those expelled diplomats was Didier Rutembesa, who was suspected of helping to organize the assassination plots.[8] Rutembesa tried to get reassigned to the Rwandan embassy in Brussels, but Belgian authorities would not give him security clearance. My Rwandan source said that, undeterred, Rutembesa continued to coordinate international crimes from Rwanda. At some point before I arrived in Europe, the Belgians had intercepted a call by Rutembesa to a Rwandan national in Belgium. During this call, Rutembesa reportedly discussed "laying a trap for Judi."

It turned out that Nicholas, who wore a tactical earpiece and carried a concealed weapon, had been Salman Rushdie's security guard when the writer visited Belgium. He didn't divulge any intelligence about my case, but he did say that "authorities would not have authorized this kind of surveillance unless the matter was very serious." He was quietly interested in the kind of work I was doing, the risks involved and how I juggled my family commitments. The entire Belgian team were professional and kind. During that stressful week, I had to go to France for a day and Nicholas rode with me on the train, got off at Gare du Nord and was there the next morning, waiting for me at the same spot. I was surprised how happy I was to see him.

I had used the wifi on the train to send my husband a Skype message. I told him that everything was going to be fine, and explained how well the Belgian security team was looking after me. His response was swift. "The rest of the world is telling you that you are at risk but you continue to push ahead," he wrote. "If something happens to you it will destroy your daughters." He called the situation crazy.

I weighed his words carefully. I thought he might even be right, and knew that if he had reacted differently I would have questioned his devotion. But it was hard to explain to him how integral the work had become to my life, how the work itself kept me sane and centered. I felt I couldn't give up now, despite the threats. I felt acute despair at the idea of Kagame's government preventing people from telling the truth. Some survivors had told me of living alone with their stories, of feeling utter desolation at not being believed, not being listened to or understood. By speaking of such things—despite the dangers in doing so—and being heard, they gained legitimacy for their experiences and their suffering. I wanted to amplify their voices and believed that telling their stories to the wider world was tantamount to their survival. Their acts of courage touched me in ways I could not convey to family and friends. How could I fall silent because of a few threats? It would be like silencing them again.

When I got back to Montreal, I spent the next few weeks with my daughters, enjoying the summer. We swam in the pool. We had barbecues on the patio. We watched movies, listened to music, danced, and read books in bed. I held them close. In August I planned another trip to Europe, this time to Spain and Italy, much to the consternation of my husband. He never told me I couldn't go, but he did ask me if I would stop traveling. I told him this would be my last trip; I believed these last few interviews might be the most important of any I had done over the years. I had not told him about Didier Rutembesa, the diplomat who I'd been told intended to lay a trap for me. My husband knew that I was keeping things from him, and as the days wore on toward my departure for Barcelona, we barely spoke—though he did tell me not to contact him while I was away, but to send messages to the girls.

Before I left, I received an urgent text message from Brian, a close friend with ties to US intelligence. He told me that Kagame himself knew I was going to Spain and that I should cancel my trip. He said he had no idea whether Kagame knew about the Italian leg of my journey, but it wouldn't surprise him if he did. He wouldn't share any more information with me, but he believed that somebody I trusted—a key Rwandan source—was probably working for Kigali. I took it all in and told him I was grateful he was looking out for me.

I trusted Brian completely and knew he was not an alarmist. I was in turmoil. I had to protect my children from injury. It is a mother's first duty. What would their lives become if I did not return? How could I justify my need to see this story through against the danger of wounding them? I fought with myself until the very last minute.

In the end, I flew to Spain. Théogène Murwanashyaka had helped me set up the meetings, and I both trusted him and relied on his excellent instincts. If someone I was going to interview in Spain had leaked the information to Kagame, or if our calls had been monitored, then so be it. I would not be alone, but with Théo for all the interviews. I'd be safe. I flew to Barcelona and my trip went exactly as I had hoped. Théo came through and I got the testimony I needed.

Next I headed to Tuscany to speak with an Italian priest who had lived in northern Rwanda before the genocide. This individual had been sympathetic to the RPF cause in 1990, but once the invasion really got going—when he saw how brutally the rebels treated the Hutu peasants—his views changed radically.

I arrived at my hotel in the evening. It was an isolated and beautiful spot, just outside the ramparts of a sixteenth-century town in the northern Apennines. My interview was scheduled for early the next morning. I called my source and left a voice mail letting him know I'd arrived. In the morning I went to the dining room to have breakfast. There was a buffet table on one side of the room and a TV screen on the wall opposite the entrance. I went to the buffet for bacon, eggs and toast, and had poured myself a coffee when I noticed that a large African man had come into the room and taken a chair close to the entrance, facing me. I ate slowly, drank my coffee and watched the news on TV. Every time I looked up from my plate or away from the TV, he was staring at me. Normally, a strange man will look away when you catch him staring. This one did not. I got up for more coffee, and his eyes were still on me. I would not turn my back to him now. I went back to my seat and took a few more sips of coffee. He kept staring. My heart pounded in panic, not for the first or last time. I got up from the table and bolted out of the breakfast room toward the elevator. I pressed the button, turned around and saw him coming my way. The elevator door opened and I rushed inside. Just then I saw a white man coming toward the elevator, presumably hoping to get on. The African was close behind him. I pressed the button, once, twice, three times, to close the door on them. The door nearly shut on the white man's nose. I got off on my floor and ran down the hallway to my room, locked the door behind me and immediately called the Italian priest I was supposed to meet. I told him what had happened and he urged me to stay calm, and said that he'd pick me up in the lobby in ten minutes.

I gathered my computer, tape recorder and notepad, then glanced through the peephole of my hotel door. No one. I opened it slowly and peered down the hall. Clear. I ran to the elevator, went down to the lobby and spotted the priest. I introduced myself and he said his car was outside. I spent most of the day with him, listening to his detailed and moving stories. When I returned to the hotel in the late afternoon, I decided to speak to the clerk at reception about the harassment at breakfast.

I asked whether any nationals from Kenya, Uganda or Rwanda were staying at the hotel. (Rwanda often uses nationals from other countries to commit crimes; Rwandan operatives can also possess multiple passports from the Great Lakes region.) The clerk said this was confidential information that he could not give me. I told him I might be in danger. He called the manager and they agreed to look at the bookings. Indeed, there were Kenyans in the hotel, and someone else from the region was arriving that night. The manager said there was something odd about that reservation, but she wouldn't say what. I thought about leaving the hotel immediately, but she insisted her hotel was safe. The locks were solid, the hotel had cameras, and no one at the reception desk would divulge my room number. I had already paid for two nights and they would not give me a refund. It was getting late and I didn't know where else to go, so I went back to my room.

Later, my friend Brian got in touch to ask how I was. I told him that I'd had no security problems whatsoever in Barcelona. But I was in Tuscany now, and had had a troubling incident in the hotel dining room. I'd also found out that Kenyans were staying here.

"Get the fuck out of there now!" he yelled. "What are the odds of Kenyans in the same hotel as you, in a small Tuscan town?"

"I can't leave now. It's dark and I don't know where to go."

"Take a cab to Milan."

"But I have a train ticket for Florence tomorrow morning, then from there—"

"Forget about your ticket. Go to Milan tonight. They could break into your room at any minute."

It was late Thursday night, August 21. I was due to fly back to Canada from Milan on the Saturday afternoon, August 23. There was no point in arguing with Brian, but the idea of going to the lobby and exposing myself in full view at this hour scared me more than staying put. If I got into a cab, they could follow me and run me off the road.

Brian asked me if I'd booked my train, plane and hotel tickets online. I had. He said if I wasn't willing to take a taxi out of there tonight, I should catch an earlier train than the one I'd booked, heading at dawn for Florence. This is what he advised me to do when I got there:

> Take a train from Florence to Milan. When you arrive in Milan do not go to the hotel you booked online. Go to another one. Make sure the receipt is not sent to your email. Do not tell anyone where you are. Just disappear. Go to the airport on Saturday, check in and there will be someone waiting for you to take you through security, by VIP access. It will avoid you hanging around the airport exposed to any Rwandan. Don't go back to Europe again.

I did everything Brian told me to do. When I arrived at the airport in Milan, I was whisked through security. I touched down in Montreal, after a stopover in Toronto, but my husband was not there at the airport to meet me. I took a cab home.

I filed for divorce two weeks later. My husband was furious but did nothing to stop it. We agreed to joint custody, and he eventually helped me and the girls move into a three-bedroom apartment. He assembled my Ikea furniture and hung up pictures on the wall. He hung the framed *Globe and Mail* article on Rwandan assassination plots over my desk in my bedroom. Now that we were no longer living under the same roof, the anger and hostility faded. We started having family dinners on Friday nights, and began to really talk again.

In early March 2015, I received a call from Emmanuel Hakizimana, a Rwandan economics professor at the Université du Québec à Montréal (UQAM). He said he'd received credible evidence that Rwandan agents working in Canada were planning to strike at critics in Montreal and Toronto, and that I was on a list of targets. The reports, while unconfirmed, were that Rwandan operatives working for Kigali planned to stage car accidents. Canada's public safety minister had been alerted. CSIS was reportedly questioning individuals. Quebec provincial police had by then called me to their headquarters. They were following my case now.

I immediately told my husband about the new threat. I thought he'd be apoplectic. This is what he said:

I've known you for more than half my life. I've seen how you make decisions and take care of the girls. You're coherent and conscientious. You're a great mother. But when it comes to Rwanda, you're different. You're unable to grasp the implications of what you're doing. It's as if you can't process what's happened. You can't see it. At first you were told that if you went back to Africa, you'd be dead. Then authorities warned you against traveling in Europe, that Kagame would get you there. Now it appears his operatives are circling around you in Montreal. They're zeroing in. I bet you still don't realize what's at stake. Let me tell you, if you get into a car accident with the girls, if something were to happen to them, I would die. My life would be over. That's the reality. You think European, Canadian or US authorities really care about you? They just want to avoid an embarrassing incident on their soil. I know you have faith in a lot of Rwandans and that your work is important to them. But if anything happened to you, those Rwandans would go on with their lives. They have families. Your death would be shocking at first. Geoffrey York would do a story in the *Globe and Mail*. People would discuss it for a few days on Twitter and that would be it. Kagame would lie low but eventually start traveling again. He'd come to Canada and the US, meet everyone he wanted to, collect his money and rewards. That's politics. In the meantime, your daughters' lives would be shattered. And they're the only ones who matter.

He was right to call me out on my judgment. I had built walls around myself in order to do this work; I now felt trapped and wanted to escape. I briefly thought of giving up—sending a message to Kigali that I was done. But if I abandoned my research, I would betray everyone I had interviewed, and myself.

In this crisis, I handed over my daughters to my husband more often, and I felt relieved yet diminished in my solitude. I drastically changed my routine. I became hypervigilant on the road and in public places, watching faces at the grocery store and the gym and in restaurants. There were moments of watchful terror when I suspected I was being stalked. We monitored every activity our children engaged in even more closely than before. They never went anywhere alone, not even to a park down the road. Considering how carefree I had been as a child, an upbringing that had fed my curiosity and shaped my personality, the costs for our daughters seemed overwhelming. I felt as though I had invited my family into a cage, where it was dark and frightening. There were moments I couldn't carry on. Moreover, I had no idea whether a book about RPF crimes, if it were ever published, would make a difference. In those bleak moments my husband was the one who reminded me of how far I'd come. He'd finally realized what the work meant. "You can do this," he said, which was what I needed to hear. He also convinced me that I had enough research for several books, and that I needed to publish the first as soon as possible: "Finish what you started."

Théo also helped me regain my grip. He insisted that the Rwandan government and its ideologues were afraid of people who told the truth. He believed that if more people came forward—out of the shadows and onto the record—and exposed what actually happened during the genocide, then Kagame's power would eventually slip away. Kagame's lock on history has had a devastating impact on the daily lives of Rwandans and Congolese. As I contemplated Théo's words, I received dozens of messages from other sources, and from people I'd never heard of in my life, urging me to keep going. I couldn't help but believe that their stories were defining mine.

Still, we knew I needed a plan to deal with the immediate danger and we decided the best thing for me to do was to go public about the harassment and threats. We believed that the risk was greater if I remained a silent target. So in 2015 I spoke to a journalist and author named Lara Santoro about my security problems while investigating Rwanda, and in September the story she wrote was published online.[9] By confronting Kigali directly, I issued a warning that if anything happened to me or my family, Kagame and his regime would be a primary suspect and the Canadian authorities would in turn be held accountable. In the end, I realized that fear, in all its power, can drive many things. A fear of failure and judgment had kept me from doing what I needed to do earlier in my life. And now the fear of death ultimately helped me focus on a task that was radically important. The same fear and danger that so many others had faced finally jolted and committed me to finish what I had started.

THE SIGNS WERE THERE
FROM THE BEGINNING

FATHER GIANCARLO BUCCHIANERI, A CATHOLIC MISSIONARY WHO worked for many years in Kiyombe commune in northern Rwanda, near the border with Uganda, had initially been sympathetic to the RPF. He understood the emotional underpinnings of the political movement: that Tutsis stripped of their land in the 1950s and 1960s and forced to flee their country had suffered a grave injustice; that many of them still languished in camps in Uganda and deserved to have a place in Rwanda. He believed that by delaying the return of these refugees, President Habyarimana was committing a colossal mistake in the pursuit of peace. But that was before the invading RPF forces laid land mines around the springs where local village children went every morning to fetch water. He still remembers the frantic calls he received from his parishioners one morning in 1991, telling him that dozens of children who had been playing near the springs had been killed, or seriously wounded, by exploding land mines.[1]

"I went to collect the corpses. It was a spectacle . . . just horrible," Father Giancarlo told me. "There were so many children. Their bodies were shredded. We filled our vehicles with bodies and drove to the hospital in Ngarama. Many were dying. We were desperate."

That atrocity was followed by the killing of about a hundred peasants in RPF attacks on the surrounding villages. From such assaults, the soldiers moved on to acts the priest described as "pure terrorism." In one instance, the RPF broke into a Catholic clinic on a hill adjacent to Father Giancarlo's church in Nyarurema, where dozens of sick children were being cared for. The soldiers shot nine of the children in the head. He got there the morning after: "Brain matter was all over the floor. I have never seen anything like it in my life." The priest, who was urged by local clergy to document the crimes because they felt it was unsafe for them to do so, soon saw a logic behind the horror. "The RPF wanted villages empty," he said. "They wanted the territory, food, livestock, everything. They also believed that Hutu peasants would provide intelligence to the Hutu army. They wanted them out."

By 1992, Kagame's troops had forced hundreds of thousands of Hutu peasants from their land and from villages in northern Rwanda into over-crowded camps. In the small vicinity that Father Giancarlo covered in the northeast, there were camps in Gakoma, Ngarama, Gituza and later Kiziguro. The Kiziguro camp ended up housing hundreds of thousands of people who had abandoned smaller camps farther north that had been shelled by Kagame's army. By February 1993, an estimated one million Hutus—or one-seventh of the entire population of Rwanda—were displaced. "It was biblical," the priest said. "There was a terrible atmosphere in the camps. Everyone was on top of one another. You cannot imagine it. There was no hygiene." The orphanage in Kiziguro, run by the Sisters of Calcutta, was full of handicapped children who had to be urgently moved to Kigali because of the continued attacks on the displaced Hutus. Many of the children died en route.

In these camps, frightened and angry Hutu youth began to organize and spread anti-Tutsi propaganda, and the seeds of extremism were planted. The deprivation and injustice bred bigotry and violence. The Hutu mayor of nearby Murambi, Jean-Baptiste Gatete, regularly came to Camp Kiziguro and began organizing political meetings at the Gabiro military barracks on the edge of the Akagera park. "These youths began to spiritually train to commit genocide," Father Giancarlo said. "They did not hand out machetes, but they were preparing a tragedy."

Then Hutus and Tutsis began coming to the priest to tell him that Tutsis in the area were disappearing. By early 1994 the situation had become explo-sive. Father Giancarlo had been carefully documenting crimes against both ethnic groups, but when he passed this information on to organizations such as Human Rights Watch, he said it seemed as if they were only interested in violations against Tutsis. Alison Des Forges came to see him with Joaquim

Vallmajo, a Spanish priest in Byumba, but she was focused almost exclusively on the killings of Tutsis in Bugesera and Kibilira. He said, "She was not interested, in any real detail, in what the RPF had done or was doing."

Academics at the University of Rwanda estimated that some forty thousand civilians had been killed by the RPF in Byumba and Ruhengeri prefectures by early 1993.[2] Yet the international community failed to take on board the serious and systematic nature of violence against Hutus before the genocide. The degree of civilian suffering at the hands of the RPF was significant yet not depicted in international reports.[3] If the RPF atrocities had been addressed—if there had been an attempt to identify and stop the rebel army's criminal acts—Rwandan history might have turned out differently.

It was also mystifying that the international community seemed to ignore the inhumane conditions in the seething displacement camps of the north. Pierre Laplante, a Canadian nurse who worked for Doctors Without Borders, provided emergency care in those camps prior to the genocide, moving from camp to camp in the northeast. The thatched huts and other makeshift shelters stretched for kilometers up the hillsides and on mountaintops, "as far as the eye could see," he said. The most pressing problem was sanitation. "Kids were pooping outside their huts. They would play in the dirt and drink from puddles." The children contracted a host of parasitic infections. Scabies, lice, diarrhea and respiratory infections such as tuberculosis were common. At one point, viral meningitis broke out and medical teams had to bring in vaccine guns to prevent an epidemic.[4]

Malnutrition was rife. People ate berries and shrubs. If they were lucky, they received beans from the UN World Food Programme. If they got sorghum, they'd beat it and ferment it into sorghum beer, get drunk on that and ingest toxins. Children exhibited the hallmarks of hunger: distended abdomens, emaciated limbs, reddish discolored hair, and alopecia—loss of hair.

People in the camps and those who had dared to stay in their villages lived in a state of hypervigilance, because of regular bombardment by the RPF. An MSF video I watched showed a school that the RPF had attacked with a rocket; it was not an isolated event.[5] The so-called demilitarized zone, supposedly monitored by the UN peacekeeping mission as part of the Arusha peace accords, was just as dangerous at night as the camps, and the RPF would send in their commandos to kill civilians still living there.[6]

In 2001, the RPF founder, Alphonse Furuma, fled Rwanda and eventually sought asylum in the United States. He gave a detailed public account to the Ugandan government and press of his army's brutal campaign prior to and after 1994, and has reconfirmed to me what he said then.[7] I've already written about much of what he claimed, but it's important to remember who was saying it. He stated:

- The RPF committed systematic massacres, laid land mines, looted properties, demolished homes and other buildings, and destroyed crops in a bid to displace the population and create a Hutu-free territory. These crimes were carried out in Muvumba, Ngarama, Bwisigye, Kiyombe, Mukarange, Cyumba, Kibali, Kivuye and Cyungo, as well as in Kinigi, Butaro, Cyeru and Nyamugari, from 1990 to 1992.

- The RPF attacked refugee camps and densely populated villages. It routinely shelled these civilian targets with 120-millimeter mortars, 107-millimeter rocket launchers and 122-millimeter guns mounted on hilltops overlooking such locations. Examples of these incidents, he said, were the shelling of Rwibare refugee camp in Muvumba, Kisaro camp in Buyoga, as well as Byumba and Ruhengeri in 1991 and 1992.

- When the Arusha peace talks started in 1992, Kagame launched a deliberate policy to create a Tutsiland through "Hutu massacres, massive population displacement, property appropriation and land grabbing in the northeast, east, southeast and central Rwanda." The policy continued in 1993, 1994 and 1995.

- The RPF routinely executed Hutu prisoners of war between 1991 and 1994. The only exceptions were those "kept alive for the purpose of showing off to journalists and for the exchange of prisoners of war with the government side in the framework of the Arusha Peace Agreement."

- The RPF assassinated Hutu elites, including its own members, such as High Command captain Donate Muvunanyambo, in addition to civilian cadres recruited in the demilitarized zone in northern Rwanda from 1992 to 1994. The most targeted districts were Muvumba, Ngarama, Bwisigye, Kiyombe, Mukarange, Cyumba, Kibali, Kivuye, Cyungo, Kinigi, Butaro, Cyeru and Nyamugari.

- The RPF carried out revenge massacres against the Hutu population whenever the Hutu regime in Kigali massacred Tutsis. These massacres

took place in the north during the RPF offensive in February 1993. During
that time, Hutus were hunted down and shot on sight. In one location in
Ngarama, at least 134 people were massacred and buried in shallow graves.

- RPF political and military cadres infiltrated government-controlled areas
  to commit terrorism, particularly in urban areas. From late December 1993,
  people were trained and given weapons and then conducted a terrorist
  campaign against civilians in Kigali City. They targeted high-profile Hutu
  politicians, among them the late president Juvénal Habyarimana, former
  minister Félicien Gatabazi, Emmanuel Gapyisi and Martin Bucyana.

- From 1990 to 1994, the Directorate of Military Intelligence, under the
  leadership of Kayumba Nyamwasa, operated centers to detain, torture,
  assassinate and bury Hutus. One of the most notorious locations was at
  Kinyami district headquarters, where hundreds of civilian Hutus were
  arrested, detained, tortured, killed and disposed of between April and July
  1994. Bodies were exhumed in 1997 by the military, and the remains were
  burnt with diesel and acid and dumped in Akagera National Park. The
  MP Evalist Burakari was assassinated because he was a witness. The
  victims were mostly Hutu elites from Kibali, Buyoga, Kinyami, Rutare,
  Muhura and Giti.

- After its capture in 1994, Gabiro barracks served as a Hutu killing ground.
  Every time there was a security crisis, Hutus in urban areas and eastern
  Rwanda were rounded up, blindfolded, packed on lorries, transported to
  Gabiro and killed.

  During RPF security operations and counterinsurgency operations,
  Hutus were rounded up, their hands were tied and their heads were covered
  tightly with plastic. They were then loaded onto containers that were locked
  and driven to the Akagera park, where those who'd survived the journey
  were forced to lie in the hot sun. The victims were left to die slowly from
  heat, thirst and suffocation.

- The RPF systematically executed Hutus who tried to join the RPF's
  military Training Wings in Nakivale, Gishuro, Karama and Gabiro from
  1990 to 1994.

Furuma had narrowly escaped execution himself when he openly opposed
Kagame's scorched-earth campaign at the outset of the war of invasion. It

would be the last time he spoke out against RPF methods until he fled the country. He said that no one had dared to take on Kagame to his face except Seth Sendashonga. Sendashonga directly and openly challenged Kagame in meetings, in front of everyone. "Only Seth dared to do this. There was no one else," Furuma said.

As I've written earlier in the book, Sendashonga was a Hutu student activist and opponent of the Habyarimana regime before he joined the RPF in 1992.[8] He became the interior minister in Rwanda's post-genocide government, but quickly condemned the continued killing and forced disappearances of Rwandans at the hands of the RPF. After RPF soldiers unleashed machine guns and rocket-propelled grenades on Kibeho, a displacement camp housing hundreds of thousands of Hutus, in April 1995—a gruesome attack in which four thousand Hutus are said to have been killed in front of UN peacekeepers and human rights monitors—Sendashonga demanded justice.[9]

But there was relatively little international outrage over the Kibeho massacre, despite the public nature of the carnage. In Philip Gourevitch's acclaimed book on the genocide, *We Wish to Inform You that Tomorrow We Will Be Killed with Our Families*, Gourevitch compared the gunning down of Hutus who had sought refuge at the camp to General Sherman's march through Georgia near the end of the American Civil War, calling it "an episode of criminal excess by agents of the state rather than . . . evidence of the fundamental criminality of the state." In trying to understand the violence, he also evoked France's killing of Nazi collaborators following the Second World War.[10] "France had been through a hellish ordeal," he wrote, "and the swift killing of collaborators was widely held to be purifying to the national soul."[11] To Gourevitch, such horrifying acts by the RPF were reprisals—emotionally driven bursts of revenge. No matter how flagrant, shocking and organized these killings were, he saw a greater evil at work: Hutu power lurking in the masses of civilians—for example, "the electric glint of insane eyes or a ragged leer of unnerving brutality" he spotted in a prison in Gitarama where inmates were subjected to inhumane conditions.[12]

Gourevitch's depiction of Kibeho as a spasm of vigilante justice was categorically wrong. Yet his use of the word "purifying" was not far off the mark. Operations in the greater area of Gikongoro, where Kibeho sat, could indeed be considered ethnic purification. In the months leading up to the Kibeho attack, Kagame's forces and Tutsi civilian cadres regularly rounded up Hutus and brought them to Gikongoro military camp, where they were promptly executed. The commander in charge of the prefecture of Gikongoro in 1995 was Patrick Nyamvumba.[13]

At the Kibeho camp, soldiers under Brigade Commander Fred Ibingira had unleashed fire not only on the makeshift dwellings but on a crowded hospital compound, and continued to fire on fleeing refugees, shooting women and children in the back. Corpses were taken at night to Butare and Nyungwe forest to be burned, reducing the body count for international observers. Many people who survived the onslaught and fled were then targeted. One survivor I met in Toronto said that he and his wife and infant son escaped to a family property in the prefecture of Kigali Rural. RPF soldiers stormed the village while he was out collecting food. When he returned home, he found his wife and child dead in their outhouse.[14]

Many Kibeho survivors were promised protection by the RPF and transported to Camp Huye. These people were put to death. A former intelligence officer told the ICTR that the killings went on for "three days, 24 hours straight." An estimated sixty soldiers were stationed at Nyungwe forest to take the bodies off trucks, dig graves and bury the corpses.[15]

But the global outcry was muted and the aid kept flowing. The Dutch government did temporarily suspend the payment of $30 million it had pledged and urged the European Union to do the same.[16] But less than three months later, the European Commission decided to lift the partial suspension and fully resume all areas of cooperation, with a view to "assisting national reconciliation . . . and rehabilitation."[17] The RPF's biggest sponsors, the United States and Britain—and to a lesser extent Canada—were in for the long haul, whatever the cost.

The truth, no matter what aid donors seem to believe, is that the RPF has never stopped the violence. Kagame killed before the genocide. He killed during the genocide. And he killed after the genocide. The West's unbridled support only fed the regime's sense of impunity. Journalists from outside the country rarely perceived the truth. And journalists inside the country could not report on RPF violence. If they tried, they faced injury or death.

In December 1994, Rwandan journalist Edouard Mutsinzi dared to call the RPF troops the "new Interahamwe" for crimes they'd committed in southern and eastern parts of the country. Kagame ordered intelligence operatives to teach the journalist a lesson by cutting out his tongue, slicing his hand and attacking his eyes. The assault took place in a bar in Nyamirambo, and was carried out by DMI agents and soldiers from the counterespionage section of the Gendarmerie. The journalist was left in a coma and eventually evacuated to Kenya. He survived but has never returned to Rwanda.[18]

And the violence has spread. As soon as the genocide officially ended in July 1994, Kagame and his senior intelligence apparatus created a war room at DMI headquarters and began planning their boldest experiment yet: the invasion of Zaire.[19] The attack on Rwanda's neighbor would allow the RPF either to eliminate many of the Hutu refugees who had fled there after the genocide or to bring hundreds of thousands of them back home, where they could be controlled. It would also destroy Hutu military bases in eastern Zaire, which were seen as an ongoing threat to the regime's security. And last (but no less important) they would overthrow President Mobutu Sese Seko, install a sympathetic or puppet government, and thereby ensure that Rwanda, a perennially poor but ambitious country, could exploit Zaire's mineral riches for years to come.

But first they had to justify such an expansion of regional conflict. A former RPF intelligence officer testified to the UN that in March 1996, Kagame, James Kabarebe and Colonel William Bagire discussed staging attacks in Rwanda in a bid to convince the international community that Hutu rebels were destabilizing the region and threatening to reignite the genocide. One of Kagame's key commanders at the time, Captain Emmanuel Ruvusha, eventually launched attacks in the region of Ruhengeri, near Birunga, and in Rubavu, near Gisenyi, according to the testimony.[20] These false flags elicited outrage from foreign governments and international media, and helped justify Kagame's foray into Zaire.

Among the members of the international community, only Amnesty International expressed skepticism, as early as August 1996:

> Armed opposition groups based in neighbouring countries continue to
> carry out deliberate and arbitrary killings of unarmed civilians in Rwanda.

The victims have included vulnerable individuals such as the elderly, children and babies. They are almost always killed at night, often in their homes. Some of these killings are characterized by especially brutal methods. However, in some instances, it seems likely that members of the RPA were in fact responsible for killings which were publicly attributed to opposition groups, as in the case of 46 detainees at the communal detention centre at Bugarama, in Cyangugu, who were killed with guns and grenades in the night of 19–20 May. "The Government of Rwanda has been quick to expose many of the recent killings as the work of armed opponents; in other instances it has claimed that civilians were caught in cross-fire between insurgents and the RPA. Yet evidence to substantiate these assertions is sometimes scarce," Amnesty International said. "Independent investigations should be carried out to establish responsibility for each incident, unless there is incontrovertible evidence as to the identity of the perpetrators." Individuals inside Rwanda who denounce human rights violations by government forces are subjected to threats, arrests, and persistent intimidation. They are publicly branded as "genocidaires" or defenders of the militia allied to the former regime.[21]

Since Rwanda's role in the bloodshed in the wider region has become clearer, Western policy makers and officials still argue that Congo's unending war is not entirely of Rwanda's making, that the Rwandan Hutu FDLR is a major troublemaker, fighting and feasting over the spoils, along with homegrown militias and predatory Congolese soldiers. Policy makers continue to split hairs about the multitude of local disputes in Congo over land, tribe, ethnicity and politics, as though state actors such as Rwanda and Uganda are beside the point in a failed state of fiefdoms. And yet the big guns in the Kivus and northern Congo have always been Rwanda and Uganda, the West's allies. Our refusal to penalize these two countries for their role has only meant more death and destruction for the Congolese people. As pernicious as the other actors are—the FDLR or Nande or Mai-Mai, to name just a few—no Western country or multilateral institution has funded these movements. Their militias find their own financing, through extortion networks, illegal trade or other illicit means. Certainly none of these militias' leaders are bestowed with awards or invited to speak at the United Nations or Ivy League universities or the Toronto Club. If any of these warlords were to set foot in the West, they would be arrested and put in jail. The West's respect for Museveni and Kagame—patrons of and actors in a war that has raged for more than two decades—is indefensible.

I've described Kagame's hijacking of the ICTR in Arusha. But how has he managed to escape prosecution by the International Criminal Court in The Hague? Why did the ICC fail to prosecute him for his direct backing of insurgencies in Congo from 2002 onward, when the crimes of his client militia clearly fell under the court's jurisdiction?

With sufficient political will, the Rwandan president could still be tried for these crimes. Kevin Jon Keller, a professor of criminal law at the University of London, told me, "The ICC could prosecute him for any criminal actions he ordered or abetted on the territory of an ICC member state, such as the DRC or Uganda. Personally, I think it's unlikely that he will ever be prosecuted, given that he still remains a darling of the West, despite his murderous, authoritarian nature. The result, no doubt, of his remarkable receptivity to Western capital." (While Rwanda relies on donors for 40 percent of its budget, the country has a high ranking on the World Bank's "ease for doing business" index, attracting foreign investment in real estate, communications technology, infrastructure and tourism.)[22]

To some extent, Kagame is shielded from prosecution by a bilateral immunity agreement his government signed with the United States.[23] This agreement ensures that no US or Rwandan national will be handed over to the ICC without the permission of the other state. Neither the US nor Rwanda is a signatory to the ICC, but Washington funds the court and wields great authority over it.

Yet reining in Kagame has been a question that ICC officials have revisited for more than a decade. An insider who worked at the ICC's Office of the Prosecutor said, "It is my opinion that Kagame should be removed from power through a well-crafted investigation and prosecution. Suffice to say that I have seen Mr. Kagame as a serious destabilizing force in Rwanda and the wider region."[24]

In the early years, the ICC was unwilling to take on Kagame because a group of powerful men decided it was more expedient to leave him alone and unrestrained. The short-term interests of mining companies and patronage networks, money and politics, counted for more than the sanctity of human life and humanitarian law. Initially, investigators avoided looking into his crimes in the Kivus, a region of eastern Congo where Rwanda's proxies operated, because the region was simply too volatile. Kagame was viewed as a "particularly dangerous actor," according to the insider at the Office of the Prosecutor, who was an investigator, and the risks were considered too great on the ground to send in staff to collect evidence. A decision was taken to investigate low-level suspects such as rebel leader Thomas Lubanga instead, in a region farther north called Ituri. "We operated on a basis of a hands-off policy vis-à-vis Rwanda's more important clients," said the investigator, who asked to remain unnamed.

South Africa, the continent's economic powerhouse, also played a role in the hands-off attitude to investigating Kagame's activities from 2003 onward. The ICC's chief prosecutor at the time, Luis Moreno Ocampo, had established a collegial relationship with South Africa's then president, Thabo Mbeki. And according to the above-mentioned investigator, the South Africans began "playing" Moreno Ocampo in pursuit of South African strategic interests in the resource extraction sector: "There was a belief that the best guarantor of stability—or relative stability—in a number of areas of importance to South African firms was the Rwandan Patriotic Army and its client militia."[25] The investigator said he and his colleagues learned that details of their operations and whereabouts in the field were somehow being leaked and Kagame's officials were being briefed on them. He added, "A number of us regarded the relationship [between] Mr. Moreno Ocampo and Mr. Mbeki as a threat to our safety in the field."

Eventually, Moreno Ocampo came under increasing pressure from NGOs and progressive media to do something about the warring militias in eastern and northern Congo, in particular the leaders of those groups loyal to Rwanda. The two biggest warlords under Kagame's control were Laurent Nkunda and Bosco Ntaganda. Eventually, Kagame nominally "neutralized" Nkunda, putting him under house arrest in Gisenyi, where, the ICC investigator told me, he remained "free to wander about town, play tennis and whatnot." But Ntaganda, the nastiest warrior in the Great Lakes, who attacked UN personnel and Congolese civilians in Ituri and the Kivus, was left alone.

In 2010, the investigator said, "Mr. Moreno Ocampo traveled to Kigali and asked Mr. Kagame point-blank for Ntaganda—and Mr. Kagame told him that this was not going to happen. The prosecutor did not object." By then, he noted, Moreno Ocampo was often referring to President Kagame as "Paul."

In 2013, less than a year after Moreno Ocampo left the ICC and Fatou Bensouda became chief prosecutor, Ntaganda surrendered to the court. (Sources have told me that Ntaganda was afraid Kagame was going to eliminate him as a potential witness in case he was ever arrested, so Ntaganda preempted that fate by walking into the US embassy in Kigali and asking to be brought to The Hague.) The Rwandan-born warlord is now standing trial, not for crimes in the Kivus but for those committed earlier, in Ituri—ordering his militia to commit murder, rape, sexual enslavement and pillaging. A lawyer for the victims said, "Victims were killed by bullets, by arrows, by nail-studded sticks. Most of them were mutilated, some were decapitated and their head borne as a trophy." [26]

Whether the ICC will be able to deliver justice in this case is not yet clear. In 2016, the court discovered records of hundreds of phone conversations indicating that Ntaganda had been involved in coaching key witnesses, obstructing the investigation and interfering with prosecution witnesses. [27]

Western nations have praised Rwanda for its technocratic governance and economic performance. Recent amendments to the constitution that would allow Kagame to rule until 2034 have drawn only tepid criticism from Washington and London. Donors like the microcosmic efficiency of Kigali, as though the rampant rights violations, the staged elections, the disappearances and assassination plots don't matter. When she was the US ambassador to the United Nations under Barack Obama's government, Samantha Power said she regretted the lack of "political space" in Rwanda and its "less impressive" record on human rights. She also nudged Kagame not to hang on to power, but to step down in 2017. Yet she still applauded Kagame for his "epic scale of achievements" since the genocide. [28]

But Kagame's true legacy in the Great Lakes region is that of a predatorial puppet master who works behind the scenes to sponsor violence. [29] He is a man who, to this day, profits from the blood-soaked disarray.

Conclusion

REMEMBERING THE DEAD

THE FRENCH HISTORIAN MAXIME RODINSON, WHOSE PARENTS DIED IN Auschwitz, said that no people is destined always to be a victim. All peoples are victims and executioners by turns, and all peoples count among their number both victims and executioners.

René Lemarchand is a political scientist and genocide scholar who has examined how states have denied access to information in the immediate aftermath of violence, and how they have manipulated the narrative of violence. He has looked at how perpetrators, their allies and researchers who are invested in the perpetrators' protection have concealed evidence or removed reports from the public record. Most importantly, with grace, precision and persistence, he has documented and patiently examined the cycle of violence in Rwanda and its sister nation, Burundi.[1] He has condemned the RPF's "hijacking of Hutu memory" and Kagame's manipulation of history to the effect that *"tous les autres sont coupables, sauf moi"* (all others are guilty, except me)—as if the only memory that matters in Rwanda is Kagame's own, very selective one.[2]

Lemarchand argues:

> The imposition of an official memory is not just a convenient ploy to mask the brutal realities of ethnic discrimination. It institutionalizes a mode of thought control profoundly antithetical to any kind of inter-ethnic dialogue aimed at recognition and forgiveness. This is hardly the way to bring Hutu and Tutsi closer together in a common understanding of their tragic past.

All sides of the story need to be told, and nothing can remain hidden, if Rwanda is ever to heal.

There is no part of this book that denies the genocide. From April to July 1994, it is a fact that Tutsis were at risk of dying in Hutu-controlled areas. They were killed, first and foremost, because of their ethnicity. Fear, terror, economic opportunity, coercion by local leaders, mistrust, ethnic hostility, political affiliation and propaganda were among the reasons that Hutus turned against Tutsis. The killers were sometimes neighbors living on the same hill. But more often they were members of a Hutu militia, the civil defense force or the military. Hard-line elements of the state apparatus steered the campaign. As the genocide expert Scott Straus has written:

> There is no question that after Habyarimana's assassination, the hardliners chose genocide. Their actions were deliberate and organized, and they used the power of the state to murder massively. It was the hardliners' fractured power that initially drove their radicalization. The hardliners had stiff resistance in the army and the political arena (the Hutu moderates) even while they faced an armed enemy (the Tutsi rebels).[3]

It is important to emphasize those pockets of Hutu resistance in government, military and civilian spheres, and in every region of Rwanda. Some Hutus risked their lives to save Tutsis, and the majority of Hutu civilians did not kill their neighbors. Yet between half a million and a million Tutsis were slaughtered in a period of three months—an unfathomable number.[4] The speed and zeal with which Tutsi lives were taken is shocking. Their individual and collective suffering will never be forgotten. The pain is felt every moment. Rwanda is a country of survivors where the dead remain close.

Whether or not various Hutus conspired to commit a genocide against Tutsis in advance of the assassination of President Habyarimana does not negate or lessen the reality that there was a clear intent to exterminate Tutsis once the presidential plane went down. But this book is not an examination of the dynamics of that 1994 genocide of Tutsis. Thousands of books, essays and articles have been written about the Hutu-on-Tutsi violence. A UN court was set up to investigate and prosecute suspects who committed the most serious crimes. The individuals whom the court tried and convicted were Hutus. None were Tutsis linked to the Rwandan Patriotic Front.

After the Holocaust, when the Polish Jewish lawyer Raphael Lemkin coined the word *genocide* and initiated the Genocide Convention, he had a powerful idea in mind: to outlaw the most egregious crimes imaginable—acts of extermination. He argued that such crimes undermined the basis of an ethnic, religious or social collectivity. These were acts that ranged from massacres and pogroms to the ruining of the economic existence of the members of a collectivity, as well as all sorts of brutalities that attack the dignity of the individual as part of the campaign of extermination of the group.[5] The legal definition of genocide has nothing to do with numbers killed. It defines genocide as the "intent to destroy, *in whole or in part*, a national, ethnical, racial or religious group, as such."

As soon as the presidential plane was shot down, the RPF's military forces immediately began rounding up and killing prominent Hutus in Remera, a Kigali neighborhood it already controlled. In northern Rwanda, the mobile units drawn from the Directorate of Military Intelligence, the Training Wing and High Command began targeting Hutus—peasants and community leaders—luring them to locations and killing them as early as April 7, 1994. They did so easily and freely throughout Byumba, a vast prefecture already under RPF control. The RPF's mobile forces operated with impunity in rear areas of battalions, rounding up Hutus for slaughter. Some were dumped in rivers and swamps. Other victims were eventually put on trucks and brought to the Gabiro barracks and other areas of the Akagera park to be killed, and then incinerated.

The RPF's military sweep into Rwanda took the form of two horseshoes, following the country's lopsided geography. By the end of April, the battalions in the north had moved down Rwanda's eastern flank to Kibungo in the south, before going up to Gitarama, down to Butare and then heading northwest. During that sweep, mobile death squads were in the rear, "cleaning up"—committing genocide against Hutus. If Tutsi peasants were in the way or did not cooperate, they were murdered too.

But the principal targets of the RPF were Hutus. Tutsi civilian cadres worked hand in hand with Kagame's intelligence agents to locate and kill prominent Hutus and their families and supporters. Despite the claim by

Western human rights organizations and media that there can be no moral equivalence between the two sides, Hutus in RPF-controlled areas faced similar risks of annihilation as Tutsis did in Hutu-controlled areas. After the genocide, waves of Hutu men were recruited into the RPF's army, brought to Gabiro and Gako barracks, and slaughtered there.

The RPF leadership was cognizant of history and appears to have studied the methods of the Third Reich. In 1941, mobile killing units followed the German army as it advanced into Soviet territory. These killing units were called Einsatzgruppen, and were composed of German SS officers and police personnel who relied on civilian support to identify Jews and eliminate them.[6] The Einsatzgruppen also targeted the Roma, the mentally ill, homosexuals and Communists. Like the mobile units of the Third Reich that fanned out across the occupied Soviet Union, the RPF's death squads ranged from Rwanda's northern border with Uganda to the south, along the border with Tanzania. The trucks carrying Hutus to Akagera National Park and the open-air crematoriums in the forest there recalled the Second World War's death wagons and extermination centers.

We know what the motives were for these ethnic-based killings because former members of the RPF have testified to their aims. One of the principal goals was to remove Hutus from political and military power, and replace them with Tutsi leaders. Once the core military, political, economic and cultural leadership of the previous regime was gone, they also targeted Hutu teachers, artists, businesspeople, lawyers and judges, so they could govern with little resistance. The RPF also ordered its military to exterminate as many Hutu peasants as possible, cleansing regions especially in the north, because it wanted not only to mold the population map but also to secure property for Tutsi returnees who had been living for decades in Uganda, Congo and Burundi.

These Rwandans who grew up in Ugandan refugee camps were mostly impoverished. They were landless and stateless. They were desperate. They had been used and abused by the Ugandan regime. Their frustration and anger had mounted. Their hatred had festered. They had waited for their moment to return.

"This is not about reprisals for the 1994 genocide against Tutsis. What the RPF did to Hutus is revenge for 1959," a prominent Tutsi opposition activist

who grew up in Uganda told me.[7] He was referring to the waves of Tutsis who
were forced to flee, who lost their family members, homes and livelihoods
during the 1959 Hutu revolution, which saw the small country transition from
a Belgian colony with a Tutsi monarchy to an independent Hutu-dominated
republic. Some Tutsis consider what happened to their families in the late
1950s and early 1960s as a kind of genocide. Many of these Tutsis have deep
scars that have never healed. The opposition activist also let a telling comment
slip in our lengthy interview. "The Hutus had it coming," he said.

That the Hutus "deserved to be massacred" is pure Tutsi hard-line dogma.
And Hutu hard-liners employed a similar ideology against Tutsis. Hutu
extremists called killing Tutsi civilians "work." It is the same word Tutsi
extremists used to describe exterminating Hutus.[8]

Kagame and his Ugandan-raised colleagues provoked and nourished
Rwanda's 1994 genocide in order to seize power and hang on to it for a very
long time. They potentiated the violence by infiltrating the Interahamwe in
Kigali, Butare and Ruhengeri, and urging these youth militia to kill even
more Tutsis.[9] RPF commandos also infiltrated Hutu political parties and
their youth militias to sow division, engage in ethnic baiting and foment
violence.[10] These commando agitators egged on the violence, murdered
Hutu politicians and killed Tutsis at roadblocks.[11] These sinister, premedi-
tated and deliberate acts fed the savagery. Infiltrating enemy ranks, fueling
violence and engaging in false flag operations were vintage tactics its young,
rebel fighters had learned while participating in Museveni's dirty rebellion
in Uganda in the 1980s.[12]

As the genocide against Tutsis and Hutu resisters gained momentum,
the RPF leadership stood back and took a big, despicable breath, slowing the
RPA's advance on the capital. The gamble to consolidate power was paying
off. Rwanda's body count soared, and the RPF was able to claim it was saving
Tutsis even as it was sacrificing them. By sharing the same ethnicity as interior Tutsi, the RPF cemented its moral status as victim and savior. To top it
off, the RPF threatened the international community, demanding that it not
intervene as Rwandans lay bleeding. And the world obliged.

Kagame warned the UN's force commander, Roméo Dallaire, that if
an intervention force were sent to Rwanda to beef up UNAMIR, his army
would fight it.[13] On April 12, the RPF warned the UN against turning the

peacekeeping force into a peacemaking force or else it would consider them "as enemies."[14] On April 30, the RPF's political bureau asked the UN Security Council not to authorize an intervention because it could no longer serve a useful purpose in halting the massacres. On May 2, after two days of international mediation, the RPF refused to sign a ceasefire agreement that Rwanda's interim government had accepted.[15]

Clearly, the RPF wanted war. And it did not want anyone to know what its troops were doing in areas under its control. Nonintervention was central to its plan. The United Nations came to realize this fact. And lawyers at the International Criminal Tribunal for Rwanda eventually understood why.

Had the ICTR investigated the causes and consequences of events in Rwanda in 1994, central Africa would be very different today. Understanding the political conspiracy that lay behind RPF crimes is essential to piercing the regime's continuing capacity to deceive. By April 1994, Rwanda had effectively become a Hobbesian trap, where fear, self-protection and a preemptive strike seemed the only option.

"There was a plan, a reason and a logic to what Kagame did," argued a prominent lawyer who worked at the Office of the Prosecutor at the ICTR.[16] In the first place, Kagame needed to cover up the crimes his troops had already committed in Byumba. "Many of the graves in Byumba predated the shooting down of the plane. He had been cleansing Byumba before that. Kagame could not have accepted a peace agreement because the crimes of the Interahamwe had not yet occurred and the crimes committed by his troops had. So if he'd had a peace-sharing process, there would have been internationals all over that region and those crimes would have been revealed pretty quickly. If the Arusha accord had been put into place, all that area would have been opened up . . . Why did they need to continue the war in 1994, instead of agreeing to Arusha? Because they had to, they did not have a choice. They could not live with the peace. They couldn't live with the power transfer because there was a massive dark secret in Rwanda that they have been the keepers of."

After seizing power, Kagame struck fear into the hearts of anyone opposed to him, especially Hutus. He destroyed every potential for power sharing and ensured that interior Tutsis became consumed in the emotionally charged genocidal process that he was part of. He put 125,000 *"génocidaires"* in jail and hundreds of thousands through the traditional *gacaca* justice process to control and scare everyone. He needed money to run the country, so he had to keep the international community on his side. He convinced donors that he was single-handedly creating stability and rebuilding Rwanda from a ruined nation.

If the UN tribunal had fully investigated and acknowledged what had happened in 1993 and 1994, it would have taken a different strategy in prosecuting the criminals. Instead, it accepted the Hollywood version of the good guys versus the bad guys. The truth is that the United States and its closest allies did not want the United Nations in Rwanda watching the violence as it was going on. Washington urged the UN to pull out. Powerful insiders have known all along what Kagame is responsible for, and have let him get away with it.

Yet the darkest secret that the RPF has kept from the wider international community is that its troops continued to commit genocide against Hutus in 1994 and in the following years. The policy of ethnic murder came from the highest level of government and military. While the scope and scale of the killing will only be known after Kagame and his clique are gone, the manner in which Hutus were targeted gives clues as to how many were killed. The RPF's victims are estimated to have been between several hundred thousand and a million human beings.[17]

I want to end with just one of those deaths. On April 11, 1994, a Hutu man named Claudien Habarushaka, a member of President Habyarimana's ruling party, was killed by an RPF firing squad near the Amahoro stadium in Kigali, the place where the UNAMIR peacekeepers were trying to keep roughly thirty thousand Tutsis and Hutus safe.[18] A Tutsi neighbor had led him to the spot, under RPF escort. "I am going to die," he said moments before being executed. "And I have done nothing wrong."

His wife, Venantie Mukarwego, was hiding with her children in another area of the capital and did not know what had happened to her husband until she met the Tutsi neighbor in Nairobi after the genocide and he gave her a detailed account. Habarushaka had been targeted by the RPF because he'd been a prefect of Kigali under the Habyarimana government. They tortured him and then brought him to the house near the Amahoro stadium, where they filled his body with bullets. In Rwanda, Habarushaka's murder is considered one of many "anonymous" crimes that happened in the heat of the violence. Yet he was targeted in the first few hours of the genocide because he had been a member of Habyarimana's inner circle. He was killed because he was Hutu.

"We cannot say Claudien was assassinated by the RPF," his widow told me. "There is no tribunal willing to prosecute his murder. We were not allowed to go to *gacaca*, Rwanda's traditional courts. There has been no memorial. We can't properly mourn his death. We don't know what happened to his body, whether he was dumped in a mass grave, taken by the wind or eaten by dogs. We can't purge our emotions. We have to pretend that nothing is wrong.

"But I will never accept it."

APPENDIX A

Structure of RPF Violence from 1994 through the Counterinsurgency

HIGH COMMAND COUNCIL
- run by Paul Kagame, along with Kayumba Nyamwasa, Steven Ndugute, Fred Ibingira, Frank Mugambage, Charles Ngoga and others
- responsible for devising military strategy for battalions, supervised DMI, worked closely with RPF Secretariat

RPF SECRETARIAT
- a political body headed by Theogene Rudasingwa* that provided ideology and policy to DMI and other intelligence departments
- drafted a code of silence equivalent to omertà that threatened death against any official, cadre or soldier who revealed crimes

ABAKADA
- later called *intore*
- comprised thousands of civilians, conducted activities according to RPF Secretariat policy
- many members participated in DMI crimes
- helped ensure Stasi-like state

DIRECTORATE OF MILITARY INTELLIGENCE (DMI)
- headed by Kayumba Nyamwasa before and during genocide; headed by Karenzi Karake from July 1994 into counterinsurgency; deputy director was Jackson Rwahama
- ordered, supervised and executed large-scale massacres of Hutu civilians; staged massacres against Tutsis and Hutus; organized selective killings of opponents

COUNTER-INTELLIGENCE
- run by Charles Karamba
- organized death squads
- planned crimes; many killers came from here

CRIMINAL INVESTIGATIONS AND PROSECUTION
- run by Joseph Nzabamwita
- helped organize and supervise crimes
- meant to investigate and prosecute crimes, but often worked with cadres to fabricate evidence

RESEARCH, RECORDS AND REGISTRY
- run by Charles Shema
- archives, analysis, surveillance
- agents involved in killing
- helped recruit at ICTR, embassies, international institutions

EXTERNAL INTELLIGENCE
- in early years run by Patrick Karegeya
- conducted targeted assassinations

HIGH COMMAND/ REPUBLICAN GUARD
- effectively headed by James Kabarebe
- later run by Alex Kagame, Tom Byabagamba
- soldiers assisted in DMI operations

TRAINING WING
- run by Patrick Nyamvumba during genocide
- worked with DMI mobile units to conduct genocide/ethnic cleansing of Hutus in RPF-controlled zones
- lured, recruited and eliminated massive numbers of Hutu male recruits after genocide
- killed Tutsi recruits deemed suspicious

GENDARMERIE
- run by Kayumba Nyamwasa after the genocide
- carried out extermination campaign against Hutus during counterinsurgency, and killings of Hutu recruits
- worked jointly with DMI, *abakada*, Training Wing and High Command

SPECIAL INTELLIGENCE
- run by Jean Jacques Mupenzi and Rugumya Gacinya
- coordinated extermination operations

CRIMINAL INVESTIGATION DEPARTMENT
- run by Emmanuel Bayingana
- organized death squads

MILITARY POLICE
- run by Augustin Gashayija prior to and during genocide
- run by Jackson Rwahama after genocide
- assisted in DMI operations

---

* Theogene Rudasingwa denies having ordered the killing of Hutus but acknowledges that he became aware in 1994 of the RPF's extermination campaign. He says the policy came from DMI, not the RPF Secretariat.

APPENDIX B

The Criminals of the Rwandan Patriotic Front

	NAME	ALLEGED CRIMES
1	Paul Kagame	He is allegedly ultimately responsible for the massacres of several hundred thousand Hutu civilians in Rwanda and a lesser number of Tutsis from April 1994 to December 1995.
		He is allegedly ultimately responsible for the killing of an estimated 200,000 Rwandan Hutu and Congolese Hutu in Zaire/DRC in 1996–97 and countless Hutus who returned to Rwanda from refugee camps between 1995 and 1998.
		He is allegedly ultimately responsible for unleashing the 1996–97 war in Zaire and supplying proxy militias in the DRC in the years thereafter. The lengthy conflict involved multiple actors and countries, and left millions of people dead from violence and war-related illnesses.
		Specifically:
		He is allegedly ultimately responsible for orchestrating and ordering the mass murder of civilians during the 1990–94 invasion war.
		He is allegedly ultimately responsible for massacring civilians in the demilitarized buffer zone, between March 1993 and April 1994, a responsibility he shared with DMI chief Kayumba Nyamwasa, Chief Political Commissar (CPC) Frank Mugambage, the RPF secretary-general Theogene Rudasingwa and the RPF political bureau.
		Kagame is allegedly ultimately responsible for shooting down the plane carrying presidents Habyarimana of Rwanda and Ntaryamira of Burundi on April 6, 1994, an operation that was prepared by Nyamwasa's DMI in conjunction with Kagame's High Command unit.
		He is allegedly responsible for the Byumba stadium mass murder of several thousand Hutu civilians in April 1994.
		He allegedly ordered large-scale civilian killings in all RPF progressively occupied areas from April 1994 to December 1995, during which upwards of 500,000 mainly Hutu civilians were massacred.
		He allegedly ordered the mass slaughter of Hutu refugees in the Congo during the invasion of 1996 and 1997.
		He allegedly approved an extermination campaign, carried out by Nyamwasa and his senior commanders, against Hutu peasants during the counterinsurgency in northwestern Rwanda from 1996 to 1998.
		He allegedly approved the killing of the Bagogwe Tutsi community and the looting of their cattle in northwestern Rwanda.
		He allegedly approved the massacres of Banyamulenge Tutsis of Zaire/DRC at Minembwe and the surrounding area in South Kivu, where several thousand Tutsis were massacred.

	NAME	ALLEGED CRIMES
	Paul Kagame (continued)	He has allegedly ordered a significant number of targeted killings of perceived critics in Rwanda and abroad, among them Théoneste Lizinde and Seth Sendashonga in Kenya in 1996 and 1998 respectively, and Théogène Turatsinze (former director general of the Banque Rwandaise de Développement) in Mozambique in October 2012.
		He allegedly ordered the assassination of Patrick Karegeya, former chief of Rwanda's external intelligence, in South Africa in December 2013.
		He is the alleged mastermind and top coordinator of killings within the RPF/RPA system from 1990 until today. He does not tolerate operations conducted without his knowledge.
2	Kayumba Nyamwasa, currently in exile	He allegedly shares responsibility with Kagame for the massacre of several hundred thousand Hutu civilians in Rwanda, and a lesser number of Tutsis, from April 1994 and December 1995.
		He is allegedly responsible, with Kagame, for the killing of an estimated 200,000 Rwandan Hutu and Congolese Hutu in Zaire/DRC in 1996–97 and countless Hutus who returned to Rwanda from refugee camps between 1995 and 1998.
		He allegedly shares responsibility for unleashing the 1996–97 war in Zaire and supplying proxy militias in the DRC in the years thereafter. The lengthy conflict involved multiple actors and countries, and left millions of people dead from violence and war-related illnesses.
		Specifically:
		He is allegedly responsible, with Kagame, for orchestrating and ordering the murders of Hutu civilians during the RPF's invasion war from 1990 to 1994.
		He is allegedly responsible for the massacres of civilians in the demilitarized buffer zone between March 1993 and April 1994, a responsibility he shared with Chief Political Commissar (CPC) Frank Mugambage and the RPF secretary-general Theogene Rudasingwa and the RPF political bureau.
		As head of DMI, he allegedly coordinated RPF technicians who were deployed throughout Kigali before President Habyarimana's plane was shot down. The technicians' tasks were sixfold: (a) to assassinate key Hutu politicians in a bid to create tensions and foment violence; (b) to assassinate civilians, lay land mines and throw grenades in order to spread terror and create confusion among the population; (c) to intentionally spread rumors that Tutsis would be killed in mass numbers in a bid to create fear among Tutsis and allow the RPF to use its propaganda machine and demonize the regime; to encourage Hutus to believe that killing Tutsis was necessary for their survival, and to exacerbate anger among Hutus against Tutsis; (d) to assassinate prominent Hutu ideologists and opinion leaders in a bid to push Hutu anger to the extreme; (e) to join extremist Interahamwe militia in killing Tutsis and fueling violence as part of a bid to secure international support for the RPF's campaign against Hutu extremists; (f) to join the ranks of the six hundred RPF troops stationed in CND, ready to fight after the plane was shot down.

NAME	ALLEGED CRIMES
Kayumba Nyamwasa (continued)	He allegedly played a direct role in the shooting down of the plane carrying presidents Habyarimana of Rwanda and Ntaryamira of Burundi on April 6, 1994. It was an operation whose preparation he allegedly coordinated in consultation with Kagame.
	He is allegedly responsible for large-scale massacres of Hutu civilians in Giti and Rutare in Byumba from April to June 1994.
	He allegedly supervised killings in two mountainous locations between Giti and Rutare, along with Jackson Rwahama and other senior RPA commanders, from April 16 to 25, 1994. Entire families were decimated—shot or hacked with hoes. Nyamwasa allegedly ordered that each victim be shot in the head to ensure death.
	He is allegedly responsible for killing civilians at Giti Communal Office, where a DMI detachment was established. Killings took place at night. Soldiers under his command allegedly screened and killed Hutus at night, sometimes burying them alive in mass graves. Victims died from being shot or hacked or from suffocation. The victims suffered immeasurably.
	He allegedly coordinated civilian killings in Muhura, Gikomero, Kibungo town and surrounding areas.
	He was allegedly responsible with Kagame for the killing of selective francophone Tutsi soldiers who joined the RPA before the genocide, in addition to Hutu recruits, who were systematically eliminated.
	He was allegedly responsible, from June 1994 onward, for coordinating mass killings at Masaka in Kigali and at other sites.
	He was allegedly involved in coordinating the massacre of Hutu refugees at Kibeho in April 1995.
	He allegedly ordered the massacre of Hutu civilians, mainly women and children, in the Kanama commune of Gisenyi in October 1997.
	He was the alleged coordinator and mastermind of an extermination campaign against Hutu peasants during the counterinsurgency war from 1996 to 1998 in northwestern Rwanda, where entire Hutu families were annihilated on the pretext they were harboring insurgents.
	He is allegedly responsible for the key assassination of RPA officers Major Birasa and Captain Eddy, an operation falsely blamed on Hutu insurgents and used to inflict more murders on the Hutu civilian population. These assassinations were allegedly carried out by Jean Jacques Mupenzi under the instructions of Nyamwasa and Kagame.
	He allegedly shares responsibility for killing hundreds of thousands of Rwandan and Congolese Hutus during the first invasion of Zaire, and later the large-scale mass murder of Hutu refugees and civilians in Congo from 1996 to 2002.
	He is allegedly responsible for killing members of the Bagogwe Tutsi community in northwestern Rwanda, and looting their cows during the counterinsurgency.

	NAME	ALLEGED CRIMES
	Kayumba Nyamwasa (continued)	He is allegedly responsible, with Kagame, for massacring several thousand Banyamulenge Tutsis of Zaire/DRC at Minembwe and the surrounding area in South Kivu.
		He is allegedly responsible for ordering the assassinations of Spanish priest Joaquim Vallmajo along with three Rwandan priests in April 1994 in Byumba prefecture, British Catholic Marist brother Chris Mannion and Rwandan Joseph Rushigajiki, also a Marist brother, in July 1994, Canadian priest Claude Simard in October 1994, Griet Bosmans, a Belgian nun, in Gisenyi in April 1997, Canadian priest Guy Pinard in Ruhengeri in February 1997, Croatian Reverend Vjeco Curic in 1998, and Spanish citizens from the NGO Medico El Mundo—Luis Valtueña Gallego, Maria Flores Sirera Fortuny and Manuel Madrazo Osuna—in Ruhengeri in January 1997.
3	Jackson Rwahama	As deputy head of DMI, he was allegedly the field coordinator of mass murders that took place in communes Giti, Rutare, Kinyami and Muhura during the genocide. He allegedly used DMI units and Training Wing troops to carry out operations. Rwahama allegedly discussed operations and strategies with Nyamwasa, how many Hutus to kill and where to find forces needed for these executions.
		He allegedly worked jointly with DMI units and those from Kagame's High Command in killing operations.
		He is allegedly responsible with Nyamwasa for massacres of civilians in the demilitarized buffer zone between March 1993 and April 1994.
		He indirectly coordinated (advising Kagame and Kayumba) the mass slaying at Byumba stadium in which several thousand Hutus perished in April 1994. He is allegedly responsible for organizing massacres of civilians in Ndera and Kigali in 1994.
		He allegedly coordinated field operations and helped execute countless civilian killings in Masaka—a DMI site—from June 1994.
		He allegedly helped coordinate the April 1995 massacres of Hutu refugees in Kibeho.
		He was allegedly the main supervisor of Kami barracks slaughters until he was appointed commander of the Military Police.
		He was considered central in crafting DMI killing and assassination techniques and strategies, in addition to hiding evidence.
4	Karenzi Karake	He was allegedly one of Kagame's most willing executioners.
		In his capacity as the RPF's liaison officer in its dealings with the UN peacekeeping mission (UNAMIR) and his previous role as a member of the African Union military observer group, Karake was able to get access to the capital, scope out sites and work with RPF commandos on infiltrating Kigali.
		He allegedly shares responsibility for the April 1994 assassination of presidents Juvénal Habyarimana of Rwanda and Cyprien Ntaryamira of Burundi.

NAME	ALLEGED CRIMES
Karenzi Karake (continued)	He is allegedly responsible for facilitating the technicians' operations in Kigali and throughout Rwanda.
	He was allegedly responsible for coordinating civilian killings after the plane crash at a number of sites (Ndera, Kigali, Kigali-Ngari, Byumba).
	As head of DMI after the genocide, he allegedly organized and ordered the killing of Canadian priest Claude Simard in October 1994.
	He allegedly organized the assassination of British Marist brother Chris Mannion and his Rwandan colleague Joseph Rushigajiki in July 1994.
	He is allegedly responsible for organizing and overseeing the assassination of Canadian priest Father Guy Pinard in Ruhengeri in February 1997.
	He is allegedly responsible with Kayumba Nyamwasa for the assassination of the Croatian-Bosnian priest Curick Vjecko in Janury 1998 in Kigali. Also involved were Jean Jacques Mupenzi, Emmanuel Bayingana, Joseph Nzabamwita and Gacinya Rugumya.
	As head of DMI, he was allegedly directly involved in the assassination of Spanish aid workers in Ruhengeri: Luis Valtueña Gallego, Maria Flores Sirera Fortuny and Manuel Madrazo Osuna.
	He allegedly helped plan and execute the assassination of Spanish priest Joaquim Vallmajo, along with other local priests, in April 1994 in Byumba.
	After the genocide, Karake allegedly transformed Kami barracks into what it is now: a slaughter pen that no independent observer, NGO or journalist had access to.
	He allegedly helped plan the attack on Kibeho refugee camp that claimed the lives of several thousand Hutus in 1995.
	He allegedly helped organize burning the bodies of Hutus killed in Rwanda between 1994 and 1998.
	He allegedly helped mastermind the invasion of Zaire and subsequent massacres of hundreds of thousands of Hutu refugees in Zaire in 1996–97.
	He allegedly ordered DMI operations in which Hutu refugees from Zaire were suffocated to death while being transported aboard trucks to sites where their bodies were burned.
	He allegedly organized the killing and burying of thousands of civilians and soldiers at Masaka, the headquarters of DMI, and other DMI killing grounds between 1994 and 1997.
	As head of DMI, he shares responsibility with Nyamwasa—who directed the Gendarmerie—for killing tens of thousands of Hutu civilians of northwestern Rwanda in regions of Gisenyi and Ruhengeri.

	NAME	ALLEGED CRIMES
	Karenzi Karake (continued)	He allegedly helped authorize the massacres of Bagogwe Tutsi and the looting of their livestock in northwestern Rwanda, under instruction of Paul Kagame and in collaboration with a number of senior commanders such as Charles Kayonga, Kayumba Nyamwasa and Mubarak Muganga.
		As chief of the National Intelligence and Security Services, he allegedly ordered the assassination of Colonel Patrick Karegeya, who was strangled to death in a hotel room in Johannesburg in December 2013.
5	Fred Ibingira	He was a member of the powerful High Command Council. As head of the 157th Battalion in 1994, he allegedly coordinated and ordered the mass killing of tens of thousands of Hutu civilians in Bugesera in southern Rwanda, and allegedly ordered the killings of Hutus in Umutara, Kibungo, Butare, Gikongoro and Gitarama, among other areas.
		He was allegedly directly responsible for the assassination of bishops and priests in Gakurazo in June 1994.
		He allegedly supervised and executed the mass murder of several thousand Hutus in Kibeho in April 1995.
		He allegedly shares responsibility for orchestrating and carrying out mass murder of Hutu refugees in Zaire in 1996–97.
		He allegedly supported Karake at DMI in operations in which countless Hutu returnees from Zaire were killed in 1996–97. The operations screened soldiers and civilians.
		He allegedly played a role in assassinating Canadian priest Father Claude Simard in October 1994 by providing soldiers and guidance for the operation ordered by Karake's DMI and Kayumba's Gendarmerie Special Intelligence.
		He allegedly shared responsibility for the assassination of British Catholic Marist brother Reverend Chris Mannion and his Rwandan colleague Joseph Rushigajiki in July 1994 in Save, Butare.
6	James Kabarebe	He allegedly helped orchestrate and order the mass murder of civilians during the RPF's scorched-earth campaign prior to the genocide.
		He allegedly assisted in massacres of civilians in the demilitarized buffer zone between March 1993 and April 1994, a responsibility allegedly shared with DMI chief Kayumba Nyamwasa, Chief Political Commissar (CPC) Frank Mugambage and the RPF secretary-general Theogene Rudasingwa of the RPF political bureau.
		As Kagame's aide-de-camp and the effective head of High Command, he allegedly played a supervising role in the massacre of an estimated several hundred thousand Hutu civilians—and some Tutsis—in Rwanda between April 1994 and December 1995. As operations coordinator for the invasion of Zaire, he was also allegedly responsible for the deaths of 200,000 Hutu refugees massacred in Zaire, in addition to countless returnees who disappeared after Rwandan troops invaded and forced their repatriation.

	NAME	ALLEGED CRIMES
6	James Kabarebe (continued)	*Specifically:*
		He shares responsibility for allegedly shooting down the plane carrying presidents Juvénal Habyarimana of Rwanda and Cyprien Ntaryamira of Burundi in April 1994.
		He allegedly helped organize large-scale civilian killings in all RPF progressively occupied areas from April 1994 to December 1995, during which several hundred thousand mainly Hutu civilians and military recruits were massacred, according to estimates.
		He was allegedly directly involved in preparing and ordering the mass killings of Hutu refugees in Zaire during the invasion and sweep of Zaire by the Rwandan army in 1996–97. Countless Congolese Hutu were also killed during this RPF campaign.
		He was allegedly involved in the killings of Bagogwe Tutsi and the looting of their herds of cows in northern Rwanda during the counterinsurgency.
		He was allegedly involved in the massacres of Banyamulenge Tutsis of Zaire/DRC at Minembwe and surrounding areas in South Kivu.
		He allegedly helped organize the assassination of Patrick Karegeya, the former chief of external intelligence, in South Africa in December 2013.
7	Patrick Nyamvumba	He was allegedly involved in the murders of hundreds of young francophone Tutsis from Rwanda, Burundi and Zaire and the very few Hutu who joined the RPA during the struggle prior to the genocide.
		He was allegedly involved in the killings of civilians in the demilitarized buffer zone between 1993 and 1994.
		As chief instructor and effective head of the Training Wing, he allegedly commanded death squad operations in which Hutu civilians in RPF-controlled areas were butchered. Training Wing troops under Nyamvumba joined DMI forces of Kayumba Nyamwsa and the High Command unit guarding Kagame to conduct the killing in all RPF-controlled zones. Nyamvumba's troops lured and killed Hutus at meetings. Some were hunted down and killed with guns or *agafuni* hoes and dumped in the Akagera River. Victims were also loaded onto trucks, taken to Akagera National Park and killed there, before being burned and incinerated.
		Nyamvumba's forces allegedly cleansed the Hutu population in areas of Umutara, southern Buganza across Muhazi, Rwamagana, Kayonza, Gahini, and Bicumbi from April to July 1994. These areas belonged to former prefectures of Byumba, Kibungo and Kigali-Ngari. Approximately 75,000 to 110,000 Hutu civilians were butchered in these areas alone, according to former DMI staff.
		He allegedly used the Training Wing at Gabiro as a slaughter site where up to hundreds of thousands of Hutus from different areas of the country were killed during and after the genocide. In this task, mobile units under the guidance of DMI agents screened and loaded civilians onto trucks that were driven to Gabiro.

	NAME	ALLEGED CRIMES
	Patrick Nyamvumba (continued)	Officers who allegedly assisted Nyamvumba in these operations were Jean Bosco Kazura (attached to the High Command unit), Emmanuel Butera, John Birasa, and Gahizi Wellars, among others.
8	Dan Munyuza	He was allegedly involved in the massacre of Hutu civilians in the demilitarized buffer zone from March 1993 to April 1994.
		He allegedly played a leading role in eliminating Hutus who attempted to join RPA ranks prior to the genocide in addition to francophone Tutsis (people perceived to be intellectuals) who joined the RPA's struggle from Burundi, Rwanda and Zaire.
		He is an alleged key organizer of assassinations and massacres that involved DMI operatives.
		He played a key role in killing several thousand Hutu civilians butchered at Byumba stadium and thousands of others massacred in Byumba between April and May 1994.
		In conjunction with DMI soldiers, Munyuza allegedly helped coordinate the 1994 killings at the Training Wing, working closely with Patrick Nyamvumba in Hutu cleansing campaigns from Byumba to Kigali-Ngari into the prefecture of Kibungo.
		He is allegedly responsible for targeted assassinations in Kigali after the RPF seized power in 1994 in Kigali and elsewhere.
		He was allegedly directly responsible for the assassination of Spanish priest Joaquim Vallmajo, killed with three local priests in April 1994 in Byumba.
		He allegedly shared responsibility for assassinating British Catholic Marist brother Chris Mannion and his Rwandan colleague, cleric Joseph Rushigajiki, in July 1994 in Save in Butare.
		He allegedly helped oversee killing operations at Kami barracks between June and August 1994.
		When he was chief of Military Police, he allegedly coordinated the deaths of a large number of former regime members throughout Rwanda and repatriated from Zaire. Many of these men were butchered in Kanombe Military Police barracks, others at Kami, Gabiro, Nasho. He allegedly oversaw tortures and killings of Hutu and Congolese prisoners of war, a responsibility shared with his predecessors from the Military Police, John Zigira and Jackson Rwahama. Hutu recruits were also killed at the Training Wing barracks in Gako.
		He allegedly helped coordinate the death by strangling of Patrick Karegeya in South Africa in December 2013.
9	Jack Nziza	He is often described as a ghost for never appearing in the field but allegedly having an invisible hand in the most egregious crimes orchestrated by the Directorate of Military Intelligence.
		As the key enforcer of DMI operations at its headquarters, Nziza was allegedly central to devising plans for the second invasion of Congo in 1998.

	NAME	ALLEGED CRIMES
	Jack Nziza (continued)	He has been allegedly directly involved in organizing most assassinations of RPA officers, government officials and cadres killed by the regime, at home or abroad, in addition to dissidents and critics.
		He has earned a reputation for allegedly going after anyone, Tutsi or Hutu, who is a potential threat to Kagame.
		He allegedly organized the assassination of RPA major Alex Ruzindana in 2003. Ruzindana was killed by DMI operatives in Nyungwe forest. Lieutenant Colonel John Karangwa, on instructions from Jack Nziza, allegedly helped devise the assassination in consultation with Emmanuel Gasana Rurayi and Faustin Kalisa, Kagame's cousin who later became deputy chief of national police.
		He allegedly oversaw, with Patrick Karegeya at External Intelligence, the Congo desk, which organized and controlled the exploitation of Congolese natural resources, following the Rwandan invasion of Zaire. They selected Rwandans and Congolese to do business on Congolese soil and set up black market foreign exchange bureaus in Kigali, with DMI agents.
		He allegedly oversees a great deal of army business, RPF political matters, local government issues, DRC business matters, the workings of governors, mayors, religious groups and churches. He allegedly oversees funds and procurement systems within the army and gets involved with big or small income generating projects.
10	Cesar Kayizari	He allegedly advises Kagame on important military operations, and is considered one of his right-hand men.
		He is allegedly responsible for overseeing massacres of hundreds of Hutu civilians in the prefecture of Ruhengeri, in 1993, as operations commander in that zone (OCO commander) before the genocide.
		He allegedly played a crucial role in facilitating the massacres of civilians in the prefecture of Cyangugu from 1994 to 1996.
		He allegedly provided soldiers and intelligence to allow DMI to kill thousands of Hutu civilians in Nyungwe forest after the genocide.
		He allegedly assisted in the killing operations at Kibeho that left several thousand Hutu refugees dead in April 1995.
		He has been allegedly involved in planning most if not all targeted assassinations of dissidents and perceived critics in foreign countries.
11	Wilson Gumisiriza	As DMI intelligence officer for the 157th Battalion, he allegedly facilitated the killing of tens of thousands of Hutu civilians during the genocide in Bugesera in southern Rwanda, and allegedly assisted killing operations in Umutara, Kibungo, Butare, Gikongoro and Gitarama.
		He was allegedly directly responsible for the assassination of Catholic bishops and priests, and an eight-year-old boy at Gakurazo in central Rwanda in June 1994.

	NAME	ALLEGED CRIMES
	Wilson Gumisiriza (continued)	He was allegedly involved in the mass murder of Hutu civilians in Mayaga, Butare, Gikongoro, Gitarama and Cyangugu between 1994 and 1995. Massacres he allegedly facilitated were also committed in Butare areas of Kibayi, Sovu and Nyanza; a smaller number of Tutsis were also killed in these operations. These Tutsis were often witnesses to the slaughter of their Hutu neighbors, and were killed to ensure the information would remain concealed. He allegedly shared responsibility for these killings with Innocent Kabandana.
		He was allegedly involved in operations of mass murder of several thousand Hutu refugees in Kibeho in April 1995.
		He was allegedly involved in organizing the killing of thousands of Hutus who returned from Zaire/DRC to Rwanda after the genocide and during the counterinsurgency.
		He was allegedly involved in organizing the mass murder of Hutu refugees in Zaire from 1996 onward.
12	John Zigira	He allegedly facilitated the mass murder of thousands of Hutu civilians and recruits from April 1994 in areas where the Training Wing operated. He allegedly collaborated with Patrick Nyamvumba in killings and helped to conceal these crimes. Corpses were often burned; ashes were thrown in rivers and lakes in Akagera National Park.
		He allegedly coordinated and supervised massacres of several tens of thousands of Hutu civilians in Save, Kabutare, Rubona, Songa, Kibayi and Gihindamuyaga, where victims were estimated between forty thousand and seventy thousand. He shares responsibility for these killings with Fred Ibingira, Wilson Gumisiriza and Innocent Kabandana. The crimes occurred between June 1994 and 1995.
		He allegedly oversaw summary executions of Hutu soldiers returning from the DRC, killed in the Military Police barracks and in Nasho-Kibungo at a special Training Wing site.
		He allegedly helped organize the assassination of Canadian priest Father Claude Simard on October 17, 1994. Simard was beaten to death with a hammer in Ruyenzi, Butare, for gathering evidence of RPF crimes.
		He allegedly shared responsibility with Brigadier General John Bagabo for the slaughter of dozens of Tutsi soldiers considered *ibipinga* (obstacles of the state). They were killed at Nasho in Akagera park and Kanombe Military Police barracks.
13	Rugumya Gacinya	He allegedly helped fuel massacres of Hutus in the demilitarized zone of Byumba in 1993 as he served in the capacity of Bravo battalion's intelligence officer. Hutus were killed with *agafuni* and by bullets. The Bravo battalion was commanded by Twahirwa Dodo.
		He allegedly assisted in large-scale massacres of Hutus who were internally displaced in Byumba and Kigali-Ngali, and in killings of Hutu in Kigali in 1994: an estimated seven to ten thousand Hutus perished, allegedly under Gacinya and Colonel Dodo's forces, in less than three weeks from April to May 1994.

	NAME	ALLEGED CRIMES
	Rugumya Gacinya (continued)	As head of the Gendarmerie's Special Intelligence, he allegedly helped mastermind the Kibeho slaughter of several thousand Hutu refugees in April 1995.
		He allegedly shared responsibility for organizing, with Jean Jacques Mupenzi, special forces to massacre Hutu peasants in Gisenyi and Ruhengeri between 1996 and 1998 in operations ordered by Kayumba Nyamwasa, as part of counterinsurgency operations under the pretext of chasing out insurgents known as *Abacengezi*.
		He allegedly helped plan the assassination of Canadian priest Guy Pinard in 1997 during Communion in Ruhengeri.
		He was allegedly involved in operations to assassinate Croatian-Bosnian Catholic priest Reverend Curick Vjeko in Janury 1998 in Kiyovu, Kigali.
		He was allegedly involved in organizing the killings of Hutu returnees from the DRC in Nyungwe and burning bodies in Nyungwe from 1996 to 2000.
		He allegedly helped plan many if not most targeted assassinations in the country, as head of Special Intelligence.
		He was allegedly responsible for the assassination of Lieutenant Colonel Augustin Cyiza, a high-profile Hutu officer from the former Habyarimana regime who was integrated into the RPA. He was killed in April 2003 in an operation allegedly coordinated by Gacinya and Jack Nziza.
		He allegedly supervised the assassination of Assiel Kabera, a presidential adviser during H.E. Pasteur Bizimungu's tenure in March 2000, an operation allegedly ordered by Nyamwasa and Kagame.
14	Charles Kayonga	As commander of RPA's battalion at the CND headquarters in Kigali prior to the genocide, he was allegedly directly responsible for shooting down the plane carrying presidents Juvénal Habyarimana of Rwanda and Cyprien Ntaryamira of Burundi in April 1994.
		He allegedly assisted in planning operations to assassinate political figures in Rwanda between 1993 and 1994; and was allegedly part of planning false flags that targeted and killed civilians in Rwanda in order to spread confusion in the population and demonize the Habyarimana regime in the eyes of the international community. Many interior Tutsis died during these operations.
		He allegedly helped direct house-to-house killings of Hutu businessmen, political figures and civil servants in areas surrounding Remera stadium and the CND in April 1994.
		He was allegedly involved in orchestrating civilian killings in all RPF progressively occupied areas from April 1994 to December 1995, when hundreds of thousands of Hutus were massacred. His area of operations was mainly in Kigali in the immediate aftermath of the plane crash but widened to other areas afterward.

	NAME	ALLEGED CRIMES
	Charles Kayonga (continued)	He was allegedly involved in the killings of Bagogwe Tutsi and the looting of their cows in northwest Rwanda during the counterinsurgency.
		He allegedly helped coordinate killings of Hutu refugees in the first invasion of Zaire, and subsequent waves of RPF-inspired violence in Congo in later years.
15	Jean Jacques Mupenzi	He allegedly assisted in masterminding the murder of civilians during the RPA's invasion war in northern Rwanda.
		He allegedly assisted in planning massacres of civilians in the demilitarized zone from 1993 to April 1994.
		He was allegedly directly involved in massacres of civilians in Giti and Rutare commune of Byumba from April to June 1994.
		He allegedly supervised killings in Giti, Kinyami, Muhura, Rutare, Gikomero, Kibungo town center and surrounding areas from April to June 1994.
		He was allegedly engaged in burning an estimated thirteen thousand corpses at Murindi wa Nasho in southeastern Rwanda. The decomposing bodies were placed in a pile by soldiers then covered with wood. Mupenzi and Jean Damascène Sekamana allegedly directed the operations in which gasoline and gas oil were used. The operations took place in late May and early June 1994.
		He allegedly supervised mass killings that took place in Masaka DMI site in June and July 1994, where tens of thousands of Hutu civilians were massacred, including "reporters" (members of the former military regime).
		He allegedly helped oversee the killing of clergy at Rwesero Catholic Minor Seminary in Giti and the surrounding areas, in addition to targeting prominent Hutus in those areas, in April 1994.
		He was allegedly involved in operations to assassinate Canadian priest Claude Simard in October 1994.
		He allegedly conducted in person—with a small commando unit—the ambush and assassination of Major Birasa of the RPA, with colleague Captain Eddy. This staged operation was falsely blamed on *Abacengezi* (Hutu insurgents) during the counterinsurgency campaign. This operation was allegedly carried out by Mupenzi and ordered by Nyamwasa and Kagame.
		As codirector of the Gendarmerie's Special Intelligence, Mupenzi coordinated operations to exterminate Hutu peasants during the counterinsurgency in northwestern Rwanda.
		He allegedly helped plan the assassination of Canadian priest Guy Pinard in Ruhengeri in February 1997.
		He was allegedly involved in operations to assassinate British Catholic Marist brother Chris Mannion and his Rwandan colleague Joseph Rushigajiki in July 1994.

	NAME	ALLEGED CRIMES
	Jean Jacques Mupenzi (continued)	He was allegedly involved in operations to assassinate Croatian-Bosnian Catholic priest Curick Vjeko in Kigali in January 1998.
		He was allegedly directly involved in the assassinations of three Spanish citizens working for the NGO Medico El Mundo, killed in January 1997 in Ruhengeri: Luis Valtueña Gallego, Maria Flores Sirera Fortuny and Manuel Madrazo Osuna.
16	Emmanuel Gasana Rurayi	He was allegedly involved in killing operations of Hutu civilians in Ruhengeri, in particular Kidaho, Nyamagumba and Kinigi, between 1993 and 1994.
		He was allegedly involved in massacres of civilians in the buffer zone from March 1993 to April 1994.
		He was allegedly involved in operations against Hutu civilians in Bugesera and Mayaga, then Butare city, where he allegedly oversaw and conducted large-scale massacres of men, women, children, babies and the elderly, from June to August 1994. The killing ground he operated in was the arboretum forest of the National University of Rwanda. Bodies were buried in mass graves, then burned and incinerated with a mixture of gas oil and gasoline.
		He was allegedly involved in preparations of operations at Kibeho where several thousand Hutu refugees were killed in April 1995.
		He allegedly helped form and supervise killing squads to operate in southwestern Rwanda (Nyungwe forest, Butare, Gikongoro, Cyangugu) from 1999 to 2000.
		He was allegedly involved in the mass murder of internally displaced refugees and returnees from the DRC, some in Nyungwe forest and others transported to Butare, where they were brutally killed with *agafuni* or suffocated.
		He was allegedly involved in planning to assassinate Alex Ruzindana in 2003, an operation by DMI operatives in Nyungwe.
17	Charles Karamba	As part of DMI, he allegedly helped devise schemes to assassinate political figures in Rwanda between 1993 and 1994 prior to the genocide. These crimes destabilized the Habyarimana regime and demonized it in the eyes of the international community. Tutsis inside Rwanda died in the RPF's destabilization campaign.
		As part of DMI, he was allegedly directly involved in preparations to shoot down the plane carrying the Rwandan and Burundian presidents in April 1994, an incident that sparked the genocide.
		As a key intelligence officer in DMI under Nyamwasa, Karamba allegedly directly oversaw the infiltration of RPF technicians in Interahamwe activities during the genocide, in particular at their presence at roadblocks in Kigali, where technicians fueled massacres and directly participated in killings of Tutsis.

	NAME	ALLEGED CRIMES
	Charles Karamba (continued)	He was allegedly among key figures who organized house-to-house killing of Hutu businessmen, political figures and civil servants in areas in and around Remera stadium and the CND in April 1994.
		He was allegedly involved in organizing large-scale civilian killings in Kigali after President Habyarimana was assassinated.
		As head of counterintelligence at DMI after the genocide, he was allegedly involved in overall planning and supervising of the killings of Hutu refugees in Zaire following the 1996–97 invasion.
		He allegedly helped plan the assassination of Canadian priest Guy Pinard in February 1997 in Ruhengeri.
		He was allegedly involved in carrying out the assassination of Croatian-Bosnian Catholic priest Reverend Curick Vjeko in January 1998 near Kagame's official residence in Kiyovu.
		As head of counterintelligence, he allegedly had a hand in the planning of many if not most targeted assassinations in the country.
18	Joseph Nzabamwita	He was allegedly directly involved in the massacres of civilians in Giti commune of Byumba from April to June 1994, and in civilian killings in Kinyami, Muhura, Rutare, Gikomero, Kibungo town and surrounding areas from April to June 1994.
		He was allegedly directly involved in mass killings in Masaka—a DMI site—in June and July 1994, where tens of thousands of Hutu civilians perished, in addition to "reporters" (members of the former regime's army who joined the RPA).
		He allegedly helped organize the killings of clergy at Rwesero Catholic Minor Seminary in Giti and other locations, and also allegedly targeted prominent Hutus in Giti and Rutare in April 1994.
		As head of the Criminal Investigations and Prosecution department of DMI after the genocide, Nzabamwita was allegedly in charge of eliminating witnesses and concocting criminal charges on the orders of Kagame and Karake. Many Hutus perished in these schemes, in particular wealthy Hutu returnees from Zaire, in a bid to confiscate properties and wealth, or for political reasons.
		He was allegedly involved in overall operations throughout the country to kill "reporters" (former troops who joined the RPA) and Hutus who returned or were repatriated from the DRC.
		He was allegedly among the top coordinators of killing operations at Kami barracks after the genocide. There were permanent agents whom Nzabamwita could replace any time with the approval of Karake.
		He was allegedly involved in planning the assassinations of Canadian Father Guy Pinard in February 1997 and Croatian-Bosnian priest Curick Vjeko, killed in January 1998.

	NAME	ALLEGED CRIMES
19	Jean Bosco Kazura	As a deputy commander under Patrick Nyamvumba during the genocide, he allegedly supervised killings of Hutu civilians in Umutara, southern Buganza across Muhazi, Rwamagana, Kayonza, Gahini, Bicumbi and other areas from May to July 1994. These areas belonged to the former prefectures of Byumba, Kibungo and Kigali-Ngali. Approximately 75,000 to 110,000 Hutu civilians were butchered in these operations, their bodies either buried in mass graves or reduced to ash from burning with gasoline and gas oil. Their ashes were thrown in the Akagera River or in lakes, or mixed with soil in Akagera National Park. He was, along with Patrick Nyamvumba, allegedly involved in the mass murder of Hutu returnees from the DRC and the elimination of Hutu recruits and young soldiers who graduated from the Training Wing. These people often suffocated in trucks or were killed at various locations, often in Akagera; their bodies were burned and incinerated.
20	Rose Kabuye	She was the most high-ranking and influential woman in the Rwandan Patriotic Army. As mayor of Kigali, she was allegedly involved in organizing massacres of Hutu civilians in areas of Kigali-Ngali and Kigali City from April 1994; she allegedly ordered Tutsi cadres and DMI to commit murders of Hutus in Ndera, Gikomero, Kabuga, Nyacyonga and Remera. She allegedly used local leaders at sector and cell levels to identify people to be killed, in particular Hutu returnees from Zaire and Hutu residents who owned decent homes and properties. She allegedly closely collaborated with DMI in night operations as entire families were abducted and brought to Kami or other killing grounds. The killings were carried out in conjunction with Kigali authorities and DMI. Many safe houses were used by DMI as secret slaughter sites. She allegedly led and coordinated local leaders of Nyumbakumi (in which the government assigns representatives to monitor every ten houses), cells, sectors, communes and the prefecture—who were mostly RPF political cadres or RPA members. She allegedly coordinated their activities at the field level in Kigali and reported directly to the RPF's Secretariat. She allegedly met the DMI, RPF Secretariat and army/Gendarmerie networks who screened and killed Hutu and anyone labeled "igipinga" (whether they were Hutu, Tutsi or foreign citizens). This system was replicated in other parts of the country as well.

ACKNOWLEDGMENTS

I'd like to express my profound gratitude to everyone who shared his or her experience of war and genocide. Although your wounds still burn, your stories form a collective memory of frailty and strength. And telling them constitutes a moral act.

To Rwandan Hutus who have suffered in silence or dared to challenge the false accounts of Paul Kagame's heroism and paid for it. Your stories have inspired me.

To Rwandan Tutsis who shared their accounts of persecution, and to former members of Kagame's army who risked their lives to tell the truth, your courage is a current that lifts us all. I'm forever grateful that you helped me discover what the RPF did and how it covered up its trail of crimes. I truly believe your actions will help heal Rwanda.

To the Congolese whose suffering and dignity I briefly witnessed, you forced me to examine my beliefs and myself. You taught me how to resist lies.

To the countless African journalists and activists who have faced merciless attacks for speaking inconvenient truths to power, your work has guided me throughout.

I would like to single out the early, critical work of documentary makers Peter Verlinden, from Belgium, and the late Yvan Patry, from Quebec. I look back at their films and am floored at what they were able to show when others refused or were unable to do so.

I wish to acknowledge Filip Reyntjens, René Lemarchand, André Guichaoua and Alan Kuperman for their combined scholarship. Each of them opened a window that helped me understand the history and politics of Rwanda.

I'd like to thank Susan Thomson and Anjan Sundaram for their poignant and chilling portraits of contemporary Rwanda.

I'm grateful to author Lara Santoro, who convinced me that my own story was worth telling.

I want to thank the *Globe and Mail*'s Africa correspondent Geoffrey York, one of the finest journalists I've ever had the privilege of working with, for tackling complex issues that take months to investigate.

I am indebted to the whistleblowers from the ICTR for their extraordinary leap of faith.

To Faustin Twagiramungu, Jean-Marie Ndagijimana and Joseph Matata, who have fought to resist tyranny and reconcile Rwandans, I appreciate their early assistance in helping me find credible witnesses.

I wish to acknowledge the authors Barrie Collins and Robin Philpot for their research on the RPF's invasion war and its propaganda campaigns prior to and after the genocide.

I'd like to thank ICTR defense lawyers Peter Erlinder and Christopher Black for providing journalists and Rwanda observers with access to important evidence from ICTR trials.

Finally, I'd like to thank my parents for raising me to value freedom and believe that anything is possible. To my children, thank you for your fortitude and patience. You are wonderful human beings and I owe you my happiness. And to their father, who gave me strength and clarity when I most needed it, I will forever be grateful.

NOTES

Throughout the notes, "ICTR top secret summary report" refers to the following: *General Report on the Special Investigations Concerning the Crimes Committed by the Rwandan Patriotic Army (RPA) during 1994*. Report submitted October 1, 2003, to Hassan Bubacar Jallow, ICTR Prosecutor, and Melanie Werret, Chief of Prosecutions.

Another ICTR top secret report, "H's case," refers to: *Special Case of Investigation: H's case*. Report submitted on May 5, 2005, to Hassan Bubacar Jallow, ICTR prosecutor and Majola Bongani, deputy ICTR prosecutor.

Introduction: Against the Grain

1. ICTR top secret summary report.
2. *Summary of Conclusions between the Government of Rwanda and the International Criminal Tribunal for Rwanda*. Document from US Ambassador for War Crimes Pierre Prosper through US embassy, signed by Ambassador Margaret McMillion.
3. Interview with former High Command soldier who was part of a DMI killing unit.

Chapter 1. Kagame's Inner Station

1. Interview with Elise, a Hutu refugee who survived attacks by Kagame's forces in Congo.
2. Alex de Waal, "No Bloodless Miracle," *Guardian*, November 15, 1996; Philip Gourevitch, "The Return," *New Yorker*, January 1997; Philip Gourevitch, "Continental Shift," *New Yorker*, August 1997.
3. Nicholas Stockton, *Rwanda: Rights and Racism*. Oxfam, Oxford, December 12, 1996; UNHCR spokeswoman Melia Sunjic, *Relief Web*, November 22, 1996.
4. Interviews with Hutu refugees, victims' families, displaced Congolese and humanitarian staff.
5. MSF, *Forced Flight: A Brutal Strategy of Elimination in Eastern Zaire*, report, May 16, 1997.
6. Interview with Jean-Bosco, Rwandan orphan in Congo.
7. Interview with Eugène, Rwandan orphan in Congo.
8. Interview with Rwandan teenage refugee in Congo.
9. Interviews with Nyana and other local aid volunteers.
10. Interviews with former Rwandan intelligence staff, Rwandan refugees and Congolese aid workers.
11. Interview with Rwandan refugee shot in backside.
12. Stephen Smith, "190,00 Hutu Refugees Are Missing in Zaire—MSF accuses," *Libération*, May 20, 1997 (translated from the French for MSF's report *Forced Flight*, cited above).
13. Interview with former Rwandan DMI soldier tasked with killing in Congo.
14. Howard W. French, "Hutu Refugees Trapped in Zaire between Tutsi and the Crocodiles," *New York Times*, March 13, 1997; James C. McKinley Jr., "Machetes, Axes and Rebel Guns: Refugees Tell of Attacks in Zaire," *New York Times*, April 30, 1997; James C. McKinley Jr., "Zaire Refugees Bear Signs of Rebel Atrocities," *New York Times*, May 2, 1997.
15. Marek Enterprise, "Zaire Watch News Briefs 16 Apr 1997," Reliefweb.int, April 16, 1997.
16. Richard C. Morais, "Friends in High Places," Forbes.com, August 10, 1998.
17. In later years, McKinney would become a staunch critic of the US backing of the Kabila–Kagame Congo and provided scathing testimony in US congressional hearings.
18. AMF investor promotion video.
19. Interview with South African mining market analyst, who tracked AFDL advance.
20. Robert Block, "As Zaire's War Wages, Foreign Businesses Scramble for Inroads," *Wall Street Journal*, April 14, 1997; "U.S. Firm Seek Deal in Central Africa," *Wall Street Journal*, October 14, 1997.
21. The *New York Times* reported in 1988: "No other private corporation in modern history has had closer ties to the Federal Government than Bechtel. In the Reagan Administration alone, the engineering

services company has supplied a secretary of state (George P. Shultz), a defense secretary (Caspar W. Weinberger) and a deputy secretary of energy (W. Kenneth Davis)." Bechtel is "one of the best connected, most powerful and most secretive companies in the world," the UK's *Independent* reported. "For a top job at Bechtel, former military personnel, ex-diplomats and retired politicians need apply," a former employee, who asked not to be identified, said. "Bechtel's ties with the American intelligence service, through its network of associates, has earned it the nickname 'the working arm of the CIA' and spawned a thousand conspiracy theories. 'Some say the firm is a "shadow government",' says one website, which goes on to claim that former Bechtel officers are part of a US cult." The mega company profited greatly from the war in Iraq, and received a request to bid on the reconstruction of Iraq even before the US invasion began.

22. Marc Pilisuk and Michael N. Nagler, eds., *Peace Movements Worldwide* (Santa Barbara, CA: Praeger, 2010).
23. Interview with Congo's finance minister.
24. Branchaud was from the 12e Régiment Blindé du Canada, a well-known armoured regiment. After his work in reconnaissance as Canadian liaison officer in Kinshasa, he became a decorated officer. In the 1980s, he had joined the British army and served in Operation Desert Storm. In 2003, he was in the Middle East, as part of Operation Telic, the second invasion of Iraq. He then went back to Africa to work as Canada's military attaché in Nairobi, before heading to Libya during the civil war, then on to Mali to help the French secure the Bamako airport from Islamist fighters. In 2015, Lieutenant-Colonel Branchaud worked with J5 Plans Africa, directing strategic plans and policy at Canadian Joint Operations Command Headquarters. From Royal Canadian Hussars Association (armoured reconnaissance regiment of the Primary Reserve in the Canadian Forces) Spring 2015 newsletter.

Chapter 2. The Rationale for War

1. Amnesty International, *Ending the Silence*, September 1997.
2. Hutu victims from northwestern Rwanda, former RPF soldiers, officers; Spanish indictment issued on February 6, 2008, by High Court Judge Fernando Andreu Merelles charging 40 current or former high-ranking Rwandan military officials with serious crimes, including genocide, crimes against humanity, war crimes and terrorism, committed over a period of 12 years, from 1990 to 2002, against the civilian population and primarily against members of the Hutu ethnic group.
3. Human Rights Watch, "Civilian Killings and Impunity in Congo," *Human Rights Watch/Africa and FIDH* 9, no. 5 (October 1997).
4. Nik Gowing, *Dispatches from Disaster Zones*, a study for the UN's Office for the Coordination of Humanitarian Affairs (OCHA). London: May 1998.
5. Human Rights Watch, *What Kabila Is Hiding*, October 31, 1997.
6. Gowing, *Dispatches*.
7. Ibid.
8. Ibid.
9. Handwritten account from witness in the Zairean forest, given to a priest who passed on a copy to me; also, Filip Reyntjens, *The Great African War: Congo and Regional Geopolitics 1996–2006* (Cambridge: Cambridge University Press, 2010).
10. Human Rights Watch, *What Kabila Is Hiding*.
11. Gowing, *Dispatches*.
12. Ibid.
13. Interview with Stephen Smith, former journalist with *Libération*.
14. Interview with Gregory Stanton.
15. These images were photogrammetry that consisted of maps and scale drawings from aerial photographs.
16. Nicholas Stockton, *Rwanda: Rights and Racism*. Oxfam, Oxford, December 12, 1996.
17. Written notes of interview with Danish researcher Phil Clark.
18. Presentation to the MNF Eastern Zaire Steering Group Meeting, December 13, 1996.

19. The killings of Hutu refugees in Congo by Rwandan-led AFDL forces were documented by UN aid workers in October, Amnesty International in November, and the French newspapers *Libération* and *Le Monde* in early December 1996, before Baril released his report to the UN.
20. Interview with Marius Bujold.
21. European Community Humanitarian Office, "Eastern Zaire: Refugees in a Desperate Plight," *ECHOnews* 14 (March 1997), http://aei.pitt.edu/83397/1/14.pdf.
22. Ibid.
23. Colum Lynch, "US Agents Were Seen with Rebels in Zaire: Active Participation Is Alleged in Military Overthrow of Mobutu," *Boston Globe*, October 8, 1997.
24. Lynne Duke, "US Military Role in Rwanda Greater Than Disclosed," *Washington Post*, August 16, 1997.
25. Howard French, "Kagame's Hidden War in the Congo" *New York Review of Books*, review September 24, 2009.
26. Gowing, *Dispatches*, citing *The International Response to Conflict and Genocide: Lessons from the Rwanda Experience by the Committee of Emergency Asssistance to Rwanda* (Danish Foreign Ministry, 1996).
27. Associated Press, "Rwandan Soldiers Attack Refugee Camp in Zaire," *Reliefweb.int*, October 27, 1996.
28. Extract from MSF report; and Amnesty International, "AFDL Alleged to Have Massacred More than 300 Hutu Refugees," November 26, 1996.
29. "Several Mass Graves Containing Bodies of Hutus Discovered in Eastern Zaire," *Le Monde*, December 8, 9, 1996; Florence Aubenas, "Zaire: Mass Graves and Dying Refugees in the Virunga Forest," *Libération*, December 7, 9, 1996.
30. Interview with Gregory Stanton.
31. Tom Masland, "Losing Africa Yet Again," *Newsweek*, October 5, 1998.

Chapter 3. Rwanda Digs In

1. Interview with former RPF soldier Théogène Murwanashyaka.
2. Pole Institute (Institut Interculturel dans la Région des Grands Lacs), *Regards Croisés*, Goma, report no. 15, December 1, 2005.
3. Amnesty International, *Democratic Republic of Congo: "Our Brothers Who Help Kill Us": Economic Exploitation and Human Rights Abuses in the East*, report, March 31, 2003, https://www.amnesty.org/en/documents/afr62/010/2003/en/.
4. UN Security Council Report of the Panel of Experts on the Illegal Exploitation of Natural Resources and Other Forms of Wealth of the Democratic Republic of Congo, 2000.
5. UN Security Council Report of the Panel of Experts on the Illegal Exploitation of Natural Resources and Other Forms of Wealth of the Democratic Republic of Congo, 2001.
6. Interview with Theogene Rudasingwa, former head of RPF Secretariat.
7. Amnesty International, *Democratic Republic of Congo*.
8. UN Security Council Report of the Panel of Experts on the Illegal Exploitation of Natural Resources and Other Forms of Wealth of the Democratic Republic of Congo, 2002.
9. Ibid.
10. Amnesty International, *Democratic Republic of Congo*.
11. Interview with human rights lawyer Luc Côté.
12. Interviews with UN staffers at Kibeho.
13. Judi Rever, "Congo Butchery Like Rwandan Genocide," AFP, August 28, 2010.
14. UN Office of the High Commissioner, *DRC: Mapping Human Rights Violations 1993–2003*, Geneva, August 31, 2010.
15. Interview with José Pablo Baraybar.

Chapter 4: Going for Broke

1. The Spanish indictment alleges that RPF intelligence ordered the killings of a Spanish priest in Byumba in 1994, four Spanish priests in Congo in 1996, three Spanish nationals in Ruhengeri, Rwanda, in 1997 and another Spanish priest in Gitarama, Rwanda, in 2000.
2. Human Rights Watch, *Leave None to Tell the Story: Genocide in Rwanda* (New York: Human Rights Watch, 1999).
3. Interviews with former RPF soldiers and officers.
4. Interview with Luc Marchal.
5. ICTR documents, top secret reports, SIU summary and H's case.
6. ICTR testimony R000281.
7. Interviews with former RPF intelligence officers.
8. ICTR documents, top secret reports, SIU summary and H's case.
9. André Guichaoua, *Butare the Rebel Prefecture*, submitted to the ICTR, 2004.
10. Interviews with former RPF soldiers and officers.
11. Interview with former senior counsel at the Office of the Prosecutor of the ICTR.
12. Testimony of former RPF soldiers to Bruguière inquiry and to ICTR Special Investigations Unit.

Chapter 5. The Deep Structures of RPF Violence

1. In Uganda, Kagame was nicknamed "Pilato," which was short for Pontius Pilate, the biblical figure responsible for the crucifixion of Christ. As head of Ugandan intelligence, Kagame is said to have inflicted brutal torture on his enemies, according to former RPF intelligence officials I've interviewed and the book *Noires Fureurs, Blancs Menteurs* by Pierre Péan.
2. ICTR documents and interviews.
3. Interviews with former DMI soldiers, officer; ICTR top secret summary report, pages 22–27.
4. ICTR SIU findings: Witnesses told investigators that DMI intelligence officers and staff carried out massacres at the following sites, in some cases with the help of soldiers: Gabiro, Kami, Masaka, Giti, Nyamirambo, Kidaho, Butaro, Kirambo, Ruhengeri City, Kinihira, Nyungwe Forest, Kabutare, Butare Arboretum, Save, Gikomero, Ndera, Runda, Musambira City, Muhura-Byumba City.
5. ICTR top secret summary report, page 25. A few other technicians were cited as having worked at roadblocks, including Lieutenants Vianney and Hitimana.
6. Interview with Théogène Murwanashyaka, former soldier active in Byumba and Kigali.
7. Former soldier in RPF intelligence.
8. DMI agents put kerosene in ears to poison people and kill them. They believe it causes brain damage, and causes victims to lose speech and hearing, before they die.
9. Interview with former DMI official.
10. ICTR top secret summary report.

Chapter 6. Getting Away with Mass Murder at the Byumba Stadium

1. Interview with Théogène Murwanashyaka. The RPF'S High Command unit was made up of bodyguards for Kagame. Many High Command soldiers were used in special operations.
2. Jack Fischel, professor emeritus of history at Millersville University, Millersville, PA, "Holocaust, Rwandan genocide compared," lecture April 3, 2006 http://lancasteronline.com/news/holocaust-rwandan-genocide-compared/article_26dd84e9-7ac0-5c7d-8061-ae459fd0ad8c.html; "Rwanda and Genocide of the 20th Century," Givelli Mikel, Washington State University, Digital History Projects, essay published on August 28, 2014.
3. Interview with former RPF Military Police soldier.
4. Interviews with former investigator, ICTR Special Investigations Unit.
5. Interview with former High Command soldier; André Guichaoua, *From War to Genocide: Criminal Politics in Rwanda*, 1990–1994 (Madison: University of Wisconson Press, 2015).
6. Interview with former Kagame military escort (1).

7. ICTR top secret summary report, page 6.

8. Ibid., page 7.

9. Ibid.

10. Interview with former Kagame military escort (2).

11. Interview with Major Alphonse Furuma, RPF founder. In early 1991, only a few months after RPA troops first invaded Rwanda, he was tried for treason in a military court for criticizing Kagame's scorched-earth policies. He narrowly escaped being executed. At the end of the trial, Kagame said: "Let the fool go." Furuma said Kagame was not ready, at that time, to kill him. "At that point, he wasn't quite what he would later become," Furuma said. After the trial, Furuma was demoted and deployed to field logistics, and he shut his mouth for the rest of the invasion war. Not only did Kagame not tolerate dissent within the RPF or the RPA, it was almost impossible to escape to a neighboring country without being tracked down and killed. Very few managed to flee and live freely and safely. By 1999–2000, when Uganda and Rwanda began to fight each other in Congo, it became safer for RPF dissidents to seek asylum in Uganda.

12. Former ICTR prosecutor Del Ponte has written, in *Madame Prosecutor: Confrontations with Humanity's Worst Criminals and the Culture of Impunity*, that Kagame had command responsibility for the entire RPF in 1994. Former officers and soldiers of the RPA, including ex–DMI staff, have confirmed that it was not possible to challenge Kagame's authority or orders. If anyone did, they were eliminated.

Chapter 7. Kagame's Roving Death Squads

1. Interview with Rwandan Hutu refugee, victim at Karambi Trading Center (1).

2. Statement by refugee submitted to NGO providing legal aid to refugees.

3. Interview with Hutu refugee, victim at Karambi Trading Center (2).

4. Interview with former RPA intelligence officer.

5. Interview with Joseph Matata, director of CLIIR, a Belgian-based Rwandan human rights organization.

6. The mass graves Matata visited were in Muhazi, Kayonza and Kabarondo.

7. James Karuhanga, "United Nations, African Union praise Nyamvumba's 'dedication' at UNAMID," *The New Times*, June 5, 2013.

8. Interviews with former officers and soldiers either involved in operations and/or with knowledge thereof.

9. Interview with Rwandan refugee who gathered livestock for Nyamvumba's death squad.

10. Scott Baldauf, "Former Rwandan Army Chief Shot in South Africa: Was It an Assassination Attempt?" *Christian Science Monitor*, June 20, 2010.

11. The three intelligence staff from the Training Wing who joined Nyamvumba in these operations after the plane was shot down were Dan Munyuza, Rwakabi Kakira and Kalemara.

12. Rwanda's last ruling king was Kigeli V Ndahindurwa, who presided over the country until 1961 and the overthrow of the monarchy. He died in 2016 in the United States, at the age of eighty.

13. Interview with former intelligence staffer who received daily updates of operations.

14. Interview with a soldier in one of Kazura's killing units.

15. Interview with junior officer present during operations in Kibungo.

16. Interview with officer and former colleague of Kazura, deployed in Rwanteru.

17. Many Rwandan men were put in containers in trucks and died en route. They died of suffocation from the exhaust, sources confirmed.

18. Interview with former SIU investigator.

19. ICTR testimony of intelligence staff from the Training Wing. Indexed page R000229.

20. ICTR testimony of intelligence staff from DMI. Indexed pages R000239, R000240.

21. The witness also participated in massacring Hutus at Kibeho, and said those responsible for planning that operation were Fred Ibingira, Colonel Nyamvumba, Dan Munyuza, and Emmanuel Gasana. Kayumba Nyamwasa, Jack Nziza and Jackson Rwahama joined their team two days into the massacres, at which time survivors were brought to Camp Huye, where they were promised protection

but killed with ropes and hammers. The bodies of Hutus killed at Kibeho and then at Camp Huye were also transported to Nyungwe and burned.

22. At the end of August 1994, the UNHCR estimated that there were 2.1 million Rwandan refugees in 35 camps in neighboring countries. Around Goma, the capital of Zaire's North Kivu province, five huge camps held at least 850,000 people. To the south, around Bukavi and Uviva, thirty camps held about 650,000 people. A further 350,000 refugees were located in nine camps in Burundi, and another 570,000 in eight camps in Tanzania.

23. The communes visited by Gersony's team amounted to 28 percent of the country.

24. US State Department cable sent to US ambassador at UN, embassies in Great Lakes.

25. See cable from Shaharyar Khan of UNAMIR in Kigali to United Nations leaders in New York, October 14, 1994: http://www.rwandadocumentsproject.net/gsdl/collect/mil1docs/index/assoc/HASHc166/6f755cde.dir/doc84106.PDF.

26. Khan went on to write that he did not believe the killings were part of a "pre-ordained, systematic massacre ordered from the top" but admitted that the UN was now "engaged in a damage limitation exercise." And two former officials of Kagame's post-genocide government who took part in discussions of Gersony's findings told me that they were asked by Kofi Annan, who went on to become secretary-general of the UN but at the time was the UN peacekeeping chief, to reject Gersony's report.

27. Raymond Bonner, "UN Stops Returning Rwandan Refugees," New York Times, September 28, 1994, http://www.nytimes.com/1994/09/28/world/un-stops-returning-rwandan-refugees.html.

28. Gérard Prunier, Africa's World War (New York: Oxford University Press, 2008), page 31.

29. Human Rights Watch, Leave None to Tell the Story: Genocide in Rwanda (New York: Human Rights Watch, 1999), page 1114.

30. The complete report can be found here: https://www.hrw.org/reports/1999/rwanda/.

31. Human Rights Watch, "Rwanda: A New Catastrophe?" Human Rights Watch/Africa 6, no. 12 (December 1994), https://www.hrw.org/reports/pdfs/r/rwanda/rwanda94d.pdf.

32. Interview with Manzi Mutuyimana, a Hutu refugee in exile.

33. ICTR top secret summary report, page 13.

34. Ibid., page 12.

35. Refugees International, excerpts from UNHCR Ngara Protection Report, May 17, 1994.

36. Donatella Lorch, "Thousands of Rwanda Dead Wash Down to Lake Victoria," NYTimes.com, May 21, 1994, https://partners.nytimes.com/library/world/africa/052194rwanda-genocide.html.

37. David Lamb, "Rwandan Dead Glut the Waters of Lake Victoria," Los Angeles Times, May 29, 1994, http://articles.latimes.com/1994-05-29/news/mn-63667_1_lake-victoria.

38. Richard Dowden, "Sweet Sour Stench of Death Fills Rwanda," Independent (London), May 6, 1994, http://www.independent.co.uk/news/world/sweet-sour-stench-of-death-fills-rwanda-richard-dowden-in-rusumo-finds-only-flies-goats-and-chickens-1434162.html.

Chapter 8. The Tutsi Fifth Column

1. Straus teaches at the University of Wisconsin–Madison, and is the author of The Order of Genocide: Race, Power and War in Rwanda. The book's findings are largely based on interviews with Rwandan prisoners.

2. Multiple interviews with former soldiers, intelligence agents and cadres.

3. ICTR top secret report, H's case, page 44.

4. ICTR testimony of soldier from 3rd Battalion, indexed page R0000281.

5. ICTR testimony of civilian who joined RPF in Byumba, indexed page R000174.

6. ICTR top secret summary report, page 23.

7. ICTR testimony from RPF civilian cadre working in refugee camp, indexed page R0000130.

8. Top secret report on Giti, Rutare: testimony of former DMI officer, page 40.

9. Interview with Abdallah Akishuli, a former RPF civilian cadre.

10. Former RPF Secretariat chairman Theogene Rudasingwa told me in an interview in 2016 that he never authorized the cadres to commit crimes. Now a dissident in exile, Rudasingwa admits, however, that

cadres participated in DMI killing schemes and that some of his colleagues at the RPF Secretariat were aware of, and authorized, these murders.

11. By July, the RPF officer in charge of the area was Major John Zigira, who had previously been a political commissar at the Training Wing, according to ICTR witness.

12. ICTR testimony of intelligence staff from Training Wing, indexed page R0000230.

13. Interview with Théogène Murwanashyaka, former soldier stationed in Byumba and Kigali.

14. Human Rights Watch, "April 1994: The Month That Would Not End," 1999 https://www.hrw.org/reports/1999/rwanda/Geno4-7-02.htm: Professor Alan Kuperman's doctoral research on the RPF revealed that "during the three years prior to its invasion, the RPF managed to create at least 36 clandestine cells in Rwanda's central and southern prefectures of Kigali, Butare, and Gitarama—the ones most strongly opposed to Habyarimana because of his favoring his own northwestern region. And by the time the Arusha accords were signed in August 1993, the rebels had infiltrated 146 supporters into Kigali alone."

15. Interview with Pierre, who was part of DMI mobile unit in Rutare, Giti and Kabungo.

16. Interview with Pierre, confirmed by Abdallah.

17. Jean-Marie Ndagijimana, "Deus Kagiraneza, ancien officier du FPR: 'les jeunes militaires tutsi francophones étaient executes sous le moindre prétexte,'" *La Tribune Franco Rwandaise* (blog), July 6, 2007, http://www.france-rwanda.info/article-23169842.html.

18. ICTR top secret summary report, pages 15–17.

19. ICTR testimony from intelligence staff from Training Wing, indexed page R0000227.

20. From interviews with former intelligence staff. The Nyumbakumi operates as an unofficial "sub cell" that is part of a larger, highly organized administrative structure that predates colonial times and has long been used to exert authority over Rwandan citizens.

Chapter 9. Spinning Lies from Truth

1. Interview with Clément, a student from Giti.

2. Ibid.

3. ICTR top secret summary report, page 6.

4. Ibid., page 5.

5. The top secret summary document stated a sergeant named Ndekewe, an aide-de-camp to the Military Police, was giving orders. "The soldiers gathered the population, mostly women and children, and Sgt Ndekewe gave the order to shoot all of them. Most of those who fled into the woods were located and shot by the soldiers. The soldiers would kill everybody in their path and on their return, bury the bodies."

6. ICTR top secret summary report, ICTR testimony from former DMI officer in Giti.

7. The witness said Nyamwasa ordered these grisly operations. Others who had roles in directing the violence were Jean Jacques Mupenzi, Habas Musonera and Joseph Nzabamwita. Mupenzi would later move up in rank and become head of Special Intelligence in the Gendarmerie. Nzabamwita became head of DMI's Criminal Investigations and Prosecution.

8. A corporal in charge of the burial teams was named Emmanuel Nkuranga.

9. ICTR witness testimony.

10. Interview with former child soldier who was part of DMI's rotating units in Giti.

11. Interview with Pierre, DMI member in Giti. The officer was part of a core team that entered Rutare and Giti with the 21st Battalion led by Martin Nzaramba. Nyamwasa was there from the beginning, staying with colleagues in a zinc corrugated shack in Rutare, not far from the Centre de Négoce, a trading center behind a series of acacia trees. A banana plantation was about 150 meters away. The officer said Nyamwasa was the commanding officer of operations in Rutare, Giti and Kinyami and that, under his direction, Lieutenant Mupenzi gave his soldiers direct orders to kill Father Gaspard Mudashimwa and other Hutu clergy at the Rwesero Seminary. "Nothing could be done without him ordering it," he said of Nyamwasa. "But Kayumba was in touch with Kagame all the time."

12. Human Rights Watch, *Leave None to Tell the Story: Genocide in Rwanda* (New York: Human Rights Watch, 1999).

Chapter 10. Scenes from a Counterinsurgency

1. As reported earlier in the book, and based on interviews with former RPF soldiers, officers and founder Theogene Rudasingwa.
2. Rwanda has long been divided along ethnic and regional lines. A previous Hutu-led government under President Grégoire Kayibanda was accused of protecting the political and economic interests of Hutus from southern Rwanda.
3. Interview with member of the Rwanda National Congress, a Rwandan opposition group in exile.
4. Interview with Paul, a Rwandan Hutu from Gisenyi.
5. Ibid.
6. "Rwanda: plusieurs militaires ex-FAR ont été tués, portés disparus, emprisonnés sans enquêtes et sans dossiers judiciaires et souvent victimes de machinations," CLIIR.org–Rwanda (website), April 14, 1999, http://www.cliir.org/detail/le-sort-des-ex-far-integres-dans-lapr.html.
7. Interview with Jérôme, a Hutu from Ruhengeri.
8. Interview with Guillaume Murere, a Rwandan Canadian.
9. Interview with Jérôme, a Rwandan in Europe.
10. Interview with a former RPF Gendarmerie officer based in northwestern Rwanda during the counterinsurgency.
11. Interview with Neza, a resident adjacent to the RPA military base Mukamira.
12. Amnesty International, "Rwanda: 'The Dead Can No Longer Be Counted,'" press release, December 19, 1997.
13. Interview with Brigitte Tuyishime, a Hutu from Gisenyi.
14. Amnesty International released a first report, "Rwanda: Ending the Silence," in September 1997; it followed with an updated report, "Rwanda: Civilians Trapped in Armed Conflict," in December 1997, https://www.amnesty.org/download/Documents/156000/afr470431997en.pdf.
15. The caves in the commune of Kanama were known locally as Nyakimana and Nyakiliba.
16. Centre de Lutte contre l'Impunité et l'Injustice au Rwanda, "L'Armée Rwandaise a massacré, dans la grotte de Nyakimana, plus de 8000 habitants de quatre secteurs de la commune Kanama (Gisenyi) entre les 24 et 27 octobre 1997," press release, November 22, 1997, http://jambonews.net/wp-content/uploads/2010/10/massacres-nyakinama-Kanama-par-kagame.pdf.
17. Interview with Serge, soldier with DMI team that attacked civilians in Kanama caves.
18. Amnesty International, "Rwanda: Civilians Trapped," pages 8–10.
19. Report on the Mudende Camp Massacre and Kanama Cave Stand-Off by David J. Scheffer, US Ambassador at Large for War Crimes Issues.
20. James C. McKinley Jr., "Machete Returns to Rwanda, Rekindling a Genocidal War," *New York Times*, December 15, 1997, http://www.nytimes.com/1997/12/15/world/machete-returns-to-rwanda-rekindling-a-genocidal-war.html.
21. Assassinations of Hutu politicians, teachers and civil society members in Rushashi and neighboring Tare at the beginning of the counterinsurgency were cleverly calculated and replicated in other communes. Apart from protests from a few vocal Rwandan human rights activists, there was next to no international opprobrium over these schemes.
22. Extensive interviews with family and friends of targets and victims in Rushashi.
23. Among the victims in Rushashi and Tare were the public prosecutor, Floribert Habinshuti, also a Hutu, along with his wife and two children, in addition to a dozen other individuals who were heading home after attending the ordination of a priest, and a beloved school principal named Laurent Bwankakeye who was murdered along a road with three of his colleagues. "Massacre de dizaines de civils par l'APR qui l'attribue aux 'infiltrés,'" CLIIR.org–Rwanda (website), July 20, 1998, http://www.cliir.org/detail/com381998-larmee-patriotique-rwandaise-massacre-plusieurs-dizaines-de-civils-non-armes-et-attrib.html.
24. One of the RPF's most brazen attacks against innocent people occurred during the World Cup soccer finals in 1998 as several hundred fans were watching a game at a popular bar, Pensez-Y, in Tare. Interviews with two former DMI members, one of whom was on-site during the operation, revealed how two platoons of soldiers from the RPA's 7th Brigade descended on the bar. The soldiers threw

grenades and sprayed the premises with machine-gun fire, before dousing the bar with gasoline and setting it ablaze with civilians inside—teachers, students, farmers and merchants. Kigali accused Hutu insurgents of attacking the bar. But residents of Tare were familiar with the violence that authorities regularly engaged in. "It was barbaric," said an intelligence staffer who brought DMI vehicles to the bar and watched the building go up in flames, as people screamed and clamored to escape and died. "This was a DMI operation ordered by Karenzi Karake," the staffer said. "There was nothing we could do. If we raised objections or complained about the level of depravity, we risked being assassinated."

25. Gaspard Musabyimana, "Épuration ethnique de la magistrature rwandaise," Musabyimana.net (website), January 28, 2008, http://www.musabyimana.net/20080128-epuration-ethnique-de-la-magistrature-rwanadaise/.

26. Correspondence between Spanish authorities and the Office of the UN High Commissioner for Human Rights. The requests were made by Spain to gather evidence for Judge Fernando Andreu Merelles' 2008 indictment against 40 Rwandan military officials.

27. Interview with Jordi Palou-Loverdos, lawyer who represented families of Spanish, Rwandan and Congolese victims in Spanish indictment against Rwandan military officials.

28. Interview with former Gendarmerie officer.

29. Interview with Nitin Mahdav, US aid worker who survived attack in Rwanda.

30. Correspondence between Spanish officials and UN Human Rights Commission.

31. According to the ICTR's top secret summary report, a witness said RPF soldiers had occupied a Catholic school in Ruhengeri, after which twenty corpses had been found in a latrine pit. They were believed to be victims of the army. Pinard was killed after he'd got access to the school and discovered the bodies. Another priest who was in charge of retrieving the bodies from the latrine pit for proper burial was also killed, according to the witness.

32. Interview with witness to murder of Guy Pinard in Ruhengeri in 1997.

33. The witness gave a copy of his statement addressed to the Canadian High Commission in Nairobi to the Globe and Mail. Roger Tessier told the newspaper that he knew the witness well and believed he was credible.

34. Geoffrey York and Judi Rever, "Families of Two Canadian Priests Killed in Rwanda Still Wait for Justice," Globe and Mail, November 14, 2014: http://www.theglobeandmail.com/news/world/families-of-two-canadian-priests-killed-in-rwanda-still-wait-for-justice/article21599090/.

35. As the Quebec head of the Society of Missionaries of Africa in 1997, Richard Dandenault was in contact with Guy Pinard's family after the murder and sought answers from Canadian authorities.

36. A UN military observer report, based on witness testimony, stated that Simard had written a letter about the problems he was having with the RPA, and that this letter, along with the cassettes exposing RPA crimes, was seized on the night of his death. An intelligence official who worked with DMI at the time confirmed to me that the RPA got access to the letter and cassettes.

37. Two-part (1994/1995) UN military observer report written by Canadian Major Tim Isberg, and UN civilian police report written by C.S.M. Brew in November 1994.

38. Interviews with satellite experts.

39. Other Westerners who have consistently framed Kagame and the RPF in a positive light include Philip Gourevitch, a writer for the New Yorker; Bernard Kouchner, France's former foreign minister; Rick Warren, a US evangelical pastor; Phil Clark, a London-based academic who has written on transitional justice; William Schabas, a Canadian professor and president of the International Association of Genocide Scholars; and Linda Melvern, a British journalist.

Chapter 11. An Illegal Deal

1. ICTR top secret summary report, pages 1–4.

2. Carla Del Ponte, Madame Prosecutor: Confrontations with Humanity's Worst Criminals and the Culture of Impunity, a memoir, co-authored with Chuck Sudetic (New York: Other Press, 2009); Lars Waldorf, "A Mere Pretense of Justice: Complementarity, Sham Trials and Victor's Justice at the Rwanda Tribunal," Fordham International Law Journal, 2011; interview with ICTR lawyer at OTP.

3. Interview with British judge Douglas Marks Moore.
4. Note written by SIU investigator.
5. Interview with former lawyer at ICTR's Office of the Prosecutor.
6. Interview with Théogène Murwanashyaka.
7. ICTR top secret summary report, page 30.
8. Summary of Conclusions between the Government of Rwanda and the International Criminal Tribunal for Rwanda, May 21, 2003; Agreement between US Ambassador for War Crimes Pierre Prosper and Rwanda's General Prosecutor to the Supreme Court Gerald Gahima; document signed by US Ambassador to Rwanda Margaret McMillion.
9. Del Ponte, *Madame Prosecutor.*
10. Former ICTR lawyer.
11. Former ICTR lawyer at OTP.

Chapter 12. The Consequences of Betrayal

1. Interview with Anaïs, whose brother Richard Shéja was killed in Gakurazo, Gitarama.
2. Interview with Espérance, whose son Richard Shéja was killed in Gakurazo, Gitarama.
3. Interview with Emmanuel Dukuzemungu, sole survivor among Rwandan clergy targeted in Gakurazo massacre.
4. Interview with former ICTR official.
5. They included, among others, Lieutenant Colonel Fred Ibingira, commander of the 157th Battalion, Major Gumisiriza, battalion IO, Major John Ntibesigwa, Sergeant Emmanuel Ruzigana, Sergeant Jimmy Muyango Mwesige, and Sam Bigabiro from the 101st Battalion.
6. Former ICTR official.
7. Kenneth Roth, Executive Director, Human Rights Watch, "Letter to ICTR Chief Prosecutor Hassan Jallow in Response to His Letter on the Prosecution of RPF Crimes," Human Rights Watch website, August 14, 2009: https://www.hrw.org/news/2009/08/14/letter-ictr-chief-prosecutor-hassan-jallow-response-his-letter-prosecution-rpf.
8. Interviews I conducted in Congo.
9. Interviews with former Rwandan prime minister Faustin Twagiramungu, a former inmate at Gitarama prison, Joseph Matata, and ex–RPF members.
10. The Gitarama lists of eighteen thousand people who disappeared under RPF occupation from June 1994 onward.
11. ICTR top secret summary report, page 11.

Chapter 13. The Assassination of Habyarimana

1. Michael Andrew Hourigan submitted his affidavit to the ICTR in November 2006 to put on record the evidence he had collected and how it was dealt with. The affidavit was accessed by defense lawyers at the tribunal.
2. Ann Garrison, "Legacies: Michael Hourigan and the ICTR," Ann Garrison website, December 9, 2013, http://www.anngarrison.com/audio/2013/12/09/477/Legacies-Michael-Hourigan-and-the-ICTR.
3. Michelle Zilio and Geoffrey York, "Kagame Government Blocked Criminal Probe, Former Chief Prosecutor Says," *Globe and Mail,* October 26, 2016.
4. The investigators independently collected their own body of evidence, based on testimony from eight informants. Their investigation, while differing in some details, matches the general conclusions reached three years later by French investigators. The French report can be viewed here: http://www. olny.nl/RWANDA/Lu_Pour_Vous/Dossier_Special_Habyarimana/Rapport_Bruguiere.pdf.
5. The officers in attendance were Colonel Kayumba Nyamwasa, Colonel Ndugute, Colonel Sam Kaka, Lieutenant Colonel James Kabarebe and Major Jack Nziza, according to testimony.
6. The team of commandos named in the Bruguière report were Eric Hakizimana, Frank Nziza, Jean Bosco Ndayisaba, Didier Mazimpaka and Patiano Ntambara.

7. Bruguière obtained confirmation from Russia's military that the two missile launchers found in Masaka were part of a batch of weapons sold from the Soviet Union to Uganda.

8. Interview with Filip Reyntjens, author of *Political Governance in Post-Genocide Rwanda*, and other books.

9. Reyntjens said that his student contacted someone at the barracks to help him locate the receipt, then was caught. The academic believes his student was set up.

10. French arrest warrants issued against Rwandan officials: Tribunal de grande instance Paris, Delivrance de mandats d'arrêt internationaux par le Juge Jean-Louis Bruguière, November 17, 2006.

11. Pierre Péan, *Le Monde Selon K.* (Paris: Fayard, 2009), page 217.

12. Interview with an individual assisting the French probe into Habyarimana's assassination.

13. The cable can be read here: https://wikileaks.org/plusd/cables/09PARIS1349_a.html.

14. Chris McGreal, "Top Rwandan Aide Chooses French Terror Trial," *Guardian*, November 10, 2008, https://www.theguardian.com/world/2008/nov/10/rwanda-congo-kabuye.

15. Pierre Péan, *Le Monde Selon K.*

16. Interview with Luc Marchal, former UNAMIR commander in Kigali.

17. Jean Pascal Serre, *Rapport Complementaire en Acoustique, Cour d'Appel de Paris, Tribunal de Grande Instance de Paris*, No d'Instruction 2272/00/13 & 1341. No de Parquet 9729523030 Procédure Criminelle, 3 janvier 2012. The report did not explain why investigators used booster rockets, which are shorter burning rockets and are unguided, rather than guided missiles. The investigators also admitted that mitigating factors such as "the effect of noise absorption by the soil or by the topology of the land, the effect of any other noise present at the time, and also of the ambient noise level when the tests were conducted, cannot be assessed with certainty." Barrie Collins, "Shooting Down the Official 'Truth' about Rwanda," *Spiked* (website), March 15, 2012, http://www.spiked-online.com/spikedplus/article/12233#.V5jVya5VC4s.

18. Pierre Péan, "J'ai assisté à la preparation de l'attentat qui a déclenché le genocide," *Marianne,* 31 mars, 2014.

19. Interview with Jean Marie Micombero, former RPF secretary-general at the Ministry of Defense.

20. Interview with Lev Forster, lawyer representing Kigali defendants in French indictment.

21. Interviews with Chryso's friends, families and lawyers at ICTR.

22. Interviews with family, survivor account from Rwandan Political Prisoners Support Network, "Kidnapping of J. Chrysostome Ntirugiribambe: Is This How a Hero Is Rewarded?" RPPSN website, undated, https://rappr-rppsn.org/kidnapping-of-j-chrysostome-ntirugiribambe-is-this-how-a-hero-is-rewarded/.

23. Interviews with Chryso's friends and RNC members.

24. Interviews with Micombero and Chryso's family members and friends.

25. Interview on BBC's *Hard Talk* program in December 2006: https://www.youtube.com/watch?v=JcmCNqmHoaw.

26. Interview with Théogène Murwanashyaka.

27. E-mails from Théogène Murwanashyaka to investigator in Bruguière inquiry.

28. Among the more high-profile witnesses to testify for Bruguière and granted asylum in Europe were former RPA soldiers Abdul Ruzibiza, Emmanuel Ruzigana and Aloys Ruyenzi.

29. Stephen Smith, "Révélations sur l'attentat qui a déclenché le génocide rwandais," *Le Monde*, March 3, 2004.

30. Emmanuel Ruzigana was an RPF technician who carried out dirty operations prior to and during the genocide, and has since maintained close ties with Rwanda, according to interviews with former intelligence staff.

31. Ruzigana issued a formal denial in a letter to Judge Bruguière obtained by the French newspaper *Libération*: http://www1.rfi.fr/actufr/articles/084/article_47956.asp.

32. Even after his death, Ruzibiza remains a controversial figure. The former RPF soldier was considered brave for exposing RPF crimes, but he lied about his role in operations linked to the killing of Habyarimana. Ruzibiza was not directly involved with the missile team.

33. Pierre-François Naudé, "Questions autour de la mort de Joshua Abdul Ruzibiza," *Jeune Afrique*

(website), September 24, 2010, http://www.jeuneafrique.com/184337/politique/questions-autour-de-la-mort-de-joshua-abdul-ruzibiza/.
34. Interview with Félix Flavien Lizinde, the son of Théoneste Lizinde who was assassinated by suspected RPF agents in Nairobi.
35. Geoffrey York and Judi Rever, "Probe Revisits Mystery of Assassination That Triggered Rwandan Genocide," *Globe and Mail*, October 11, 2016, http://www.theglobeandmail.com/news/world/probe-revisits-mystery-of-assassination-that-triggered-rwandan-genocide/article32316139/.

Chapter 14. Becoming a Target
1. Tim Reid had been deployed by the UN in several countries, including the DRC, as a senior peacekeeper, working as a military observer and senior adviser. He also worked for the UN Human Rights Field Operation in Rwanda during the counterinsurgency, and has been concerned by the consistent pattern of human rights violations by the RPF in the Great Lakes region and the increasing number of RPF officials working for UN agencies.
2. The Spanish indictment against the RPF, 2008, can be read here: http://www.friendsofthecongo.org/pdf/spanish_indictment.pdf. Colum Lynch, "US Backs UN Official in Darfur Indicted in Rwanda Deaths," *Washington Post*, June 29, 2008.
3. Interview with Jordi Palou-Loverdos, lawyer for Spanish, Congolese and Rwandan victims of RPF crimes.
4. Judi Rever, "What Is Happening to Rwandan Refugees in Uganda?" *Le Monde Diplomatique* (online), June 5, 2013.
5. Judi Rever, "Rwandan Generals Accused of War Crimes in UN Employ," *Foreign Policy Journal* (online), December 10, 2013.
6. Judi Rever and Geoffrey York, "Rwanda's Hunted. Assassination in Africa: Inside the Plots to Kill Rwanda's Dissidents," *Globe and Mail*, May 2, 2014.
7. Geoffrey York, "Rwandan Officer Who Leaked Assassination-List Evidence Becomes a Target," *Globe and Mail*, November 19, 2015.
8. "Rwanda, SA Diplomatic Rift Gets Wider," *Sunday Independent* (Cape Town), March 9, 2014.
9. Lara Santoro, "Terror as Method: A Journalist's Search for Truth in Rwanda," *Foreign Policy Journal* (online), September 25, 2015, https://www.foreignpolicyjournal.com/2015/09/25/terror-as-method-a-journalists-search-for-truth-in-rwanda/.

Chapter 15. The Signs Were There from the Beginning
1. Interview with Catholic missionary Giancarlo Bucchianeri.
2. "Victimes des massacres du RPR en préfectures de Ruhengeri et de Byumba en février 1993," Table reproduced by James Gasana in *Rwanda : du parti-Etat à l'Etat-garnison* (Paris: Editions L'Harmattan, 2002). Barrie Collins, *Rwanda 1994, The Myth of the Akazu Genocide Conspiracy and Its Consequences* (Basingstoke: Palgrave Macmillan, 2014), page 105.
3. *Report of the International Commission of Investigation on Human Rights Violations in Rwanda since October 1, 1990* (ICI). The 1993 report, written by Alison Des Forges and William Schabas, appeared to mirror the claims of one side only: the RPF. "I remember this report vividly," said Theogene Rudasingwa, the RPF's former secretary-general, now in exile. "As RPF's roving ambassador, this was a treasure in my hands. In Africa, Europe and here in the US it was a powerful weapon. I disseminated it more than anybody else. At that time we were active in convincing the international community and human rights organizations that the massacres of Tutsis in Bugesera, Kibilira and Bigogwe were acts of genocide. The word *genocide* started appearing in our vocabulary as early as 1993," he told me.
   One of the most salient revelations in the report came from an informant named Janvier Afrika, a man who wore many hats. He said he had been a former agent of Rwanda's secret service. He was also a journalist and member of the Interahamwe. From his jail cell, he gave investigators detailed

testimony that he had attended meetings in which President Habyarimana and several officials authorized anti-Tutsi death squads throughout the country. Afrika named *bourgmestres* and ministers involved in organizing the slaughter of Tutsis, in particular the Bagogwe Tutsis in Ruhengeri. Afrika would also claim that French soldiers trained Interahamwe to carry out killings.

The problem with Afrika was his lack of credibility: he was suspected of having infiltrated Hutu militia on behalf of the RPF and admitted he had close ties with its members. He said the RPF helped him escape prison in February 1994, and that after its troops seized power in July, he lived with Kagame's aunt in Kigali. Afrika eventually encountered problems with the RPF and fled the country, revealing he'd been encouraged by the RPF to give false testimony about Habyarimana-directed death squads. He was also known to be one of Kayumba Nyamwasa's close contacts, according to a former DMI intelligence officer.

More fundamentally—yet revealing of the investigative team's bias—the ICI report gave curt treatment to massive human rights violations against Hutus in RPF zones. The investigators spent little time in RPF areas and interviewed individuals only under RPF escort.

4. Interview with Pierre Laplante, former MSF nurse in northern Rwanda, prior to genocide.
5. MSF footage dated 1992 from northern Rwanda.
6. Interviews with Hutu victims, Catholic priests and former RPF soldiers.
7. Alphonse F. Furuma, "Crimes Committed by Kagame," Ishyaka Banyarwanda-Banyarwanda . . . (blog), January 23, 2009, http://banyarwandapoliticalparty.org.over-blog.com/2014/03/crimes-committed-by-kagame-by-major-furuma-alphonse.html.
8. Interview with RPF founder Alphonse Furuma.
9. Office of the High Commissioner for Human Rights report, Operation Kibeho. United Nations and Rwanda: 1993–1996, United Nations Bluebook Series.
10. Philip Gourevitch, *We Wish to Inform You that Tomorrow We Will Be Killed with Our Families: Stories from Rwanda* (New York: Farrar, Straus and Giroux, 1998), page 187.
11. Ibid., page 188.
12. Ibid., page 248.
13. ICTR testimony from former DMI agent, R0000239.
14. Interview with Hutu survivor from Kibeho.
15. ICTR testimony from former DMI agent, R0000240.
16. Donatella Lorch, "Rwandan Killings Set Back Effort to Provide Foreign Aid," *New York Times*, April 26, 1995, http://www.nytimes.com/1995/04/26/world/rwandan-killings-set-back-effort-to-provide-foreign-aid.html.
17. European Commission, press release, July 13, 1995, http://europa.eu/rapid/press-release_IP-95-756_en.htm.
18. ICTR testimony from former RPF Training Wing, DMI officer, R0000232.
19. Interviews with former RPF intelligence staff and former head of RPF Secretariat Theogene Rudasingwa.
20. ICTR testimony from former DMI agent, R0000241.
21. Amnesty International, "Rwanda: Sharp Increase in Killings Could Plunge Rwanda Back Into a Cycle of Violence," Reliefweb (website), August 12, 1996, http://reliefweb.int/report/rwanda/rwanda-sharp-increase-killings-could-plunge-rwanda-back-cycle-violence.
22. US Department of State, Bureau of Economic and Business Affairs, "2017 Investment Climate Statements: Rwanda," US State Department website, June 29, 2017, /www.state.gov/e/eb/rls/othr/ics/2017/af/269769.htm.
23. Yvonne Dutton, *Rules, Politics, and the International Criminal Court: Committing to the Court* (New York: Routledge, 2013), pages 132–133.
24. Interview with former investigator at the Office of the Prosecutor at the International Criminal Court.
25. See also Denis Tull, *The Reconfiguration of Political Order in Africa: A Case Study of North Kivu* (Hamburg: Institute of African Affairs, 2005); Gregory Mthembu Salter, "Baseline study two: Mukungwe artisanal mine, South Kivu, Democratic Republic of Congo," OECD report, 2014

https://www.oecd.org/daf/inv/mne/Gold-Baseline-Study-2.pdf; Minerals Yearbook, Area Reports, International, 2008 (US Dept of the Interior, US Geological Survey); Human Rights Watch, *The Curse of Gold*, report, June 2005, https://www.hrw.org/reports/2005/drc0505/9.htm.

26. David Smith, "Congo Warlord Bosco Ntaganda Led Ethnically Motivated Murder, ICC Told," *Guardian*, February 10, 2014, https://www.theguardian.com/world/2014/feb/10/congo-warlord-bosco-ntaganda-war-crimes-hague.

27. "ICC Prosecutors Say Congolese Rebel Leader Coached Witnesses from Prison," Reuters, November 10, 2016.

28. Remarks at a UN Security Council Open Debate on Prevention and Resolution of Conflicts in the Great Lakes Region by Samantha Power, US representative to the UN, March 21, 2016. http://www.ugandandiasporanews.com/2016/03/23/diplomacy-remarks-by-amb-samantha-powers-u-s-permanent-representative-to-the-united-nations-on-conflict-prevention-in-the-great-lakes-region-feature-uganda/

29. By mid-2017, more than five thousand people had been killed and a million others displaced in Congo's diamond-rich Kasai, where a Congolese warrior named Eric Ruhorimbere has emerged as a central figure behind the violence. Ruhorimbere's background is significant: he fought in three of Kagame's brutal militias over the last twenty years. As part of misguided internationally brokered peace agreements, Ruhorimbere and thousands of other mainly Tutsi rebels later joined the ranks of Congo's army, and have fueled chaos and fought over local land and resources ever since.

Ruhorimbere has maintained close ties with Kagame through senior RPF officers James Kabarebe and Jack Nziza, according to former intelligence staff. He secretly kept collaborating with DMI agents even when the RPF was staging attacks against the Banymulenge, a Tutsi tribe to which Ruhorimbere belongs.

Conclusion: Remembering the Dead

1. René Lemarchand, *The Dynamics of Violence in Central Africa* (Philadelphia: University of Pennsylvania Press, 2008).

2. From French novelist Louis-Ferdinand Céline, cited by Pascal Bruckner, *La Tentation de l'Innocence* (Paris: Grasset, 1995).

3. Scott Straus, *The Order of Genocide: Race, Power, and War in Rwanda* (Ithaca, NY: Cornell University Press, 2006), pages 62–63.

4. Ranges of estimates from Human Rights Watch, media, the United Nations and the Rwandan government.

5. Raphael Lemkin, "Raphael Lemkin's History of Genocide and Colonialism," paper prepared for United States Holocaust Memorial Museum, 2004, https://www.ushmm.org/confront-genocide/speakers-and-events/all-speakers-and-events/raphael-lemkins-history-of-genocide-and-colonialism.

6. Holocaust Encyclopedia, "Einsatzgruppen: Mobile Killing Units," United States Holocaust Memorial Museum website, https://www.ushmm.org/wlc/en/article.php?ModuleId=10005130.

7. Interview with Tutsi opposition activist who grew up in Uganda before joining the RPF.

8. Interviews with former RPF intelligence, soldiers.

9. Interviews with former RPF officers and soldiers, and ICTR testimony from top secret documents (summary, Giti, Rutare).

10. Interahamwe were the youth wing of the ruling MRND; Abakombozi were the youth wing of the PSD; Ikuba were the youth wing of the MDR; Impuzamugambi were the youth wing of the CDR.

11. The "political mob" murders of Hutu politicians Félicien Gatabazi (PSD) and Martin Bucyana (CDR) in February 1994 were part of RPF commando operations, according to ICTR testimony and multiple interviews with former RPF members.

12. ICTR testimony, interviews with former RPF intelligence.

13. Roméo Dallaire, *Shake Hands with the Devil: The Failure of Humanity in Rwanda* (Toronto: Random House Canada, 2003), page 342.

14. *International Prosecutors* Luc Reydams, Jan Wouters & Cedric Ryngaert eds. (Oxford: Oxford University Press, 2012), page 31.
15. Ibid.
16. Interview with former official from OTP at ICTR.
17. The rate of killing depended on the capacity and effectiveness of RPF personnel in a given area and their access to the civilian population. This killing capacity was in turn a function of the opportunities the RPA had to conceal these crimes or in some cases blame them on Hutu forces. On the rare occasions that NGOs or UN staff or independent journalists did travel in or enter RPF-controlled areas, these individuals were escorted and their movements tightly controlled.

The RPA could easily load victims onto trucks or take them to isolated locations in the bush or to enclosed buildings, without observers knowing. Where possible, house-to-house searches were conducted and people were killed on the spot. Luring and entrapment—promising of food, supplies or transport to safe areas—was central to these schemes.

Evidence from dozens of interviews with former members of battalions, its High Command unit, Training Wing and intelligence network provide different and occasionally contrasting scenarios of killing squad capacity. The testimonies provide rough estimates on the numbers of victims who perished:

- DMI mobile units comprised between fifty and sixty men who operated in the rear of military battalions. Mobile units were present in every area under RPA control, suggesting a dozen to fourteen units matching the number of battalions on the ground, sources involved in these operations said. Conservative estimates from intelligence sources suggest that as many as five hundred Hutus were killed per day by these units, over at least a two-month period during the genocide. Over a mere sixty days, that suggests upwards of **420,000 Hutu civilians killed** by DMI units in the dozen rear areas seized and controlled by the RPA. Over ninety days, that would mean an estimated **630,000** Hutus killed by DMI units in RPF zones.

- More conservatively, some sources indicated that DMI operated smaller, more [platoon-sized] detachments. Civilian and other military sources have estimated that these smaller DMI platoons managed to kill at least a hundred people per day, over a two- to three-month period, in villages under RPF control. If, at a minimum, a dozen or so detachments operated across Rwanda during the genocide, this would suggest **72,000 at a minimum and 108,000 at a maximum were killed** by smaller DMI detachments alone. This figure does not include estimates of civilians killed by RPA battalions. A former DMI staffer operating in Ruhengeri estimated that his unit killed between 150 and 200 people a day with ropes, knives, machetes and pangas (a kind of ax). Men, women and children were put in mass graves and burned. He estimated that between May 1993 and August 1994, his unit killed **100,000** people.

- Testimony from soldiers and officers in battalions indicates that up to two hundred civilians were killed daily by a dozen or so RPA battalions fanning out all over Rwanda. Over a two-month period, this would suggest regular troops killed at least **144,000 Hutu civilians**; over three months, the number of victims could have risen to **216,000**.

- Luring and loading people onto trucks enabled the RPA's DMI agents to kill easily, discreetly and in vast numbers. Dozens of military sources testified on this method, but one High Command intelligence official said he was receiving reports that one hundred to two hundred people were being loaded onto between five to ten trucks and brought to Akagera National Park daily. Over the course of two months, this would at a minimum (one hundred people on five trucks a day) suggest **30,000** people transported to their death. If up to two hundred people were put onto ten trucks every day, for three months, the total maximum number of victims brought to Akagera to be burned and incinerated would be **180,000**.

- Sources from the Training Wing have provided rough estimates of numbers of Hutu civilians and Hutu male recruits killed during and after the genocide. They estimated up to **half a million** people perished in these schemes.

- A UN investigator who probed RPF crimes for nearly a decade said Kagame's troops were responsible for **"at least half a million"** deaths in Rwanda during and after the genocide.

- Theogene Rudasingwa, former head of the RPF's political Secretariat, has accused Kagame and his former colleagues of committing genocide against Hutus in 1994. He alleges that approximately **one million** Hutu civilians died from April 1994 onward.

18. Interview with Habarushaka's widow Venantie Mukarwego, and a witness standing at the gate of Amahoro stadium who saw Habarushaka brought into a house nearby.

INDEX

JUDI REVER is a freelance print and broadcast journalist who started her career with Radio France Internationale before working for the wire service Agence France-Presse, reporting from Africa and the Middle East. Her reporting on Rwanda has been featured in seven front-page stories in *The Globe and Mail* over the past four years, and she has been named a country of origin information expert on Rwanda by the Rights in Exile Programme, which promotes the legal protection of refugees. Her work has also appeared in *Foreign Policy Journal*, *Le Monde Diplomatique*, *Humanosphere*, *Digital Journal* and *The Africa Report*. @judirever